D1615727

FREE WILL AND LUCK

Free Will and Luck

ALFRED R. MELE

OXFORD
UNIVERSITY PRESS

2006

OXFORD
UNIVERSITY PRESS

Oxford University Press, Inc., publishes works that further
Oxford University's objective of excellence
in research, scholarship, and education.

Oxford   New York
Auckland   Cape Town   Dar es Salaam   Hong Kong   Karachi
Kuala Lumpur   Madrid   Melbourne   Mexico City   Nairobi
New Delhi   Shanghai   Taipei   Toronto

With offices in
Argentina   Austria   Brazil   Chile   Czech Republic   France   Greece
Guatemala   Hungary   Italy   Japan   Poland   Portugal   Singapore
South Korea   Switzerland   Thailand   Turkey   Ukraine   Vietnam

Copyright © 2006 by Oxford University Press, Inc.

Published by Oxford University Press, Inc.
198 Madison Avenue, New York, New York 10016

www.oup.com

Oxford is a registered trademark of Oxford University Press.

Library of Congress Cataloging-in-Publication Data

Mele, Alfred R., 1951–
Free will and luck / Alfred R. Mele.
p.   cm.
Includes bibliographical references and index.
ISBN-13 978-0-19-530504-3
ISBN 0-19-530504-3
1. Chance.   2. Fortune.   3. Fate and fatalism.   4. Free will and determinism
5. Libertarianism.   I. Title.

BD595.M45 2006
123'.5—dc22   2005051261

3 5 7 9 8 6 4 2

Printed in the United States of America
on acid-free paper

For Dannil and Perrin

Preface

I believe that human beings sometimes act freely and are morally responsible for some of what they do. If free will is the power to act freely, then I believe in free will. In this book, I try to make salient the most difficult conceptual problems that my belief encounters, and I develop solutions to those problems. I also expose some pseudo-problems along the way.

Portions of this book derive from some of my published articles. Chapter 1 incorporates material from "Agnostic Autonomism Revisited," in J. Taylor, ed., *Personal Autonomy* (Cambridge: Cambridge University Press, 2005); "Libertarianism, Luck, and Control," *Pacific Philosophical Quarterly* (2005) 86: 395–421; and "Agents' Abilities," *Noûs* (2003) 37: 447–70. Chapters 2 and 3 draw, respectively, on "Decisions, Intentions, Urges, and Free Will: Why Libet Has Not Shown What He Says He Has," in J. Campbell, M. O'Rourke, and D. Shier, eds., *Explanation and Causation: Topics in Contemporary Philosophy* (Cambridge, Mass.: MIT Press, 2005) and "Libertarianism, Luck, and Control." Section 3 of chapter 4 is based partly on "Soft Libertarianism and Frankfurt-Style Scenarios," *Philosophical Topics* (1996) 24: 123–41 and "Ultimate Responsibility and Dumb Luck," *Social Philosophy & Policy* (1999) 16: 274–93. Section 2 of chapter 6 derives from "A Critique of Pereboom's 'Four-Case Argument' for Incompatibilism," *Analysis* (2005) 65: 75–80. Parts of sections 1 and 2 of chapter 7 are based on "Dennett on Freedom," *Metaphilosophy* (2005) 36: 414–26 and "Agnostic Autonomism Revisited."

I owe a special debt to Randy Clarke, Ish Haji, Neil Levy, Eddy Nahmias, and Derk Pereboom for providing helpful written comments on a draft of this book. I am grateful to many people for useful comments on parts of this book: Helen Beebee, Dan Dennett, Matthew Elton, John Fischer, Josh Gert, Carl Ginet, Alan Goldman, Risto Hilpinen, Chris Hitchcock, Jamie Hobbs, Bob Kane, Tomis Kapitan, Pekka Mäkelä, Cei Maslen, Hugh McCann, Michael McKenna, Tim O'Connor, Sue Pockett, Michael Quante, Piers Rawling, Mike Ridge, Dave Robb, Helen Steward, Steve Sverdlik, Pekka Väyrynen, David Widerker, Gideon Yaffe, and Aaron Zimmerman.

Drafts of sections or chapters were presented at meetings of the North Texas Philosophical Association and the Pacific Division of the American Philosophical Association, at the Catholic University of America, Cornell University, Florida State University, the Jean Nicod Institute, the Max Planck Institute for Psychological Research (Munich), Southern Methodist University, State University of New York–Stony Brook, Texas Tech University, Tilburg University, University College London, Washington State University, and the Universities of Bucharest, Calgary, Cincinnati, Colorado at Boulder, Dundee, Edinburgh, Florida, Helsinki, Glasgow, Manchester, Miami, Oregon, Oxford, Stirling, and Zurich. I am grateful to my audiences for their help. I also am grateful to students in seminar discussions of a draft of this book at Florida State University and the University of Helsinki.

Contents

FREE WILL AND LUCK

ONE

Introduction

Is it true that at least some human beings sometimes act freely and are morally responsible for some of what they do? Some philosophers answer *yes* and others *no*. Philosophical defenses of these answers traditionally include a defense of a judgment about whether free action and moral responsibility are compatible or incompatible with determinism. I make no such judgment in this book: I am agnostic about the issue. Introducing some standard definitions facilitates an explanation of my departure from tradition:

1. *Determinism.* "The thesis that there is at any instant exactly one physically possible future" (van Inwagen 1983, p. 3). More fully, at any instant exactly one future is compatible with the state of the universe at that instant and the laws of nature. (There are more detailed definitions of *determinism* in the literature; but this one will do for my purposes. An exception may be made for instants at or near the time of the big bang.)

2. *Compatibilism.* The thesis that free action and moral responsibility are compatible with the truth of determinism. (A compatibilist may or may not hold that there are free and morally responsible human beings and may or may not hold that determinism is true.)[1]

3. *Incompatibilism.* The thesis that neither free action nor moral responsibility is compatible with the truth of determinism. (An incompatibilist may or may not hold that there are free

and morally responsible human beings and may or may not hold that determinism is true.)

4. *Libertarianism.* The conjunction of incompatibilism and the thesis that some human beings act freely and are morally responsible for some of what they do.

Obviously, libertarianism and compatibilism are mutually exclusive. Even so, in an earlier book, *Autonomous Agents* (Mele 1995), I advanced both libertarian and compatibilist views, and I will do the same here. How can that be? Well, I was then, and still am, officially agnostic about the truth of compatibilism. Also, I took my primary opponents to be theorists who argue that both compatibilism and libertarianism are false and, accordingly, that there are no free and morally responsible human beings. In Mele 1995, I defended a position that I called *agnostic autonomism*, the conjunction of the agnosticism just identified with the assertion that, as I have elected to put it in this book, there are free and morally responsible human beings.

I argued in Mele 1995—and continue to believe—that agnostic autonomism is more credible than the view that there are no free and morally responsible human beings (NFM). Consider the following propositions:

a. Some human beings sometimes act freely and are morally responsible for some of what they do, and determinism is compatible with that (compatibilist belief in free, morally responsible human beings).

b. Some human beings sometimes act freely and are morally responsible for some of what they do, and determinism is incompatible with that (libertarianism).

c. Either a or b (agnostic autonomism).

d. No human beings ever act freely, and no human beings are morally responsible for anything (NFM).

Imagine that each proposition has a subjective probability greater than 0 and less than 1 for an arbitrarily selected informed reader, Rita. Then *c* should have for her a higher subjective probability than *a* and a higher subjective probability than *b*, because *c* is the *disjunction* of *a* and *b*.[2] So what about *d*? I argued that the case for NFM is no better than the case for *a* and no better than the case for *b* (1995, ch. 13). If Rita is persuaded by my arguments, then because *c* should have a higher subjective probability for her than each of *a* and *b*, *c* should have a higher subjective probability for her than *d*: agnostic autonomism beats nonautonomism! The nature of the claimed victory is such as to call for further work on all sides. Part of my aim in Mele 1995 was to motivate such work. Since then, much good work of this kind has been published. (I am not claiming any responsibility for motivating it.) In this book, I respond to some of it—the work that is most directly relevant to my concerns here.

Libertarians argue that determinism precludes free action and moral responsibility by, for example, precluding an agent's being ultimately responsible for anything (Kane 1996). Some compatibilist believers in freedom argue that libertarians rely on indeterminism in a way that deprives us of the kind of control over our decisions that we need for free and morally responsible action (Berofsky 1995). Proponents of NFM can benefit from arguments on both sides, alleging that libertarians show that free action and moral responsibility are incompatible with determinism and that compatibilist critics of libertarianism show that essentially indeterministic notions of free action and moral responsibility are incoherent or unsatisfiable.

My plan in Mele 1995 was to use the resources both of libertarianism and of compatibilism in defending agnostic autonomism and to do that partly by developing the best compatibilist and libertarian positions I could develop. Part of my strategy was to construct an account of an ideally self-controlled agent (where self-control is understood as the contrary of *akrasia*: roughly, weakness of will), to argue that even such an agent may fall short of autonomy (or free agency), and to ask what may be added to ideal self-control to yield autonomy (or free agency). I offered two answers, one for compatibilists and another for libertarians. I then argued that a disjunctive thesis associated with both answers— agnostic autonomism—is more credible than NFM.

My strategy in this book is different. I believe that close attention to Frankfurt-style scenarios and especially to agential luck sheds considerable light on the theoretical problems that philosophers who believe that there are free, morally responsible agents encounter and therefore assists in surmounting those problems. I explore the significance of Frankfurt-style cases in chapter 4. Luck is a thread running through chapters 1, 3, 4, and 5. (Chapter 2 is a critique of some neuroscientific work on free will.) In Mele 1995, I raised some luck-based problems for libertarian views and offered a libertarian resolution of them. Since then, there have been significant developments in libertarian views. For example, Robert Kane has developed his event-causal libertarianism in considerable detail (1996, 1999b), and Randolph Clarke (2003) and

Timothy O'Connor (2000) have done the same for agent-causal libertarianism. In chapter 3, I challenge these recent libertarian positions, and in chapter 5, I argue that an alternative libertarian view is superior. I then turn to compatibilism, criticizing, in chapter 6, the major objections to compatibilism in general, and replying, in chapter 7, to objections to my compatibilist proposal in Mele 1995. Chapter 8 wraps things up with some brief summaries and a discussion of a pair of thought experiments about imagined empirical discoveries. As in Mele 1995," I offer readers a disjunction of libertarianism and compatibilist belief in free, morally responsible agents.

The following two sections sketch themes from Mele 1995: a serious problem luck poses for libertarians (sec. 1), and my modest libertarian proposal for dealing with it (sec. 2). (I offer a considerably bolder libertarian proposal in chapter 5.) The sketches are offered as background for subsequent chapters. Sections 3 and 4 provide additional background: their topics are deciding, the timing of actions, the expression "free will," and agents' abilities.

1. A Problem about Luck for Libertarians

Libertarians have the option of endorsing either stronger, nonhistorical requirements on free action or weaker, historical requirements (Mele 1995, pp. 207–9). For example, they can claim that an agent freely A-ed at t only if, at t, he could have done otherwise than A then or claim instead that an agent who could not have done otherwise at t than A then may nevertheless freely A at t, provided that he earlier performed some relevant free action or actions at a time or times at which he could have done otherwise than perform those actions. I call any free A-ings that occur at times at which the past (up to those times) and the laws of nature are consistent with the agent's not A-ing then *basically free actions*. In principle, libertarians can hold that an agent's basically free actions that are suitably related to his subsequent A-ing confer freedom on his A-ing, even though he could not have done otherwise than A then. It is open to libertarians to accept or reject the thesis that the only free actions are what I am calling basically free actions. Exactly parallel options are open on morally responsible action.[3] These issues may safely be skirted in parts of this book, and to simplify exposition, I sometimes frame the discussion in terms of basically free actions and actions for which agents have basic moral responsibility.

Now for luck. Agents' *control* is the yardstick by which the bearing of luck on their freedom and moral responsibility is measured. When luck (good or bad) is problematic, that is because it seems significantly to impede agents' control over themselves or to highlight important gaps or shortcomings in such control. It may seem that to the extent that it is causally open whether or not, for example, an agent intends in accordance with his considered judgment about what it is best to do, he lacks some control over what he intends, and it may be claimed that a positive deterministic connection between considered best judgment and intention would be more conducive to freedom and moral responsibility.

This last claim will be regarded as a nonstarter by anyone who holds that freedom and moral responsibility require agential control and that determinism is incompatible with such control. Sometimes it is claimed that agents do not control anything at all if determinism is true. That claim is false. When I drive my car (in normal conditions), I control the turns it makes, even if our universe happens to be deterministic. I certainly control my car's turns in a way in which my passengers and others do not. A distinction can be drawn between compatibilist or "proximal" control and a kind of control that requires the falsity of determinism—"ultimate" control.[4] My controlling a turn my car makes is at least an instance of the former kind of control, and it might be an instance of the latter kind as well, depending on what the actual laws of nature are. Ultimate control might turn out to be remarkably similar to the control that many compatibilists have in mind; the key to its being *ultimate* control might be its indeterministic setting (Mele 1995, p. 213).[5] I return to this distinction in section 2.

I illustrate a salient worry about luck for libertarians with a fable.[6] Diana, a libertarian goddess in an indeterministic universe, wants to build rational, free human beings who are capable of being very efficient agents. She believes that proximal decisions—typically, decisions to *A* straightaway—are causes of actions that execute them, and she sees no benefit in designing agents who have a chance of not even trying to *A* when they have decided to *A* straightaway and the intention to *A* formed in that act of deciding persists in the absence of any biological damage.[7] The indeterministic fabric of Diana's universe allows her to build a deterministic connection between proximal decisions and corresponding attempts, and she does. Now, because Diana is a relatively typical libertarian, she believes that free decisions cannot be deterministically caused—even by something that centrally involves a considered judgment that it would be best to A straightaway. She also believes that agents can make free decisions based on such judgments. So Diana designs her agents in such a way that, even though they have just made such a judgment, and even though the judgment persists in the absence of biological damage, they may decide contrary to it.

Given Diana's brand of libertarianism, she believes that whenever agents freely perform an action of deciding to A, they could have *freely* performed some alternative action.[8] She worries that her design does not accommodate this. Her worry, more specifically, is that if the difference between the actual world, in which one of her agents judges it best to A straightaway and then, at t, decides accordingly, and any possible world with the same past up to t and the same laws of nature in which he makes an alternative decision while the judgment persists is just a matter of luck, then he does not freely make that decision in that possible world, W. Diana suspects that his making that alternative decision rather than deciding in accordance with his best judgment— that is, that difference between W and the actual world—is just a matter of bad luck or, more precisely, of worse luck in W for the agent than in the actual world. After all, because the worlds do not diverge before the agent decides, there is no difference in them to account for the difference in decisions. This suspicion leads Diana to suspect that, in W, the agent should not be blamed for the decision he makes there.[9] And that he should not be blamed, she thinks, indicates that he did not freely make it. Diana searched for grounds other than unfreedom for not blaming this agent and found none. She believes that if the agent had freely made the decision he made in W, he would have been morally responsible for it and blameworthy.

I am not privy to the details of Diana's design, but readers who need assistance in understanding her worry may consider the following story. As soon as any agent of hers judges it best to A, objective probabilities for the various decisions open to the agent are set, and the probability of a decision to A is very high. Larger probabilities get a correspondingly larger segment of a tiny indeterministic neural roulette wheel in the agent's head than do smaller probabilities. A tiny neural ball bounces along the wheel; its landing in a particular segment is the agent's making the corresponding decision. When the ball lands in the segment for a decision to A, its doing so is not *just* a matter of luck. After all, the design is such that the probability of that happening is very high. But the ball's landing there is *partly* a matter of luck. And the difference at issue at t between a world in which the ball lands there at t

and a world with the same past and laws of nature in which it lands in a segment for another decision at *t* is just a matter of luck.

Diana can think of nothing that stops her worry from generalizing to all cases of deciding, whether or not the agent makes a judgment about what it is best to do. In the actual world, Joe decides at *t* to *A*. In another world with the same laws of nature and the same past, he decides at *t* not to *A*. If there is nothing about Joe's powers, capacities, states of mind, moral character, and the like in either world that accounts for this difference, then the difference seems to be just a matter of luck. And given that neither world diverges from the other in any respect before *t*, there is no difference at all in Joe in these two worlds to account for the difference in his decisions. To be sure, something about Joe may explain why it is *possible* for him to decide to *A* in the actual world and decide not to *A* in another world with the same laws and past. That he is an indeterministic decision maker may explain this. That is entirely consistent with the difference in his decisions being just a matter of luck.

All libertarians who hold that *A*'s being a free action depends on its being the case that, at the time, the agent was able to do otherwise freely then should tell us what it could possibly be about an agent who freely *A*-ed at *t* in virtue of which it is true that, in another world with the same past and laws of nature, he freely does something else at *t*.[10] Of course, they can *say* that the answer is "free will." But what they need to explain then is how free will, as they understand it, can be a feature of agents—or, more fully, how this can be so where free will, on their account of it, really does answer the question. To do this, of course, they must provide an account of free will—one that can be tested for adequacy in this connection.

2. A Modest Libertarian Proposal

According to typical event-causal libertarian views, the proximate causes of free actions indeterministically cause them. This is a consequence of the typical event-causal libertarian ideas that free actions have proximate causes and that if an agent freely *A*-s at *t* in world *W*, he does not *A* at *t* in some other possible world with the same laws of nature and the same past up to *t*. Now, the proximate causes of actions, including actions that are decisions, are internal to agents. Even a driver's sudden decision to hit his brakes in an emergency situation is not proximately caused by events in the external world. Perception of whatever the source of the emergency happens to be—for example, a dog darting into traffic—is causally involved. And how the driver decides to react to what he sees depends on, among other things, his driving skills and habits, whether he is aware of what is happening directly behind him, and his preferences. A driver who likes driving over dogs and is always looking for opportunities to do that would probably react very differently than a normal person would. In light of the general point about the proximate causation of actions, typical event-causal libertarianism encompasses a commitment to what may be termed *agent-internal indeterminism*.

What I call *modest libertarianism* (see Mele 1995, pp. 211–21) embraces that commitment, too, even though it rejects the idea that the *proximate* causes of free actions indeterministically cause the actions. Indeterministic worlds in which every instance of causation within any agent is deterministic are hostile environments for libertarian freedom. What libertarians want that determinism precludes is not merely that agents have open to them more than one future that is compatible with the combination of the past and the laws of nature, but that, on some occasions, which possible future becomes actual is in some sense and to some degree up to the agents. They want something that seemingly requires that agents themselves be indeterministic in some suitable way—that some relevant things that happen under the skin are indeterministically caused by other such things. The focus is on psychological events, of course (as opposed, for example, to indeterministically caused muscle spasms), and, more specifically, on psychological events that have a significant bearing on action.

Requiring internal indeterminism for free action and moral responsibility is risky. To be sure, quantum mechanics, according to leading interpretations, is indeterministic. But indeterminism at that level does not ensure that any human brains themselves sometimes operate indeterministically, much less that they sometimes operate indeterministically in ways appropriate for free action and moral responsibility. One possibility, as David Hodgson reports, is that "in systems as hot, wet, and massive as neurons of the brain, quantum mechanical indeterminacies quickly cancel out, so that for all practical purposes determinism rules in the brain" (2002, p. 86). Another is that any indeterminism in the human brain is simply irrelevant to free action and moral responsibility. Modest libertarians join other event-causal libertarians in taking this risk.

Suppose that Ann, on the basis of careful, rational, informed deliberation, judges it best to *A*. And suppose that, on the basis of that judgment, she acquires an intention to *A* and then acts accordingly, intentionally *A*-ing. Suppose further that Ann has not been subjected to freedom-thwarting mind control or relevant deception, that she is perfectly sane, and so on. To make a long story short, suppose that her *A*-ing satisfies a set of alleged sufficient conditions for free action that a sophisticated compatibilist would endorse and that many sophisticated folks who have no commitment to incompatibilism would find very attractive (see Mele 1995, pp. 186–91). Now add one more supposition to the set: while Ann was deliberating, owing to her being internally indeterministic, it was causally open that she would not come to the conclusion she in fact reached.

In principle, an agent-internal indeterminism may provide for indeterministic agency while blocking or limiting our proximal control over what happens only at junctures at which we have no greater proximal control on the hypothesis that our universe is deterministic.[11] Obviously, in those cases in which we act on the basis of careful, rational deliberation, what we do is influenced by at least some of the considerations that "come to mind"—that is, become salient in consciousness—during deliberation and by our assessments of considerations. Now, even if determinism is true, it is false that, with respect to *every* consideration—every belief, desire, hypothesis, and so on—that comes to mind during our deliberation, we are in control of its coming to mind, and some considerations that come to mind without our being in control of their so doing may influence the outcome of our deliberation. Furthermore, a kind of internal indeterminism is imaginable that limits our control only in a way that gives us no less proximal control than we would have on the assumption that determinism is true, while opening up alternative deliberative outcomes. (Although, in a deterministic world, it would never be a matter of genuine chance that a certain consideration came to mind during deliberation, it may still be a matter of luck relative to the agent's sphere of control.) As I put it in Mele 1995, "Where compatibilists have no good reason to insist on determinism in the deliberative process as a requirement for autonomy, where internal indeterminism is, for all we know, a reality, and where such indeterminism would not diminish the nonultimate control that real agents exert over their deliberation even on the assumption that real agents are internally deterministic—that is, at the *intersection* of these three locations—libertarians may plump for ultimacy-promoting indeterminism" (p. 235). Modest libertarians try to stake out their view at this intersection.

One kind of possible deliberator may be so constituted that no beliefs and desires of his that are directly relevant to the topic of his current deliberation have a chance of not coming to mind during his deliberation, whereas it is causally open whether some of his indirectly relevant beliefs and desires will come to mind. The causally open possibilities of this kind do not need to be extensive to secure the possibility of more than one deliberative outcome. Modest libertarians both need and fear internal indeterminism, and they are disposed to constrain it when engaged in the project of inventing indeterministic agents who can act freely and morally responsibly.

The modest indeterminism at issue allows agents ample control over their deliberation. Suppose a belief, hypothesis, or desire that is indirectly relevant to a deliberator's present practical question comes to mind during deliberation but was not deterministically caused to do so. Presumably, a normal agent would be able to *assess* this consideration. And upon reflection, he might rationally reject the belief as unwarranted, rationally judge that the hypothesis does not merit investigation, or rationally decide that the desire should be given little or no weight in his deliberation. Alternatively, reflection might rationally lead him to retain the belief, to pursue the hypothesis, or to give the desire significant weight. That a consideration is indeterministically caused to come to mind does not entail that the agent has no control over how he responds to it. Considerations that are indeterministically caused to come to mind (like considerations that are deterministically caused to come to mind) are nothing more than input to deliberation.[12] Their coming to mind has at most an indirect effect on what the agent decides, an effect that is mediated by the agent's assessment of them. They do not settle matters. Moreover, not only do agents have the opportunity to assess these considerations, but they also have the opportunity to search for additional relevant considerations before they decide, thereby increasing the probability that other relevant considerations will be indeterministically caused to come to mind. They have, then, at least sometimes, the opportunity to counteract instances of bad luck—for example, an indeterministically caused coming to mind of a misleading consideration or a chance failure to notice a relevant consideration. And given a suitable indeterminism regarding what comes to mind in an assessment process, there are causally open alternative possibilities for the conclusion or outcome of that process.

Compatibilists who hold that we act freely even when we are not in control of what happens at certain specific junctures in the process leading to action are in no position to hold that an indeterministic agent's lacking control at the same junctures precludes free action. And, again, real human beings are not in control of the coming to mind of everything that comes to mind during typical processes of deliberation. If this lack of perfect proximal control does not preclude its being the case that free actions sometimes issue from typical deliberation on the assumption that we are deterministic agents, it also does not preclude this on the assumption that we are *indeterministic* agents.

Is a modest indeterminism of the kind I have sketched useful to libertarians? Elsewhere, I have suggested that what at least some libertarians might prize that no compatibilist account of freedom offers them is a species of agency that gives them a kind of independence and an associated kind of explanatory bearing on their conduct that they would lack in any deterministic world (Mele 1996, 1999b). The combination of the satisfaction of an alleged set of sufficient conditions for free action that a sophisticated compatibilist finds compelling, including all the proximal control that involves, and a modest agent-internal indeterminism of the sort I have described might give some such libertarians what they want. Agents of the imagined sort would make decisions and perform other actions that are not deterministically caused by things outside the agent. They would have no less control over these decisions and other actions than we do over our decisions and other actions, on the assumption that we are deterministic agents. Given that they satisfy robust alleged sufficient conditions for responsibility for certain of these decisions and other actions that a sophisticated compatibilist finds convincing, there are some grounds for viewing them as responsible agents, and owing to the indeterministic aspect of their deliberation, a kind of "ultimacy" attaches to the responsibility that they may have. The decisions and other actions at issue have, in Kane's words, "their ultimate sources in" the agents (1996, p. 98), in the sense that the collection of agent-internal states and events that explains these decisions and other actions is not deterministically caused by anything outside the agent.

Now, even if garden-variety compatibilists can be led to see that the problem of luck is surmountable by a libertarian, how are theorists of other kinds likely to respond to the libertarian position that I have been sketching? There are, of course, philosophers who contend that moral responsibility and freedom are illusions and that we lack these properties whether our universe is deterministic or indeterministic—for example, Richard Double (1991) and Galen Strawson (1986). I will not criticize Double's and Strawson's arguments again here (see Mele 1995, chs. 12 and 13 for criticism). In chapter 6, I examine an important element of Derk Pereboom's (2001) more recent defense of this view.

Modest libertarians can also anticipate trouble from traditional libertarians, who want more than the modest indeterminism that I have described can offer. Clarke, who has done as much as anyone to develop an agent-causal libertarian view, criticizes event-causal libertarianism on the grounds that it adds no "positive" power of control to compatibilist control but simply places compatibilist control in an indeterministic setting (2000, p. 35).[13] Of course, given that combining compatibilist control with indeterminism in a certain psychological sphere was my explicit strategy in constructing a modest libertarian position (Mele 1995, pp. 212–13, 217), I do not see this as an objection. In any case, traditional libertarians need to show that what they want is coherent. That requires showing that what they want does not entail or presuppose a kind of luck that would itself undermine moral responsibility.[14] The typical libertarian wants both indeterminism and significant control at the moment of decision. That is the desire that prompts a serious version of the worry about luck I sketched earlier. In chapter 3, I argue that neither agent causationists nor event-causal libertarians have laid the worry to rest. In the absence of a plausible resolution of the worry, it is epistemically open that a modest libertarian proposal of the sort I sketched is the best a libertarian can do. (In chapter 5, I develop this proposal further as a way of setting the stage for a considerably less modest one.) Of course, even if I happen to hit on the best libertarian option, it does not follow that I have hit on the best option for believers in free action and moral responsibility—as long as compatibilism is still in the running.

3. Deciding, the Time of Action, and Free Will

A brief discussion of deciding, the timing of actions, and the expression "free will" will prove useful as background. Some philosophers take moral responsibility and the freedom most closely associated with it "to apply primarily to decisions" (Pereboom 2001, p. xxi). Many philosophers have claimed or argued that to decide to A is to perform a mental action of a certain kind—an action of forming an intention to

A.[15] Elsewhere, I have defended the view that deciding is a momentary mental action of intention formation and it resolves uncertainty about what to do (Mele 2003a, ch. 9). In saying that deciding is momentary, I mean to distinguish it from, for example, a combination of deliberating and deciding. A student who is speaking loosely may say, "I was up all night deciding to major in English" when what he means is that he was up all night deliberating or fretting about what major to declare and eventually decided to major in English. Deciding to A, on my view, is not a process but a momentary mental action of forming an intention to A, "form" being understood as an action verb. Not all intentions are formed in this sense, or so I have argued elsewhere. For example, "When I intentionally unlocked my office door this morning, I intended to unlock it. But since I am in the habit of unlocking my door in the morning and conditions . . . were normal, nothing called for a *decision* to unlock it" (Mele 1992, p. 231). If I had heard a fight in my office, I might have stopped to consider whether to unlock the door or walk away, and I might have decided to unlock it. But given the routine nature of my conduct, there is no need to posit an act of intention formation in this case. My intention to unlock the door may have been acquired without having been actively formed.

I turn now to the timing of actions.[16] Consider the common libertarian claim that an agent freely A-ed at time t in world W only if he was able at the time to do otherwise than A at t. According to a standard incompatibilist interpretation of this requirement, its consequent is true if and only if in another possible world with the same past up to t and the same laws of nature, the agent does otherwise than A at t. I assume for present purposes that this interpretation is correct. Obviously, some actions take more time than others to perform. Running a marathon takes a lot longer than flipping a coin. An agent who ran a marathon might have performed an alternative action by quitting after several miles or several yards or by watching the whole race from the sidelines. In the case of extended actions, an agent's being able "at the time" to do otherwise than A at t, where A is what he did in world W at t, is secured only by there being a possible world with the same laws of nature as W and the same past as W up to a moment at which the agent's conduct first diverges from his A-ing. This initial divergence can happen at a moment at which the agent is A-ing in W or at the moment at which his A-ing begins in W.

Except in the case of momentary A-ings, "t," in "S A-ed at t," marks a stretch of time longer than a moment. So such expressions as "same past up to t," where t is the time of an A-ing, are potentially misleading. A natural reading of this expression treats t as a moment or as a stretch of time up to the *beginning of which* the past stretches. I considered using the expression "same past up to t_d," where the d signifies the moment of first divergence—a moment identical with t in the case of momentary actions and during t in the case of all other actions. This would solve the problem of potential misleadingness, but it would also depart from tradition and introduce some unnecessary stylistic complexities. I have decided simply to say what I mean by t when it designates the time of an action, to make the point just made about initial divergence, and to stick with traditional usage.

Given the plausibility of the idea that overt intentional actions—that is, intentional actions essentially involving peripheral bodily motion—are explained partly by intentions that come on the scene at least some fraction of a second before the actions begin, decisions or choices naturally receive a lot of attention in the free will literature. Libertarians who say that an agent who, in executing a hand-raising decision he made, intentionally raised his hand at t was able at the time to do otherwise at the time may mean, more precisely and more fully, that shortly before t, when he decided to raise his hand straightaway, he was able to make an alternative decision, and if he had made such a decision, he would not have raised his hand at t and would have performed an intentional alternative then. In this case, the moment at which the agent decides to A is the moment of initial action divergence. In the actual world, he decides at that moment to A; in some relevant possible world, he performs, or begins performing, an intentional alternative action. For example, it may be that in some relevant possible world he decides at that moment not to A.

Presumably, all decisions are at least partially based on or influenced by some psychological states or other—beliefs, desires, recognitions of reasons, or whatever. Anything of this kind that emerges simultaneously with a decision made at t arrives too late for that decision to have been based, even partly, on it, and too late for the decision to have been influenced by it. The upshot is this: in the case of a decision to A that an agent makes at a moment t, her having at the time a libertarian ability to do otherwise requires that there be a possible world that does not diverge from the actual world before t in which she does otherwise than make that decision at t.

Early in this chapter, I offered some standard definitions of common terminology in the literature on free will and moral responsibility. I did not offer a definition of "free will": that expression has no standard definition. A comment is in order about how I use "free will" in this book. Whatever, exactly, free will is, it is, most fundamentally, the power or ability to act freely. So one can try to understand free will by ascertaining what it is to act freely. One can develop an account of free action and define *free will* as the power or ability to perform actions that satisfy the account. For a combination of reasons, including the following, I would like to think that this approach is viable. First, I often cannot tell what authors mean by "will" in "free will";[17] second, I am blameless for this ignorance, as far as I can tell; third, I seem to have been able on various occasions to write about acting freely without using the expression "free will." In any case, if free will may be simply defined in terms of free action—as the power or ability to act freely—one can go about the business of trying to understand free action without worrying about what (the) will is supposed to be. I find that thought liberating.

I close this section with an announcement about my use of "free action" and its cognates. There are readings of "freely *A*-ed" on which the following sentence is true: "While Bob was away on vacation, mice ran freely about his house." These readings do not concern me in this book. My interest is in what might be termed *moral-responsibility-level free action*—roughly, free action of such a kind that if all the freedom-independent conditions for moral responsibility for a particular action were satisfied without that sufficing for the agent's being morally responsible for it, the addition of the action's being free to this set of conditions would entail that he is morally responsible for it.[18]

4. Agents' Abilities

Claims about agents' abilities—practical abilities—are common in the literature on free will and moral responsibility. It is often difficult to be sure what the contributors to this literature mean by "able" in, for example, assertions that an agent who did not *A* was able to *A*. In this section, using *A* as an action variable, I distinguish among two kinds or levels of practical ability: simple ability to *A* and ability to *A* intentionally. The discussion provides guidance on what, in this book, I mean by "able" in various contexts.

Although I have not golfed for years, I am able to golf. I am not able to golf just now, however. I am in my office now, and it is too small to house a golf course. The ability to golf that I claimed I have may be termed a *general* practical ability. It is the kind of ability to A that we attribute to agents, even though we know they have no opportunity to A at the time of attribution and we have no specific occasion for their A-ing in mind. The ability to golf that I denied I have is a certain *specific* practical ability—in this case, an ability to golf now.[19] My specific concern in this section is specific abilities.

There is an ordinary sense of "able" according to which agents are able to do whatever they do.[20] In this sense of "able," an agent's having A-ed at a time is conceptually sufficient for his having been able to A then. If Sanna backed her car into mine, she was able to do that, in this sense. That is so whether she intentionally or accidentally backed her car into mine. Similarly, if Sanna threw a basketball through a hoop from a distance of ninety feet, she was able to do that in this sense, and that is so whether she was trying to throw it through the hoop, or simply to hit the backboard, or merely to throw it as far as she could. Yesterday, Sanna rolled a six with a fair die in a game of chance. She was able to do that, in the sense of "able" at issue.

I said that there is a sense of "able" in which these claims are true. It can also be said that there is a kind of ability about which claims such as these are true. I call it *simple ability*. I have not claimed that simple ability to A is found *only* in cases in which agents A. Rather, my claim is that an agent's A-ing at a time is sufficient for his having the simple ability to A at that time. Another condition that may be sufficient for this is discussed shortly.

Being simply able to A is distinguishable from being able to A *intentionally*. It is controversial how much control an agent who A-s must have over his A-ing in order to A intentionally. Even so, there are clear illustrations of a difference between control that is appropriate for intentional action and control that falls short. Pilvi has enough control over her body and dice to roll a die intentionally, but, like any normal human being, she lacks control over dice needed for rolling a six intentionally with a single toss of a fair die. Therefore, although she is able to roll a six with a single toss of a fair die, she is not able to do that intentionally. Her throwing a six now owes too much to luck to be intentional. Even if, wrongly thinking that she has magical powers over dice, Pilvi *intends* to throw a six now and does so, she does not intentionally throw a six. A proper account of being able to A intentionally hinges on a proper account of A-ing intentionally and the control that involves. Paul Moser and I have offered an analysis of intentional action (Mele and Moser 1994), but there is no need to insist on that analysis here. However intentional action is to be analyzed, being able to *A* intentionally entails having a simple ability to *A*, and the converse is false.[21] Noticing that the former ability is stronger than the latter in this sense suffices for present purposes. I have no need here for an *analysis* of being able to *A* intentionally nor of the control intentional action requires.

It will be useful to have an easy way of moving back and forth between "ability" claims and "able" claims in terms of the distinction I sketched. I abbreviate "simple ability to *A*" as "*S*-ability" and "ability to *A* intentionally" as "*I*-ability." Corresponding "able" expressions are "*S*-able" and "*I*-able."[22]

I turn now to a pair of views about agents' abilities: a commonsense view and a view favored by libertarians. Again, typical libertarians maintain that acting freely requires being able to perform an alternative action and that determinism precludes this ability. I will motivate the suggestion that a commonsense view of *S*- and *I*-ability might be silent on the question whether determinism precludes this. The suggestion's plausibility enables me to move forward without attempting to resolve a long-standing dispute between libertarians and traditional compatibilists.

Here are two pronouncements of common sense (CS, for short). First, we have both general and specific abilities to do things we never do. Although Bev was able to buy a plane ticket to Beijing, she never did. Thirty years ago, on her seventieth birthday, she was tempted, for the first time, to book a flight to Beijing and was able then to do so straightaway, but she decided against the purchase and never again considered flying there. Second, we occasionally try and fail to do things we are *S*-able to do and things we are *I*-able to do. A skilled putter may fail to sink the next three-foot putt she attempts, even though she was *S*-able and *I*-able to sink it.

According to libertarians and other incompatibilists, an agent who did not *A* at *t* was able at *t* to *A* at *t* only if in a possible world with the same laws of nature and the same past up to *t*, he *A*-s at *t*. On this view, if agents in deterministic worlds are able to do anything at all, they are able to do only what they actually do. For in any world with the same past and laws as *S*'s deterministic world, *Wd*, *S* behaves exactly as he does in *Wd*. For my purposes in this section, I have no stake in accepting or rejecting this view, provided that it can be understood as a view about a *species* of ability. I will suppose that there is a species of ability—*L*-ability—such that, by definition, an agent *S* in *W* has, at the relevant time, the *simple L*-ability to *A* at *t* if and only if there is a possible world with the same past and laws as *W* (either *W* itself or another world) in which *S A*-s at *t*.[23] Similarly, I will suppose that, by definition, an agent *S* in *W* has, at the relevant time, the *L*-ability to *A* *intentionally* at *t* if and only if there is a possible world with the same past and laws as *W* in which *S A*-s intentionally at *t*. One virtue of these accounts is their precision.

It may be argued that any view of *S*- and *I*-ability that makes the two pronouncements I identified presupposes that determinism is false. But such an argument may expect too much of CS views of these abilities. Consider a basketball player, Peta, who is a superb free-throw shooter. Owing to years of practice and the skills she developed, she sinks about 90% of her free throws and typically is *I*-able to sink a free throw. Sometimes, when Peta misses, she has been fouled very hard and sees stars or is dizzy. Normally, however, things just do not go quite right when she misses. Peta may release the ball a little too early or too late, throw it a little too hard or too soft, push a bit too much or too little with her legs, or the like. If Peta's world is deterministic, all occurrences of these problems are deterministically caused. But what CS says about *I*-abilities may not be metaphysically deep. Perhaps, on a CS view of *I*-ability, that, under normal conditions, an agent intentionally *A*-s in the great majority of instances in which he attempts to *A* and the conditions under which he just now tried to *A* were normal is sufficient for his having had the ability to *A* intentionally at the time—even if his attempt failed. If what CS says about *I*-ability is inseparable from its alleged claims about *freedom-level ability*, discussion of familiar issues dividing compatibilists and incompatibilists would be in order now.[24] However, it is conceivable that a CS view of *I*-ability is silent on freedom-level ability, that it takes no explicit stand on whether determinism is true or false, and, indeed, that it ignores the topic of determinism.

What about simple ability—in particular, an *S*-ability to *A* possessed by an agent who is not able to *A* intentionally? When Pekka tosses a fair die, he tosses a six about a sixth of the time. He has experimented with ways of trying to roll a particular number—a six, for example—but he has not developed any special dice-rolling skills. Just now, Pekka is playing a board game and is about to roll a die. If his world is deterministic, then whatever number he tosses, his tossing that number is deterministically caused. Suppose he throws a five. Was he able to throw a six? Perhaps, according to CS, that, under normal conditions, an agent *A*-s (e.g., rolls a six) about a sixth of the time he *B*-s (e.g., rolls a die) and that the conditions under which he just now *B*-ed were normal is sufficient for his having been *S*-able to *A* at the time.[25]

The conditions that I suggested may suffice, according to CS, for Peta's being *I*-able to sink her free throw and for Pekka's being *S*-able to toss a six on his next roll are compatible with Peta's missing her shot and with Pekka's rolling a five, as in fact they did. CS folks should welcome this point. After all, an agent's being able to *A*, intentionally or otherwise, is not commonly deemed sufficient for his *A*-ing. (I am able to wear a kilt, but I doubt I ever will. Just now, a friend gave me a kilt and dared me to wear it to lunch. I declined.) If we know that Peta's and Pekka's world is deterministic, then we know, given how things turned out, that the state of their world millions of years ago and the laws of nature are such that, at *t*, Peta misses her shot and Pekka rolls a five. But "*S* does not *A* at *t*" is not commonly regarded as entailing "*S* is unable at *t* to *A* at *t*." Its being causally determined that *S* will not *A* at *t* does entail that *S* lacks certain *L*-abilities. However, conceivably, some CS folks who are compelled to think about determinism may judge, consistently with their CS view of *S*- and *I*-ability, that *L*-abilities have compatibilist analogues—that is, analogues compatible with determinism. Other CS folks may judge that there can be no such analogous abilities. But such a judgment may reach beyond their CS view of *S*- and *I*-ability rather than being an implicit pronouncement of it.

Philosophers happy to talk in terms of possible worlds will say that an agent in a world *W* is *S*-able to *A* at *t* if and only if he *A*-s at *t* in some relevant possible world, and is *I*-able to *A* at *t* if and only if he *A*-s intentionally at *t* in some relevant possible world. One way to see the disagreement between incompatibilists and compatibilists about determinism and being able to do otherwise is as a disagreement about what worlds are relevant. According to incompatibilists, all and only worlds with the same past and natural laws as *W* are relevant; they hold the past and the laws fixed. Compatibilists disagree. I have been suggesting, in effect, that a representative of CS who is forced to think about possible worlds may take the following position on an agent who, at *t*, tried and failed to *A* or played a game of chance in which he "took a chance" at *A*-ing but did not *A*, *A* in both cases being a kind of action the agent has often performed: relevant worlds include all worlds with a very similar past and natural laws in which the agent has the same "*A*-rate" under normal conditions (e.g., the same rate of intentionally sinking a free throw and the same rate of throwing a six when he throws a fair die) and in which conditions are normal at the relevant time. This is not to say, of course, that these are the *only* worlds that may be deemed relevant. After all, one would want to leave room for agents' being able to do things in abnormal circumstances. For example, Peta presumably is able to sink a free throw, and may be able to sink it intentionally, even when the hoop's circumference is slightly smaller than normal. One would also want to leave room for abilities to do new things—for example, sinking one's first free throw or putt.

The expression "normal conditions" cries out for attention. CS may not say anything very detailed about it, however. Presumably, normal conditions in Pekka's case exclude such things as a lopsided die and a properly shaped and weighted die that is being controlled by fancy machines. But perhaps as CS understands normal conditions, they do not exclude a combination of normal gravitational forces and normal velocities, trajectories, spins, and bounces of normal dice that may be a major part of a deterministic cause of Pekka's die's landing five-up. Similar points may be made about Peta's case. Normal conditions exclude a deformed basketball, a smaller than normal hoop, dizziness, blurred vision, and the like. However, perhaps normal conditions, as CS understands them, do not exclude various small-scale bodily events that are in the normal range for Peta when she is attempting a free throw but may add up to a major part of a deterministic cause of her shot's hitting the rim and bouncing away.

The simplicity of the accounts I suggested of simple *L*-ability to *A* and *L*-ability to *A* intentionally is attractive. I doubt that equally simple, promising accounts of *S*-ability and *I*-ability are accessible from the commonsense perspective on these abilities that I have been discussing.[26] In the literature, what looks like the most promising account, from this perspective, of something resembling *I*-ability—an analysis of a kind of responsiveness to reasons—is intricate. Incidentally, it comes, not from traditional compatibilists, but from semicompatibilists, philosophers who hold that determinism is compatible with free action and moral responsibility, even if it is incompatible with agents' ever having been able to act otherwise than they did (Fischer 1994; Fischer and Ravizza 1998).[27] Semicompatibilists contend that free action and moral responsibility do not require an ability of this kind, and they need not be in the business of providing an analysis of being able to *A*. In any case, although simplicity has its virtues, a true appeal to greater simplicity would not show that there are not, in addition to simple

L-ability to *A* and *L*-ability to *A* intentionally, non-*L* analogues of these abilities in some deterministic worlds.

I mentioned that it is often difficult to be sure what the contributors to the literature on free will and moral responsibility mean by "able." A brief discussion of a case in point is appropriate. A central plank in Peter van Inwagen's argument against the theoretical utility of agent causation is, roughly, the claim that an agent who knows that "it is undetermined" (2000, p. 17) whether he will *A* is not able to *A*—claim *C*, for short. Van Inwagen's defense of this claim features a scenario in which he knows, perhaps because God told him, that there are "exactly two possible continuations of the present, . . . in one of which" he reveals a damaging fact about a friend to the press "and in the other of which" he keeps silent about his friend (p. 17). He also knows that "the objective . . . probability of [his] 'telling' is 0.43 and that the objective . . . probability of [his] keeping silent is 0.57." Van Inwagen says that he does not see how he can "be in a position to" promise his friend that he will keep silent. He adds:

> But if I believe that I am able to keep silent, I should, it would seem, regard myself as being in a position to make this promise. What more do I need to regard myself as being in a position to promise to do X than a belief that I am *able* to do X? Therefore, in this situation, I should not regard myself as being able to keep silent. (And I cannot see on what grounds third-person observers of my situation could dispute this first-person judgment.) (pp. 17–18)

This, van Inwagen says, is an "argument for the conclusion that it is false that I am able to keep silent" (p. 18).[28]

Two sources of distraction should be eliminated. First, some people understand sincere promising as one species of promising and insincere promising as another. If the distinction is granted, van Inwagen's claims about promising should be understood to be about *sincere* promising. Second, there may well be a significant difference in many cases between the objective probability that an agent will keep silent and the objective probability that he will keep silent given that he sincerely promises to do so. I will assume that the 0.57 objective probability van Inwagen has in mind is the probability of the latter. After all, even if the objective unconditional probability that an agent will keep silent about a friend is 0.57, the objective probability that he will keep silent given that he sincerely promises to may be 1. An agent who knows that conditional fact about himself certainly seems to be in a position sincerely to promise to keep silent, other things being equal.[29]

There are many things I believe I am able to do that I do not "regard myself as being in a position to promise [sincerely] to do"—for example, toss heads now with the quarter I am holding. My belief that I am able to do this is an utterly ordinary belief. The kind of ability it is about is what I called simple ability. Van Inwagen's belief that he is not able to keep silent in the imagined scenario presumably is not about simple ability. We who believe that "the objective...probability of [his] keeping silent is 0.57" can easily imagine that he does keep silent. If he keeps silent, he is *S*-able to keep silent; that he is so able is entailed by his keeping silent.[30] And because what we are imagining is a direct "continuation of the present," it is natural to infer that van Inwagen has that ability already.

Some readers may think that the 0.57 objective probability that van Inwagen will keep silent if he sincerely promises to do so is too low for him to be *I*-able to keep silent, and others may disagree. Is a basketball player whose success rate at the free-throw line is 57% and who now, owing primarily to his pertinent skills, has a 0.57 objective probability of sinking the free throw he is about to attempt able to sink it intentionally? Readers' opinions may diverge; some may have higher standards than others regarding levels of control or reliability required for intentional action. However, for my purposes, disagreements of this kind can be set aside. Van Inwagen's argument, if it succeeds at all, should succeed even when the objective probabilities are significantly altered—for example, from 0.57 versus 0.43 to, say, 0.95 versus 0.05. (Recall claim *C*, that an agent who knows that "it is undetermined" whether he will *A* is not able to *A*. If *C* is true, it is true of an agent who knows that it is undetermined whether he will keep silent about a friend, even if he promises to do so and knows that the objective probability of his keeping silent given that he promises is 0.95.) Few people would deny that an extraordinary player with a success rate of 95% and a 0.95 objective probability of sinking the free throw he is about to attempt is able to sink it intentionally, other things being equal, and my guess is that few would deny that van Inwagen is able to keep silent intentionally in a version of the case with the new probabilities I mentioned.

Either *C* is false or van Inwagen means something by "able" that is more restrictive than "*S*-able" and "*I*-able," even on libertarian readings of these expressions. I speculated elsewhere about what he might

mean (Mele 2003b) and will not do so again here. In light of what I
have said about agents' abilities in this section, readers will find that
there is relatively little need to speculate about what I mean by "able."
Whatever restrictive meaning van Inwagen might have had in mind
for "able," it is worth noting that if there are free actions, agents can
freely *A* in some scenarios without being even *I*-able to *A*. Here are the
facts about Al.[31] Intending to vote for Gore, he pulled the Gore lever in a
Florida voting booth. Unbeknownst to Al, that lever was attached to an
indeterministic randomizing device: pulling it gave him only a 0.001
chance of actually voting for Gore. Luckily, he succeeded in producing a
Gore vote. It is very plausible that Al's voting for Gore was too lucky to
count as an intentional action (see Mele and Moser 1994) and that,
given his circumstances, Al was not *I*-able to vote for Gore—that is, to
produce a Gore vote—at the time. However, if there are free actions, it is
difficult to see why Al's voting for Gore is not among them, other things
being equal. If the action is free and if what I said is very plausible is true,
Al freely voted for Gore while not being *I*-able to vote for him.

Henceforth, in this book, the default reading of "able" in sentences
about agents' abilities is "*S*-able." If actions of some kinds can only be
performed intentionally, then, of course, an agent who is able to perform an action of one of these kinds is *I*-able to perform it.

NOTES

1. In principle, a theorist can be a compatibilist about determinism and free
action while being an incompatibilist about determinism and moral responsibility, and vice versa. One can be more fine-grained in one's use of "compatibilism" when discussing such views. For stylistic reasons, the broader
definition of "compatibilism" to which this note is appended is preferable for
the purposes of this book.
2. This is not to say that *every* disjunction of propositions with subjective
probabilities between 0 and 1 should have a higher subjective probability than
each of the disjuncts: consider the disjunction "*p* or *p*." My claim is about the
propositions at issue here.
3. Incidentally, it is possible to take a historical line on moral responsibility
while embracing the nonhistorical requirement I mentioned on free action (see
Kane 1989 for an instance of this.)
4. This distinction is similar to Fischer's distinction between "guidance"
and "regulative" control (1994, pp. 132–35).
5. That the difference between deterministic and indeterministic control is
just a difference in setting may be what Susan Hurley has in mind when she

remarks that "although control is compatible with indeterminism," no kind of control requires indeterminism and what Fischer calls "'regulative control' is not a kind of control at all" (2003, p. 44). She remarks that "there could be deterministic or indeterministic realizations of a given control system" (p. 72), and her thought seems to be that the same *kind* of control is associated with both realizations. However, just as I see nothing wrong with saying that deterministic and indeterministic widget makers are two different kinds of widget maker (even if they differ only in this way and in any ways entailed by this difference), I see nothing wrong with saying that deterministic and indeterministic control are two different kinds of control. I place no special weight on the word "kinds" in this connection.

6. For relatively recent luck-based worries about libertarian accounts of free action or moral responsibility, see Almeida and Bernstein 2003; Cohen forthcoming; Haji 1999; Mele 1995, pp. 195–204, 1999a, 1999b; and Strawson 1994.

7. Proximal decisions and intentions also include decisions and intentions to continue doing something that one is doing and decisions and intentions to start *A*-ing (e.g., start running a mile) straightaway.

8. On the actional nature of deciding to *A*, see section 4.

9. Diana toys with the thought that the agent may be blamed for the decision if past free decisions of his had the result, by way of their effect on his character, that there was a significant chance that he would decide contrary to his best judgment. But she quickly realizes that the same worry arises about past free decisions the agent made.

10. Worries about luck are not eliminated by replacing the "could have done otherwise *freely*" requirement with a requirement that the agent could have done otherwise (even if only unfreely) or with a requirement that something else could have happened at the time than that the agent *A*-ed. See chapter 3.

11. See Mele 1995, ch. 12. Also see Dennett 1978, pp. 294–99; Ekstrom 2000, pp. 103–29; Fischer 1995; and Kane 1985, pp. 101–10.

12. Regarding the parenthetical clause, notice that not all deterministically caused events need be part of a deterministic chain that stretches back even for several moments, much less to a time close to the big bang. Imagine that a Geiger counter is used as a trigger for a powerful bomb that is located in a wooden shed (see Schrödinger 1983, p. 157). As it happens, a radioactive particle decays at *t* in the vicinity of the Geiger counter. The decay event, which was not deterministically caused, causes the Geiger counter to click, which in turn causes the bomb to explode, and the explosion blows the shed to bits. This may happen in a world with laws of nature such that in any world with the same laws in which things are just as they are when the bomb begins to explode, the shed is blown to bits. The shed's destruction may be deterministically caused by the explosion, even though an important cause of the explosion was not deterministically caused.

13. On modest libertarianism in particular, see Clarke 2003, pp. 61–66.

14. Just as I distinguished between ultimate and proximal control, one may distinguish between ultimate and proximal *luck*. Perhaps millions of years ago, in a deterministic universe, conditions were such that their combination with the laws of nature entails that today Karl is an exceptionally kind person whereas Carl is a ruthless killer. Here we have ultimate luck—good and bad. Libertarians have been much more impressed by it than by proximal luck.

15. See, for example, Frankfurt 1988, pp. 174–76; Kane 1996, p. 24; Kaufman 1966, p. 34; McCann 1986a, pp. 254–55; Mele 1992, p. 156; 2003a, ch. 9; Pink 1996, p. 3; and Searle 2001, p. 94.

16. This paragraph and two of the next three derive from Mele 2004.

17. Kane 1996, ch. 2, is a notable exception.

18. Pereboom sometimes applies the expression "free in the sense required for moral responsibility" to actions (2001, p. 1). This is problematic. Suppose that actions of a certain kind are such that, necessarily, agents are morally responsible for them only if they perform them freely, in some relatively strong sense of "freely," and that, necessarily, any action that is free in that strong sense also is free in the much weaker sense in which some actions of mice are free. Then an agent's being morally responsible for actions of this kind also requires that he performed them freely in the weaker sense, and no action is free in *the* sense required (because there is not just one sense of "free" in which being morally responsible for actions of this kind requires that they be free actions). The expression "free in the *strongest* sense required" avoids this problem.

19. Although I am not able to golf just now, nor to golf two minutes from now, I am able to get to a driving range in about twenty minutes. It is very natural to say that I am able now to start hitting golf balls in twenty minutes or so.

20. J. L. Austin writes, "Of course it follows merely from the premise that he does it, that he has the ability to do it, according to ordinary English" (1970, p. 227).

21. Tomis Kapitan notes a similar distinction between abilities (1996, pp. 102–4).

22. In ordinary English, people sometimes balk at moving from "able" claims to corresponding "ability" claims. Ann rolled a six with a fair die. It is natural to say that she was able to do that, and it is perhaps less natural to say that she had an ability to do that. However, notice the awkwardness of the following assertion: "Ann was able to roll a six, but she had no ability to roll a six." Of course, a speaker who makes this assertion can draw a distinction in light of which what he means to assert is true. For example, he can say that he understands "*S* was able to *A*" in such a way that it is entailed by "*S A*-ed" and that he understands having an ability to *A* as entailing being able to *A* intentionally. For my purposes in this chapter, attention to alleged differences between "able" claims and "ability" claims would be a source of distraction.

28 • *Free Will and Luck*

23. The *L* stands for "libertarian," because libertarians and other incompatibilists typically favor an understanding of ability along these lines. The analysis offered of simple *L*-ability can be strengthened as follows for a libertarian who holds that even an agent who *A*-ed (intentionally) was not able to *A* unless he was also able at the time not to *A*: *S* has, at the relevant time, the simple *L**-ability to *A* at *t* if and only if either (1) *S A*-s at *t* and there is a possible world with the same past and laws in which *S* does not *A* at *t* or (2) *S* does not *A* at *t* and there is a possible world with the same past and laws in which *S A*-s at *t*.

24. Freedom-level ability may be understood as a kind of ability such that if, setting aside ability conditions, everything necessary for an action's being free were present, adding a suitably exercised ability of this kind would yield sufficient conditions for the action's being free.

25. *B*, like *A*, is to be read as an action variable. I will not take a stand on how actions are to be individuated—for example, on whether Pekka's rolling the die and his rolling a five are the same action under different descriptions or different actions. For a useful discussion of various positions on action individuation, see Ginet 1990, ch. 3. (Notice that if Pekka's rolling the die and his rolling a five are the same action under different descriptions, the same action can be intentional under one description and not intentional under another.)

26. The difficulty of producing an *analysis* of ability from this perspective has been a thorn in the side of traditional compatibilists, who agree with libertarians that freely *A*-ing and being morally responsible for *A*-ing require that one is able to do otherwise than *A* but disagree with them about the nature of this ability.

27. John Fischer describes his semicompatibilism as the view that "moral responsibility is compatible with causal determinism, even if causal determinism is incompatible with freedom to do otherwise" (1994, p. 180). It also is a view about free action. Fischer asserts that "guidance control is the freedom-relevant condition necessary and sufficient for moral responsibility" (p. 168), and he reports that his "account of guidance control (and moral responsibility) ... yields 'semicompatibilism'" (p. 180). Thus, I take semicompatibilism to encompass the thesis that free action is compatible with determinism (as traditional compatibilists assert), even if "determinism is incompatible with freedom to do otherwise" (which traditional compatibilists deny).

28. Van Inwagen's claim about agent causation is that the further knowledge that he "will be the agent-cause" of his conduct in this scenario would not undermine his belief that he is not able to keep silent (2000, p. 18).

29. Some readers may be distracted by the idea that free actions can have objective probabilities or by the idea that these probabilities can be known. However, for van Inwagen's purposes, nothing stronger is needed than a person's believing of herself that, because she is an indeterministic agent, there is a significant chance that she will not *A* even if she promises to *A*.

30. The abilities that concern me in this chapter, as I said, are *actional* ones. It is not clear that keeping silent is an action, even when one intentionally keeps silent (Mele 2003a, pp. 146–54). For the purposes of this chapter, however, the simplifying assumption that intentional "not-doings" (e.g., not telling on one's friend, not voting in today's election) are actions is harmless.

31. For a similar case, see Mele 1995, p. 14, n. 11.

Free Will and Neuroscience

I have what may be an irresistible urge to include in this book a chapter on neurobiologist Benjamin Libet's work on free will. This work has attracted a great deal of attention in a variety of fields, including philosophy.[1] Psychologists Patrick Haggard, Chris Newman, and Elena Magno (1999, p. 291) describe an article by Libet and colleagues (Libet, Gleason et al. 1983) as "one of the most philosophically challenging papers in modern scientific psychology." A striking thesis of that 1983 article is that "the brain . . . 'decides' to initiate or, at the least, prepare to initiate [certain actions] at a time before there is any reportable subjective awareness that such a decision has taken place" (p. 640; also see Libet 1985, p. 536).[2] In a recent article, Libet pointedly asserts: "If the 'act now' process is initiated unconsciously, then conscious free will is not doing it" (2001, p. 62; also see 2004, p. 136).

Elsewhere, I have used some of Libet's results to shed light on some philosophical questions about self-control and akrasia (Mele 1997; 2003a, ch. 8). What I found useful were the data, not Libet's interpretation of them. To use his data without misleading my readers, I found it necessary to criticize a certain central element of Libet's interpretation of them that is directly relevant to the thesis I quoted from Libet, Gleason et al. 1983. In setting the stage for my own use of Libet's data in understanding our prospects for exercising self-control in the face of temptation at roughly the time of action, I argued that they fall well short of justifying his thesis, and I defended an alternative interpretation of them. Part of the problem is that Libet and his colleagues ignore a directly relevant conceptual distinction between deciding and intending, on the one hand, and motivational states like wanting, on the other.

Patrick Haggard, in his contribution to a recent discussion with Libet, says: "Conceptual analysis could help" (Haggard and Libet 2001, p. 62). Haggard is referring specifically to conceptual differences between "will (generation of action) and choice (selection of action)" (p. 61). My conceptual focus in this chapter is on another pair of phenomena: wanting and intending. Drawing partly from Mele 1997, I criticize Libet's defense of his thesis about decisions and extend the criticism to his conclusions about free will.

1. Conceptual Matters

Because Libet uses such terms as "intention," "decision," "wanting," "wish," and "urge" interchangeably, some conceptual preliminaries are in order in interpreting his work.[3] I start with a distinction between wanting and intending. Its relevance to interpreting Libet's results will become clear in section 2.

Wanting to do something is distinguishable from intending to do it. One can want (or desire, or have an urge) to A without being at all settled on A-ing. Yesterday, I wanted to meet a friend at a 7:00 movie and I wanted to join another friend at a 7:00 lecture. I knew that I could do either but not both. I needed to make up my mind about what to do. In forming an intention to go to the movie, I made up my mind to do that. To intend to do something is, at least in part, to be settled (but not necessarily irrevocably) on doing it (Mele 1992, chs. 9 and 10). Wanting to do something is compatible with being unsettled about whether to do it. In normal scenarios, the transition from wanting to A to intending to A is progress toward A-ing (Mele 1992, pp. 72–73 and chs. 9 and 10). For reasons of convenience, one may use the verbs *want* and *desire* interchangeably, and it is natural to treat the noun *urge* as a label for a kind of desire. If wanting and intending have importantly different functional roles in the production of intentional actions, as I and others have argued they do, failing to distinguish intending from wanting can lead to serious errors.[4]

It should also be noted that some of our decisions and intentions are for the nonimmediate future and others are not. I might decide on Tuesday to attend a meeting on Friday, and I might decide now to phone my father now. The intention formed in the former decision is aimed at action three days in the future. (Of course, if I need to prepare for the meeting—or need to write a note on my calendar to remind myself of it—the intention may motivate relevant overt conduct sooner than that.) The intention I form when I decide to phone my father now is about what to do now. I call intentions and decisions of these kinds, respectively, *distal* and *proximal* intentions and decisions (Mele 1992, pp. 143–44, 158). Proximal decisions and intentions also include decisions and intentions to continue doing something that one is doing and decisions and intentions to start *A*-ing (e.g., start climbing a hill) straightaway.

A distinction between *relatively specific* and *relatively unspecific* intentions also is in order. Bob now intends to attend next week's departmental meeting. That is a more specific intention than the intention he had, at the beginning of the academic year, to attend at least a few departmental meetings during the year. He had the latter intention without being settled on any specific meetings to attend. In another illustration, Cathy has agreed to be a subject in an experiment in which subjects are instructed to salute whenever they feel like it on at least forty occasions during a two-hour period. When Cathy begins her participation in the experiment she has a relatively unspecific intention to salute many times during the next two hours. At various times during the experiment, she has specific proximal intentions to salute.

I claimed that it is risky to ignore functional differences between wanting and intending. It is plausible that effective proximal intentions play roles in the initiation, guidance, and sustaining of intentional actions and that effective proximal desires to *A* help generate proximal intentions to *A* (Mele 1992, chs. 8 and 10). On this view of things, the primary causal contribution such desires make to the production of intentional actions is mediated by associated proximal intentions.[5]

2. Libet's Work

This section develops an interpretation of Libet's work that is sensitive to the conceptual points just made. In some of his studies, subjects are instructed to flex their right wrists or the fingers of their right hands whenever they wish. Electrical readings from the scalp—averaged over at least 40 flexings for each subject—show a "negative shift" in "readiness potentials" (RPs) beginning at about 550 milliseconds (ms) before the time at which an electromyogram shows relevant muscular motion to begin (1985, pp. 529–30).[6] Subjects are also instructed to "recall . . . the spatial clock position of a revolving spot at the time of [their] initial awareness" (p. 529) of something, *x*, that Libet variously describes as an "intention," "urge," "wanting," "decision," "will," or "wish" to move (see n. 3). On the average, "RP onset" preceded what the subjects reported to be the time of their initial awareness of *x* (time W) by 350 ms. Time W, then, preceded the beginning of muscle motion by about 200 ms.

Diagram 1

−550 ms	−200 ms	0 ms
RP onset	time W	muscle begins to move

(Libet finds independent evidence of a slight error in subjects' recall of the times at which they first become aware of sensations [pp. 531, 534]. Correcting for that error, time W is −150 ms.)

At what point, if any, does a specific intention to flex arise in Libet's subjects? Again, Libet, Gleason et al. write: "the brain . . . 'decides' to initiate or . . . prepare to initiate the act . . . before there is any reportable subjective awareness that such a decision has taken place" (1983, p. 640). If we ignore the second disjunct, this quotation (given its context) apparently offers the answer that a specific intention to flex appears on the scene with "RP onset" about 550 ms before relevant muscular motion and about 350 to 400 ms before the agent becomes aware of the intention (see Libet 1985, p. 539); for to decide to initiate an act is to form an intention to initiate it.[7] But are decision and intention the most suitable mental items to associate with RP onset? Again, Libet describes the relevant occurrence of which the agent later becomes aware not only as a "decision" and the onset of an "intention" to move but also as the onset of an "urge," "wanting," and a "wish" to move. This leaves it open that at −550 ms, rather than acquiring an intention or making a decision of which he is not conscious, the agent instead acquires an *urge* or *desire* of which he is not conscious—and perhaps an urge or desire that is stronger than any competing urge or desire at the time, a *preponderant* urge or desire. It is also left open that what emerges around −550 ms is a pretty reliable causal contributor to an urge.

I believe that if Libet himself were to distinguish between intending and wanting (including having an urge) along the lines I sketched, he might find it more credible to associate the readiness potentials with the latter than with the former. To explain why, I turn to another experiment reported in Libet 1985 (and elsewhere).

Libet proposes that "conscious volitional control may operate not to initiate the volitional process but to select and control it, either by permitting or triggering the final motor outcome of the unconsciously initiated process or by vetoing the progression to actual motor activation" (1985, p. 529; also see 1999, p. 54; 2004, pp. 139, 142–43, 149). "In a veto, the later phase of cerebral motor processing would be blocked, so that actual activation of the motoneurons to the muscles would not occur" (1985, p. 537). Libet offers two kinds of evidence to support the suggestion about vetoing. One kind is generated by an experiment in which subjects are instructed both to prepare to flex their fingers at a prearranged time (as indicated by a revolving spot on a clock face) and "to veto the developing intention/preparation to act . . . about 100 to 200 ms before the prearranged clock time" (p. 538). Subjects receive both instructions at the same time. Libet writes:

> A ramplike pre-event potential was still recorded . . . resembl[ing] the RP of self-initiated acts when preplanning is present. . . . The form of the "veto" RP differed (in most but not all cases) from those "preset" RPs that were followed by actual movements [in another experiment]; the main negative potential tended to alter in direction (flattening or reversing) at about 150–250 ms before the preset time. . . . This difference suggests that the conscious veto interfered with the final development of RP processes leading to action. . . . The preparatory cerebral processes associated with an RP can and do develop even when intended motor action is vetoed at approximately the time that conscious intention would normally appear before a voluntary act. (1985, p. 538)[8]

Keep in mind that the subjects were instructed in advance *not* to flex their fingers, but to prepare to flex them at the prearranged time and to "veto" this. The subjects intentionally complied with the request. They intended from the beginning not to flex their fingers at the appointed time. So what is indicated by the RP? Presumably, not the acquisition or presence of an *intention* to flex; for then, at some point in time, the subjects would have both an intention to flex at the prearranged time and an intention not to flex at that time. And how can a normal agent simultaneously be settled on A-ing at t and settled on not A-ing at t?[9] That is, it is very plausible that Libet is mistaken in describing what is vetoed as "*intended* motor action" (p. 538, my emphasis).

If the RP in the veto scenario is not associated with an intention to flex at the appointed time, with what might it be associated? In the passage I quoted from Libet 1985 (p. 538), Libet compares "the 'veto'

RP" with (*a*) " 'preset' RPs that were followed by actual movements" and (*b*) "the RP of self-initiated acts when preplanning is present." The RP referred to in *a* is produced in experiments in which subjects are instructed to watch the clock and flex when the revolving spot reaches "a pre-set 'clock time' " (Libet et al. 1982, p. 325). "The subject was encouraged to try to make his movement coincide as closely as possible with the arrival of the spot at the pre-set time." The RP referred to in *b* is produced in two kinds of studies: (1) studies in which subjects instructed to flex spontaneously are not regularly encouraged to aim for spontaneity (Libet et al. 1982, pp. 324–26) and (2) studies in which subjects who did receive such encouragement reported that they experienced "some 'pre-planning,' " even if only in "a minority of the 40 self-initiated acts that occurred in the series for that averaged RP" (p. 328). "Even when some pre-plannings were recalled and reported, subjects insisted that the more specific urge or intention to actually move did not arise in that pre-planning stage" (p. 329). Reports of "pre-planning" seem to include reports of thoughts about when to flex and reports of anticipations of flexing (pp. 328–29). Libet and his coauthors remark that "Subject S.B. described his advance feelings [of pre-planning] as 'pre-tensions' rather than pre-plannings to act" (p. 329). This subject may have meant that he occasionally experienced tension that he expected to result in flexing.

The RPs referred to in *a* and *b* have a very similar form (Libet et al. 1982, pp. 330, 333–34; Libet 1985, p. 532). RPs with that form are called "type I RPs" (p. 326). They have significantly earlier onsets than the RPs produced in studies of subjects regularly encouraged to aim for spontaneity who report that they experienced no "pre-planning"— "type II RPs." "The form of the 'veto' RP" is the form of type I RPs until "about 150–250 ms before the preset time" (1985, p. 538). What does the veto group (group V) have in common until that time with the three kinds of subjects who produce type I RPs: those with a preset time for flexing (group PS), those who are not regularly encouraged to aim for spontaneity (group N), and those who are regularly encouraged to aim for spontaneity but who report some "pre-planning" (group PP)?

Presumably, subjects in group PS are watching the clock with the intention of flexing at the preset time. But it certainly does not follow from that and the similar RPs in groups N and PP—and V for a time— that members of each of these groups are watching the clock with a similar intention to flex. For one thing, as I have explained, it is very likely that group V—subjects instructed in advance to prepare to flex and then veto the preparation—are watching the clock *without* an intention to flex at the targeted time. Given that the members of group V lack this intention, we should look for something that groups V and PS actually have in common that might be signified by the similarity in the RPs until "about 150–250 ms before the preset time." One possibility is that members of both groups have *urges* to flex (or to prepare to flex) soon—or undergo brain events that are pretty reliable relatively proximal causal contributors to such urges—that are associated with an RP and regularly play a role in generating subsequent flexings in the absence of "vetoing."[10] In the case of group V, perhaps a subject's wanting to comply with the instructions—including the instruction to prepare to flex at the appointed time—together with his recognition that the time is approaching, produces a growing urge to (prepare to) flex soon, a pretty reliable causal contributor to such an urge, or the motor preparedness typically associated with such an urge. A related possibility is suggested by the observation that "the pattern of brain activity associated with imagining making a movement is very similar to the pattern of activity associated with preparing to make a movement" (Spence and Frith 1999). The instructions given to group V would naturally elicit imagining flexing very soon. Finally, the "flattening or reversing" of the RP "at about 150–250 ms before the preset time" might indicate a consequence of the subject's "vetoing" his preparation.

What about groups N and PP? It is possible that they, along with the subjects in groups PS and V, begin acquiring urges to flex at a greater temporal distance from 0 ms than do subjects encouraged to flex spontaneously who report no preplanning. That difference may be indicated by type I RPs' having significantly earlier onsets than type II RPs. Another possibility is consistent with this. Earlier, I distinguished proximal from distal intentions, and Libet himself recognizes the distinction (see Libet et al. 1982, pp. 329, 334; Libet 1989, pp. 183–84). Presumably, subjects in group PS respond to the instruction to flex at a preset time with an intention to flex at that time. This is a distal intention. As the preset time for flexing draws very near, that intention may become, help produce, or be replaced by a proximal intention to flex, an intention to *flex now*, as one naturally says (see Libet 1989, p. 183; 1999, p. 54; 2004, p. 148). That may happen around the time subjects in group V veto their urge to flex or closer to 0 ms. And it may happen at or around the time subjects in groups N and PP acquire a proximal intention to flex. They may acquire such an intention without having had a distal intention to flex soon: recall that members of group V probably had no distal intention to flex soon and that their RPs are very similar to those of groups N, PP, and PS until "about 150–250 ms before the preset time." All this is consistent with the similarities in RPs in the various groups of subjects, on the assumption that no segment of the RPs before about −150 to −250 ms for subjects in group PS specifically represents subjects' distal intentions to flex at the preset time— as opposed, for example, to something that such intentions have in common with distal urges to flex (or to prepare to flex) at the preset time—even though those intentions are present.

The main difference between type I and type II RPs, in Haggard's words, is that the former have "earlier onsets than" the latter (Haggard and Libet 2001, p. 49). The earlier onsets may be correlated with earlier acquisitions of urges to flex soon—urges that may be brought on, variously, by the instruction to flex at a preset time (group PS), the instruction to prepare to flex at a preset time and to veto that later (group V), unsolicited conscious thoughts about when to flex (groups N and PP), or unsolicited conscious anticipations of flexing (groups N and PP). (Of course, it is possible that some such thoughts and anticipations are instead products, in part, of urges to flex soon.) These urge inciters (or perhaps urge products, in the case of some experiences in groups N and PP) are absent in subjects encouraged to flex spontaneously who report no "pre-planning"—at least, if their reports are accurate. If type I RPs indicate urges, or urges together with proximal intentions that emerge later than the urges do, the same may be true of type II RPs. The difference in the two kinds of RP may mainly be a matter of when the urge emerges—that is, how long before 0 ms. Once again, Libet describes in a variety of ways the mental item that is indicated by RPs. Even if "intention" and "decision" (to flex) are not apt choices, "urge" and "wanting" are still in the running.

If "RP onset" in cases of "spontaneous" flexing indicates the emergence of an urge to flex soon, proximal intentions to flex may emerge at some point between RP onset and time W, *at* time W, or *after* time W: at time W the agent may be aware only of an urge that has not yet issued in a proximal intention. Again, Libet asserts, "In a veto, the later phase of cerebral motor processing would be blocked, so that actual activation of the motoneurons to the muscles would not occur" (1985, p. 537). Perhaps, in nonveto cases, activation of these motoneurons is the direct result of the acquisition of a proximal intention (Gomes 1999, pp. 68, 72; Mele

1997, pp. 322–24). Libet suggests that this activation event occurs between 10 and 90 ms before the muscle begins moving and apparently favors an answer in the 10- to 50-ms range (p. 537). Elsewhere, he asserts that the activation event can occur no later than 50 ms before the onset of muscle motion (2004, pp. 137–38).

Although I will not make much of the following point, it merits mention that urges that may be correlated with RP onset at −550 ms might not be *proximal* urges, strictly speaking. Possibly, they are urges to flex *very soon*, as opposed to urges to flex straightaway. And perhaps they evolve into, or produce, proximal urges. Another possibility is that urges to flex very soon give rise to proximal intentions to flex without first evolving into or producing proximal urges to flex. Some disambiguation is in order. A smoker who is rushing toward a smoking section in an airport with the intention of lighting up as soon as he enters it wants to smoke soon. That want or desire has a specific temporal target—the time at which he enters the smoking section. A smoker walking outside the airport may want to smoke soon without having a specific time in mind. Libet's subjects, like the latter smoker, might at times have urges or desires to flex that lack a specific temporal target. Desires to *A* very soon, or to *A*, beginning very soon, in this sense of "very soon," are *roughly proximal* action-desires.

I have been using a (roughly) proximal urge to flex as an *example* of something that might be indicated by type II RPs beginning around −550 ms. The alternatives I mentioned are (roughly) proximal urges to prepare to flex, brain events that are pretty reliable relatively proximal causal contributors to such urges or to (roughly) proximal urges to flex, relevant motor preparedness, and imagining flexing very soon. It would be helpful to have a name for this collection of alternatives: I opt for the name *(roughly) proximal urge**. What I dub the *urge* hypothesis* is the hypothesis that one or another of these things is indicated by type II RPs beginning around −550 ms. "Urge" sans asterisk continues to mean "urge"—not "urge*."

Libet's experimental design promotes consciousness of urges and intentions to flex, because his subjects are instructed in advance to be prepared to report on them—or something like them—later, using the clock to pinpoint the time they are first noticed. For my purposes, what is of special interest are the relative times of the emergence of a (roughly) proximal urge* to flex, the emergence of a proximal *intention* to flex, and consciousness of the intention. If RP onset indicates the emergence of proximal, or roughly proximal, urges* to flex, and if acquisitions of corresponding intentions directly activate the moto-neurons to the relevant muscles, we have the following picture of subjects encouraged to flex "spontaneously" who report no "pre-planning"—subjects who produce type II RPs:

Diagram 2

a. −550 ms: proximal or roughly proximal urge* to flex emerges
b. −90 to −50 ms: acquisition of corresponding proximal intention[11]
c. 0 ms: muscle begins to move.[12]

Possibly, the intention is *consciously* acquired. My point here is simply that this diagram is *consistent* with Libet's data on type II RPs and on time W.

I mentioned that Libet offered a second kind of evidence for "veto control." Subjects encouraged to flex "spontaneously" (in nonveto experiments) "reported that during some of the trials a recallable conscious urge to act appeared but was 'aborted' or somehow suppressed before any actual movement occurred; in such cases the subject simply waited for another urge to appear, which, when consummated, constituted the actual event whose RP was recorded" (1985, p. 538). RPs were not recorded for suppressed urges. But if these urges fit the pattern of unsuppressed urges* in cases of "spontaneous" flexing, they appeared on the scene about 550 ms before the relevant muscles would have moved if the subjects had not "suppressed" the urges, and subjects did not become conscious of them for about another 350 to 400 ms. Notice that it is *urges* that these subjects are said to report and abort or suppress. This coheres with my urge* hypothesis about groups V, PS, N, and PP. In group V (the veto group), as I have explained, there is excellent reason to believe that no proximal *intention* to flex is present, and the RPs for this group resembled the type I RPs for these other three groups until "about 150–250 ms before the preset time." If it is assumed that these RPs represent the same thing for these four groups until the RPs for group V diverge from the others, these RPs do *not* represent a *proximal intention* to flex before the point of divergence, but they might represent a growing urge to (prepare to) flex or other items in the urge* collection. And if at least until about the time of divergence there is no proximal intention to flex in any of these groups, we would need a special reason to believe that the type II RPs of the spontaneous flexers indicate that proximal intentions to flex emerge in them around

−550 ms. In section 4, I show that there is independent evidence that their proximal intentions emerge much later than this.

Does the brain decide to initiate actions "at a time before there is any reportable subjective awareness that such a decision has taken place" (Libet, Gleason et al. 1983, p. 640)? Libet and his colleagues certainly have not shown that it does, for their data do not show that any such decision has been made before time W or before the time at which their subjects first are aware of a *decision* or *intention* to flex. Nothing justifies the claim that what a subject becomes aware of at time W is a *decision* to flex that has already been made or an *intention* to flex that has already been acquired, as opposed, for example, to an *urge* to flex that has already arisen. Indeed, the data about vetoing, as I have explained, can reasonably be used to argue that the urge* hypothesis about what the RPs indicate is less implausible than the decision or intention hypothesis. Now, there certainly seems to be a connection between what happens at −550 ms and subsequent muscle motion in cases of "spontaneous" flexing. But it obviously is not a temporally direct connection. Between the former and latter times, subjects apparently form or acquire proximal intentions to flex, in those cases in which they do intentionally flex. And for all Libet's data show, those intentions may be consciously formed or acquired.

3. Free Will

When Libet's work is applied to the theoretically subtle and complicated issue of free will, things can quickly get out of hand. The abstract of Haggard and Libet 2001 opens as follows: "The problem of free will lies at the heart of modern scientific studies of consciousness. An influential series of experiments by Libet has suggested that conscious intentions arise as a result of brain activity. This contrasts with traditional concepts of free will, in which the mind controls the body" (p. 47). Now, only a certain kind of mind-body dualist would hold that conscious intentions do *not* "arise as a result of brain activity." And such dualist views are rarely advocated in contemporary philosophical publications on free will. Moreover, contemporary philosophers who argue for the existence of free will typically shun substance dualism. If Libet's work is of general interest to philosophers working on free will, the source of the interest must lie elsewhere than the theoretical location specified in this passage.

In a recent article, Libet writes that "it is only the final 'act now' process that produces the voluntary *act*. That 'act now' process begins in the brain about 550 msec before the act, and it begins unconsciously" (2001, p. 61).[13] "There is," he says, "an unconscious gap of about 400 msec between the onset of the cerebral process and when the person becomes consciously aware of his/her decision or wish or intention to act." (Incidentally, a page later, he identifies what the agent becomes aware of as "the intention/wish/urge to act" [p. 62].) Libet adds: "If the 'act now' process is initiated unconsciously, then conscious free will is not doing it."

I have already explained that Libet has not shown that a decision to flex is made or an intention to flex acquired at −550 ms. But even if the intention emerges much later, that is compatible with an "act now" process having begun at −550 ms. Regarding processes of many kinds, it is hard to be confident when they begin. Did the process of my baking my frozen pizza begin when I turned my oven on to preheat it, when I opened the door of the preheated oven five minutes later to put the pizza in, when I placed the pizza on the center rack, or at some other time? Theorists can argue about this, but I would prefer not to. One might say that "the 'act now' process" in Libet's spontaneous subjects begins with the formation or acquisition of a proximal intention to flex, much closer to the onset of muscle motion than −550 ms, or that it begins earlier, with the beginning of a process that issues in the intention.[14] I will not argue about that. Suppose we say that "the 'act now' process" begins with the unconscious emergence of a (roughly) proximal urge to (prepare to) flex—or with a pretty reliable relatively proximal causal contributor to such an urge—at about −550 ms and that the urge plays a significant role in producing a proximal intention to flex many milliseconds later. We can then agree with Libet that, given that the "process is initiated unconsciously,... conscious free will is not doing it"—that is, is not initiating "the 'act now' process." But who would have thought that conscious free will has the job of producing urges (or causal contributors to urges)? In the philosophical literature, free will's primary locus of operation is typically identified as deciding (or choosing), and for all Libet has shown, his subjects make their decisions (or choices) consciously.

Libet asks (2001, p. 62), "How would the 'conscious self' initiate a voluntary act if, factually, the process to 'act now' is initiated unconsciously?" In this paragraph, I offer an answer. One significant piece of background is that an "'act now' process" that is initiated unconsciously may be aborted by the agent; that apparently is what happens in instances of spontaneous vetoing, if "'act now' processes" start when Libet says they do.[15] Now, processes have parts, and the various parts of a process may have more and less proximal initiators. A process that is initiated by an unconscious urge* may have a subsequent part that is directly initiated by the conscious formation or acquisition of an intention.[16] "The 'conscious self'"—which need not be understood as something mysterious— might more proximally initiate a voluntary act that is less proximally initiated by an unconscious urge*. (Readers who, like me, prefer to use "self" only as an affix may prefer to say that the acquisition or formation of a relevant proximal intention, which intention is consciously acquired or formed, might more proximally initiate an intentional action that is less proximally initiated by an unconscious urge*.)

Recall that Libet himself says that "conscious volitional control may operate . . . to select and control ['the volitional process'], either by permitting or triggering the final motor outcome of the unconsciously initiated process or by vetoing the progression to actual motor activation" (1985, p. 529). "Triggering" is a kind of initiating. In "triggering the final motor outcome," the acquisition of a proximal intention would be initiating an action in a more direct way than does the urge* that initiated a process that issued in the intention. According to one view of things, when proximal action-desires help to initiate overt actions, they do so by helping to produce pertinent proximal intentions, the formation or acquisition of which directly initiates actions (Mele 1992, pp. 71–77, 143–44, 168–70, 176–77, 190–91).[17] What Libet says about triggering here coheres with this.

4. Further Testing

I have argued that the urge* hypothesis about what the type II RPs indicate in Libet's studies is less implausible than the decision or intention hypothesis. Is there an independent way to test these hypotheses—that is, to gather evidence about whether it is (roughly) proximal urges* that emerge around −550 ms in Libet's studies or instead decisions or intentions? One line of thought runs as follows: (1) all overt intentional actions are caused by decisions (or intentions), (2) the type II RPs, which emerge around −550 ms, are correlated with causes of the flexing actions (because they regularly precede the onset of muscle motion), so (3) these RPs indicate that decisions are made (or intentions acquired) at −550 ms.

I have shown that this line of thought is unpersuasive. A lot can happen in a causal process that runs for 550 ms, including a subject's moving from having an unconscious roughly proximal urge* to flex to consciously deciding to flex "now" or to consciously acquiring a proximal intention to flex. One can reply that, even so, 3 *might* be true. And, of course, I can run through my argumentation about the veto and related matters again to remind the imaginary respondent why 3 is improbable. But what about a test?

If makings of proximal decisions to flex or acquisitions of proximal intentions to flex (or the physical events that realize these things) cause muscle motion, how long does it take them to do that? Does it take about 550 ms? Might reaction time experiments show that 550 ms is too long a time for this? Some caution is in order here. In typical reaction time experiments, subjects have decided in advance to perform an assigned task—to "*A*," for short—whenever they detect the relevant signal. When they detect the signal, there is no need for a proximal *decision* to *A*.[18] (If all decisions are responses to uncertainty about what to do and subjects are not uncertain about what to do when they detect the signal, there is no place here for proximal decisions to *A*.)[19] However, it is plausible that after they detect the signal, they acquire an *intention* to *A* now, a proximal intention. That is, it is plausible that the combination of their conditional intention to *A* when they detect the signal (or the neural realizer of that intention) and their detection of the signal (or the neural realizer of that detection) produces a proximal intention to *A*. The acquisition of this intention (or the neural realization of that event) would then initiate the *A*-ing.[20] And in at least one reaction time experiment (described shortly) that is very similar to Libet's main experiment, the time between the "go" signal and the onset of muscle motion is much shorter than 550 ms. This is evidence that proximal intentions to flex—as opposed to (roughly) proximal urges* to flex—emerge much closer to the time of the onset of muscle motion than 550 ms. There is no reason, in principle, that it should take people any longer to start flexing their wrists when executing a proximal intention to flex in Libet's studies than it takes them to do this when executing such an intention in a reaction time study. More precisely, there is no reason, in principle, that the interval between proximal intention acquisition and the beginning of muscle motion should be significantly different in the two scenarios.[21]

The line of reasoning that I have just sketched depends on the assumption that, in reaction time studies, proximal intentions to *A* are at work. An alternative possibility is that the combination of subjects' conditional intentions to A when they detect the signal and their detection of the signal initiates the A-ing without there being any proximal intention to A. Of course, there is a parallel possibility in the case of Libet's subjects. Perhaps the combination of their conditional intentions to flex when they next feel like it—conscious intentions, presumably—together with relevant feelings (namely, conscious proximal urges to flex), initiates a flexing without there being any proximal intentions to flex. (They may treat their initial consciousness of the urge as a "go" signal, as suggested in Keller and Heckhausen 1990, p. 352.) If that possibility is an actuality, then Libet's thesis is false, of course: there is no intention to flex "now" in his subjects and, therefore, no such intention is produced by the brain before the mind is aware of it.

The reaction time study I mentioned is reported in Haggard and Magno 1999:

> Subjects sat at a computer watching a clock hand ... whose rotation period was 2.56 s. ... After an unpredictable delay, varying from 2.56 to 8 s, a high-frequency tone ... was played over a loudspeaker. This served as a warning stimulus for the subsequent reaction. 900 ms after the warning stimulus onset, a second tone ... was played. [It] served as the go signal. Subjects were instructed to respond as rapidly as possible to the go signal with a right-key press on a computer mouse button. Subjects were instructed not to anticipate the go stimulus and were reprimanded if they responded on catch trials. (p. 103)

"Reaction times were calculated by examining the EMG signal for the onset of the first sustained burst of muscle activity occurring after the go signal" (p. 104). "Reaction time" here, then, starts *before* any intention to press "now" is acquired: obviously, it takes some time to detect the signal, and if detection of the signal helps to produce a proximal intention, that takes some time, too. The mean of the subjects' median reaction times in the control trials was 231 ms (p. 104). If a proximal intention to press was acquired, that happened nearer to the time of muscle motion than 231 ms and, therefore, much nearer than the 550 ms that Libet claims is the time proximal intentions to flex are unconsciously acquired in his studies. Notice also how close we are getting to Libet's time W, his subjects' reported time of their initial awareness of something he variously describes as an "intention," "urge," "wanting," "decision," "will," or "wish" to move (−200 to −150 ms). If proximal intentions to flex are acquired in Libet's studies, Haggard and Magno's results make it look like a better bet that they are acquired around time W than that they are acquired around −550 ms.[22] How seriously we should take his subjects' reports of the time of their initial awareness of the urge, intention, or whatever is a controversial question, and I will say nothing about it here.[23]

5. Conclusion

In a recent article, after writing that "many of the world's leading neuroscientists have not only accepted our findings and interpretations, but have even enthusiastically praised these achievements and their experimental ingenuity" and naming twenty such people, Libet adds: "It is interesting that most of the negative criticism of our findings and their implications have come from philosophers and others with no significant experience in experimental neuroscience of the brain" (2002, p. 292). Later in the article, he writes of one of his critics, "As a philosopher Gomes exhibits characteristics often found in philosophers. He seems to think one can offer reinterpretations by making unsupported assumptions, offering speculative data that do not exist and constructing hypotheses that are not even testable" (p. 297).[24] When I first read the latter passage, I experienced an urge to point out that one does not need any "experience in experimental neuroscience of the brain" to realize that there is a difference between deciding and intending, on the one hand, and wanting—including having an urge— on the other. Also, one who understands Libet's data and the studies that generate them can see that nothing warrants his claim that the RPs at issue are correlated with decisions or intentions rather than with urges strong enough to issue pretty regularly in related intentions and actions or relatively proximal causes of such urges. Incidentally, as is obvious, I eventually made the transition from having an urge to comment on the quoted remarks to intending to do so.

Recall Haggard's assertion that "conceptual analysis could help" (Haggard and Libet 2001, p. 62). This chapter may be read as a test of his assertion. In my opinion, the result is positive. Attention not only to the data but also to the concepts in terms of which the data are analyzed makes it clear that Libet's striking claims about decisions, intentions, and free will are not justified by his results. Libet asserts that his "discovery that the brain unconsciously initiates the volitional process well before the person becomes aware of an intention or wish to act voluntarily... clearly has a profound impact on how we view the nature of free will" (2004, p. 201). Not so. That, in certain settings, (roughly) proximal urges to do things arise unconsciously or issue partly from causes of which the agent is not conscious—urges on which the agent may or may not subsequently act—is a cause neither for worry nor for enthusiasm about free will.

NOTES

1. Philosophers who have discussed Libet's work include Dennett (1991, pp. 154–66; 2003, pp. 228–45), Flanagan (1996, pp. 59–62), and Rosenthal (2002).

2. In a later article, Libet writes: "The brain has begun the specific preparatory processes for the voluntary act well before the subject is even aware of any wish or intention to act" (1992, p. 263).

3. Some passages in which two or more of these terms are used interchangeably are quoted later in this section and in section 3. Libet, Gleason et al. report that "the subject was asked to note and later report the time of appearance of his conscious *awareness of 'wanting' to perform* a given self-initiated movement. The experience was also described as an 'urge' or 'intention' or 'decision' to move, though subjects usually settled for the words 'wanting' or 'urge'" (1983, p. 627).

4. See Mele 1992, pp. 71–77, 142–46, 166–70, 175–94. Also see Brand 1984, pp. 121–27; Bratman 1987, pp. 18–20; and McCann 1986b, pp. 193–94.

5. Our desires and intentions, in my view, are realized in physical states and events, and their causes are or are realized in physical states and events. I forgo discussion of the metaphysics of mental causation, but see Mele 1992, ch. 2. I leave it open here that although desires and intentions enter into causal explanations of actions, the causal clout is carried, not by them (qua desires and intentions), but by their physical realizers.

6. For background on the generation, analysis, and use of electroencephalograms (EEGs) and "event-related brain potentials," including readiness potentials, see Coles and Rugg 1995.

7. I say "apparently," because an author may wish to distinguish an intention to flex one's wrist from an intention to initiate a flexing of one's wrist. I discuss initiation in section 3. For completeness, I observe that if we instead ignore the quotation's first disjunct, it makes a claim about when an intention to *prepare* to flex—or to prepare to initiate a flexing of one's wrist—arises.

8. For a more thorough discussion of the experiment, see Libet, Wright et al. 1983 or Libet, Gleason et al. 1983.

9. Try to imagine that you intend to eat some pie now while also intending not to eat it now. How would you act? Would you reach for it with one hand and grab the reaching hand with your other hand? People who suffer from anarchic hand syndrome sometimes display behavior of this kind (see Marcel 2003, pp. 76–81). Sean Spence and Chris Frith suggest that these people "have

conscious 'intentions to act' [that] are thwarted by . . . 'intentions' to which the patient does not experience conscious access" (1999, p. 24).

10. Another is that they have an intention to prepare to flex, if *preparing* is understood in such a way that so intending does not entail intending to flex.

11. Recall that Libet suggests that the activation event occurs between 10 and 90 ms before the onset of muscle motion (1985, p. 537) and later revises the lower limit to 50 ms (2004, pp. 137–38).

12. In an alternative picture, the acquisition of a proximal intention to flex sends a signal that may be regarded as a command to flex one's wrist (or finger), and that signal helps produce finer-grained signals that directly activate the motoneurons to the relevant muscles. This picture moves the time of the acquisition of a proximal intention further from 0 ms, but it does not move it anywhere near −550 ms. See section 4.

13. When does the *action* begin in all this—that is, the person's flexing his wrist or fingers? This is a conceptual question, of course: how one answers it depends on one's answer to the question "What is an action?" Libet identifies "the actual time of the voluntary motor act" with the time "indicated by EMG recorded from the appropriate muscle" (1985, p. 532). I favor an alternative position, but there is no need to disagree with Libet about this for my purposes here. Following Brand 1984, Frederick Adams and I have defended the thesis that overt intentional actions begin in the brain, just after the acquisition of a proximal intention; the action is proximally initiated by the acquisition of the intention (Adams and Mele 1992). (One virtue of this view is that it helps in handling certain problems about deviant causal chains; see Mele 2003a, ch. 2.) The relevant intention may be understood, in Libet's words, as an intention "to act now" (1989, p. 183; 1999, p. 54; 2004, p. 148), a proximal intention. (Of course, for Libet, as for me, "now" need not mean "this millisecond.") If I form the intention now to start running now, the action that is my running may begin just after the intention is formed, even though the relevant muscular motions do not begin until milliseconds later.

14. A central point of disagreement between Haggard and Libet is usefully understood as a disagreement about when the " 'act now' process" begins (see Haggard and Libet 2001). Haggard apparently views the onset of lateralized response potentials (LRP), which happens "later than RP onset," as the beginning of the process (Haggard and Libet 2001, p. 53; also see Trevena and Miller 2002).

15. Notice that in addition to "vetoing" urges for actions that are not yet in progress, agents can abort attempts, including attempts at relatively temporally "short" actions. When batting, baseball players often successfully halt the motion of their arms while a swing is in progress. Presumably, they acquire or form an intention to stop swinging while they are in the process of executing an intention to swing.

16. Readers who believe that some item or other in the collection designated by "urge*" cannot be unconscious should exclude that item from consideration when they read "unconscious urge*."

17. Those who view the connection as direct take the view that actions begin in the brain. See n. 13.

18. It should not be assumed that detecting the signal is a conscious event (see Prinz 2003).

19. In a reaction time study in which subjects are instructed to A or B when they detect the signal and not to decide in advance which to do, they may decide between A and B after detecting the signal.

20. Hereafter, the parenthetical clauses should be supplied by the reader. They serve as a reminder of a point made in n. 5.

21. Notice that the interval at issue is distinct from intervals between the time of the occurrence of events that cause proximal intentions and the time of intention acquisition.

22. In a study by Day et al. of eight subjects instructed to flex a wrist when they hear a tone, mean reaction time was 125 ms (1989, p. 653). In their study of five subjects instructed to flex both wrists when they hear a tone, mean reaction time was 93 ms (p. 658). The mean reaction times of both groups of subjects—defined as "the interval from auditory tone to onset of the first antagonist EMG burst" (p. 651)—were much shorter than those of Haggard and Magno's subjects. Day et al.'s subjects, unlike Haggard and Magno's (and Libet's), were not watching a clock.

23. For an instructive review of the literature on this, see van de Grind 2002.

24. Incidentally, Gilberto Gomes has informed me that he works in a psychology department.

THREE

Libertarianism, Luck, and Control

A familiar claim made against various libertarian accounts of free action
and action for which agents are morally responsible is that they subject
agents to luck in a way that renders action of these kinds impossible
(Nagel 1986, pp. 113–14; Strawson 1994). A more modest claim is that
these accounts subject agents to luck in undesirable ways that do not
promote free action and moral responsibility (Mele 1995, chs. 11–13;
1999a; 1999b). Sometimes these claims are elaborated in terms of *control*. For example, I have argued, on the basis of some points about luck,
that certain libertarian accounts of free and morally responsible agency
generate some undesirable limitations on agents' control that are unnecessary for agency of these kinds (Mele 1995).

Randolph Clarke, the author of an important body of work defending a kind of agent-causal libertarianism against various objections,
has replied to these claims in several places (2000, 2002, 2003, 2005a).[1]
An examination of some themes linking Clarke's replies with work by
Robert Kane (1996, 1999b), an event-causal libertarian, and Timothy
O'Connor (2000), an agent-causal libertarian, will help clarify issues
about luck and control that are central to the debate between conventional libertarians (agent causationists and others) and their critics.[2]
Such clarification is the aim of this chapter. As matters come into focus,
it will become clear that luck poses an as yet unresolved problem for
conventional libertarians.

Agent-causal accounts of free action and moral responsibility often are motivated partly by arguments that event-causal libertarian

accounts fall short of the mark. One alleged shortcoming concerns control. In section 1, I summarize a task for libertarians regarding a worry about luck and control. Kane's emended event-causal libertarian reply (1999b) to a worry of that kind is the topic of section 2. In section 3, I consider a control-focused objection that O'Connor (2000) raises against event-causal libertarianism, and I examine his agent-causal position on control. Work on control and luck in Clarke 2000, 2002, 2003, and 2005a is the central topic of sections 4 through 6. After a brief review in section 7 of some recent work on the luck problem, I conclude in section 8 that luck and control lie at the heart of important unfinished business for all believers in free, morally responsible agency. Because I have argued elsewhere that actions are, essentially, events with a causal history of a certain kind (Mele 2003a, ch. 2), I set aside noncausal accounts of free action in this book.[3]

1. A Task for Libertarians

In chapter 1, after motivating a worry about luck for libertarians with my fable about the libertarian goddess, Diana, I reported that all libertarians who hold that A's being a free action depends on its being the case that, at the time, the agent was able to do otherwise freely then should tell us what it could possibly be about an agent who freely A-ed at t in virtue of which it is true that, in another world with the same past and laws of nature, he freely does something else at t. I mentioned that if they say that the answer is "free will," they need to explain how free will, as they understand it, can be a feature of agents—or, more fully, how this can be so where "free will," on their account of it, really does answer the question. To do this, of course, they must provide an account of free will—one that can be tested for adequacy in this connection.

A libertarian can duck my question by claiming that an agent's freely A-ing at t in a world W requires that it be possible, given W's past and laws of nature, that the agent not A at t but does not require that he be able at t freely to perform some alternative to A then or freely to refrain from A-ing then. In section 4, I motivate a similar worry about luck for a libertarian view that makes the possibility I just identified a requirement for freely A-ing without requiring the ability I just mentioned.

2. Kane on Luck and Control

Robert Kane, a libertarian who shuns agent causation, finds special importance in scenarios in which we struggle with ourselves about what to do (1996, 1999b). In some cases of this kind, he says, we simultaneously try to make each of two competing choices or decisions (1999b).[4] Because the agent is trying to make each, she is morally responsible for whichever of the two decisions she makes and makes it freely, Kane claims (pp. 231–40), provided that "she endorse[s] the outcome as something she was trying and wanting to do all along" (p. 233). Someone who takes this position can consistently hold that even if the agent's deciding to *A*, as she in fact did, rather than her instead deciding to *B*, as she did at the same time in another world with the same past and laws of nature—that is, that difference, *D*, between the two worlds—is just a matter of luck, the agent decides freely and is morally responsible for her decision. At least, that is so if, as it seems, this agent's satisfying Kane's alleged sufficient condition for free and morally responsible decision is consistent with *D*'s being just a matter of luck.[5] What matters, in Kane's view, is that the agent tries to make each decision (in both worlds) and endorses the outcome in the way just mentioned. If Kane is right, he has provided a successful answer to the challenge about luck voiced in the preceding section—at least in scenarios of a certain kind.

Part of the inspiration for Kane's position is the point that "indeterminism [sometimes] functions as an obstacle to success without precluding responsibility" and freedom (1999b, p. 227). In one of his illustrations, "an assassin who is trying to kill the prime minister ... might miss because" his indeterministic motor control system leaves open the possibility that he will fire a wild shot. Suppose the assassin succeeds. Then, Kane says, he "was responsible" for the killing "because he intentionally and voluntarily succeeded in doing what he was *trying* to do—kill the prime minister." It may be claimed, similarly, that the indeterminism in the scenario does not preclude the killing's being a free action. If these claims are true, they are true even if the difference between the actual world at the time of the firing and any wild-shot world that does not diverge from the actual world before that time is just a matter of luck.

As Clarke observes, Kane's point does not get him far, for the presumption of those who judge that the assassin freely killed the prime minister is that he *freely tried* to kill him (2002, pp. 372–73): if we are told that perhaps the assassination attempt was not free, all bets are off. Kane does not claim that in cases of dual efforts to choose, the choices made are products of freely made efforts. Nor has he put himself in a position to claim this, for he has not offered an account of what it is for an effort to choose to A to be freely made. Thus, there is a salient disanalogy between cases like that of Kane's assassin and Kane's dual trying cases: there is no presumption that the dual efforts to choose are freely made. And if the agent's efforts to choose in a dual trying scenario—unlike the assassin's effort to kill the prime minister—are not freely made, it is hard to see why the choice in which such an effort culminates should be deemed free.

Readers who need help in appreciating this last point should imagine that a manipulator compels an agent, Antti, simultaneously to try to choose to A and to try to choose to B, where A and B are competing courses of action that, in the absence of manipulation, Antti would abhor performing. Imagine also that the manipulator does not allow Antti to try to choose anything else at the time and that the manipulation is such that Antti will endorse either relevant "outcome as something [he] was trying and wanting to do all along." The tryings are internally indeterministic, but Antti does not freely try to make the choices he tries to make. Apparently, whatever he chooses, he does not freely choose it—especially when the sort of freedom at issue is the sort most closely associated with moral responsibility. To be sure, in this scenario the unfreedom of the efforts is tied to serious monkey business. But take the monkey business away: if the efforts to choose still are not freely made, why should a corresponding choice count as free? The combination of trying and endorsement that Kane describes does not suffice for freely making the decision one makes: that combination is present in Antti's case. It may be claimed that this combination would turn the trick in the absence of monkey business. When I see an argument for that claim, I will try to assess it. An argument by analogy from such cases as the assassin's will not fly as long as the disanalogy I mentioned is in place. One way to eliminate the disanalogy is to produce an acceptable account of the freedom of an effort to choose to A and show that efforts at work in some dual trying scenarios satisfy the account. Of course, one would also have to deal with the strangeness of the suggestion that rational free agents try to choose to A while also trying to choose another course of action that they know is incompatible with A-ing (on this problem, see Clarke 2002, p. 372; 2003, p. 88).

Kane has suggested in conversation that it suffices for an effort to choose to *A* to be a free action that it satisfies a good compatibilist set of sufficient conditions for free action.[6] The freedom at issue is moral-responsibility-level freedom (see ch. 1, sec. 3). The suggestion poses an obvious threat to libertarianism—an essentially *incompatibilist* position. Kane is not thinking that for a deterministically caused effort to choose to *A* to be a free action, it must be preceded by some indeterministically caused free action (that confers some freedom on it). Indeed, he suggested that any agent's *first* free actions are dual efforts to choose. Now, if a compatibilist account of the freedom of these actions is true, the actions may be free even if they are deterministically caused. And if we should believe that that is true of these actions, why should we not believe that it is true of all free actions that do not depend for their freedom on earlier indeterministically caused free actions? It is difficult to see why it should be thought that efforts to choose to *A* differ from actions in general in such a way that even though compatibilism is true of these efforts, it is not true of actions in general.

3. O'Connor on Active Power

Timothy O'Connor regards the apparent failure of event-causal libertarian views as motivation for libertarians to embrace agent causation. "Active power" is O'Connor's name for the power exercised in agent causation. This power, he writes, "is the power to freely choose one's course of action for reasons" (2000, p. 95; italics eliminated). Now, what is it about active power in virtue of which it is the power to choose freely for reasons? O'Connor says that "exerting active power is intrinsically a direct exercise of control over one's own behavior" (p. 61). In this, exerting active power is supposed to differ from what happens when allegedly free choices are made according to libertarians (e.g., Kane) who hold that such choices are indeterministically caused by internal states and events. O'Connor contends that, on these event-causal libertarian views, agents do not directly control the outcome. He writes: (*O*) "There are objective probabilities corresponding to each of the [possible choices], but within those fixed parameters, which choice occurs on a given occasion seems, as far as the agent's direct control goes, a matter of chance" (p. xiii; cf. p. 29). This resembles my suggestion in chapter 1 (sec. 1) that the difference at *t* between the actual world, in which Joe decides then to *A*, and any world with the same past and laws in which he instead decides then not to *A* is just a matter of luck. Of course, I made no exception for agents who exercise "active power" or "direct control."

What is the connection between my suggestion and *O*? Consider a scenario O'Connor describes (2000, p. 74). Tim deliberates about whether to keep working or to take a break and decides to continue working. Obviously, it is not just a matter of chance that he decides to do that, and O'Connor does not claim that it is. After all, Tim had significant reasons and motivation to continue working, and he chose for those reasons. Also, in virtue of the fact just reported about Tim's motivation and, for example, the fact that he had no motivation at all for smashing his computer monitor with his coffee mug, it was much more likely that he would decide to continue working than that he would decide to smash his monitor with his mug. What O'Connor claims in *O* to be a matter of chance, "as far as [Tim's] direct control goes" given event-causal libertarian views of the sort at issue, seems to be the following cross-world difference: Tim's choosing at *t* to continue working rather than choosing at *t* to do something else, as he does in some possible worlds with the same past and laws of nature.

O'Connor's own agent-causal view is supposed to avoid this consequence. Assume that Tim chose freely in the scenario under consideration. Then, on O'Connor's view, Tim "had the power to choose to continue working or to choose to stop, where this is a power to cause either of these mental occurrences. That capacity was exercised at *t* in a particular way (in choosing to continue working), allowing us to say truthfully that Tim at time *t* causally determined his own choice to continue working" (2000, p. 74). Suppose that the position reported in the preceding two sentences is true. Why should we suppose that the following cross-world difference is not a matter of chance or luck: that Tim exercised the capacity at issue at *t* in choosing to continue working rather than in choosing to do something else, as he does in some possible worlds with the same past and laws of nature? Grant that Tim "causally determined his own choice to continue working." Why aren't the differences in his causal determinings at *t* across worlds with the same past and laws of nature a matter of chance or luck? Tim was able to causally determine each of several choices, whereas a counterpart who fits the event-causal libertarian's picture was able to make—but not to causally determine—each of several choices. If it is a matter of chance that the latter agent chooses to keep working rather than choosing to do something else, why is it not a matter of chance that the former agent causally determines the choice he causally determines rather than causally determining a choice to do something else?

Perhaps O'Connor is thinking that the conceptual relation between control and chance is such that the fact that Tim exercised direct control over which choice he makes answers each of these questions. Should his readers find this thought persuasive? I do not see why. Even if the fact that Tim exercised direct control in choosing to continue working is incompatible with its being just a matter of luck that he chose to continue working, this does not show that a relevant cross-world difference between his exercising direct control "in [this] particular way" (2000, p. 74) and his exercising it in choosing to do something else is not just a matter of luck. The reader should bear two points in mind. First, as I explained, it is not just a matter of luck that Tim chose to keep working, even on event-causal libertarian views. Second, O'Connor does not place cross-world differences in agents' doings out of bounds in the context of free will; in fact, such differences are *featured* in his objection from chance to event-causal libertarians. A third point also is worth making. Kane claims that agents exercise direct control over some of their choices (1996, p. 144). In these cases, Kane says, the agent's exercise of control is not "antecedent" to the choice; rather, it occurs "then and there," when and where the choice is made. O'Connor's critique of event-causal libertarianism makes it plain that he does not believe that what Kane conceives of as an exercise of direct control here solves the problem of cross-world luck at the time of action, and there is a parallel worry about exercises of direct agent-causal control.

O'Connor can say that even if, in scenarios featuring agent causation, cross-world differences of the kind I mentioned *are* matters of chance, that does not stand in the way of freedom and moral responsibility. In assessing the event-causal libertarian view advanced in Kane 1996, he contends that, owing to the specific kind of chanciness involved, "the kind of control that is exercised is too weak to ground [the agent's] responsibility for which of the causal possibilities is realized" (2000, p. 40). O'Connor can claim that the chanciness involved in whether an agent causally determines one choice rather than another is very different, and so different that the control that is exercised in Tim's causally determining his choice to continue working is sufficiently strong to ground his responsibility for that choice. But I find no argument for this thesis about chance and control in O'Connor 2000.

Perhaps it will be objected that I have neglected O'Connor's claim that "Active power is the power to *freely* choose one's course of action for reasons" (2000, p. 95; italics altered). I may be asked to concentrate on the thought that O'Connor is arguing that "the power to freely choose one's course of action"—the *F-power*, for short—is a possible power. It is true that he argues for this thesis, but he also contends that the *F*-power is the power of an agent directly to causally determine his choices—the *D-power*—a power that "in suitable circumstances is freely exercised by the agent himself" (p. 72).[7] What I have not been able to ascertain is why it should be believed that (in whatever circumstances are deemed "suitable") having the *D*-power suffices for having the *F*-power and exercising the *D*-power in choosing to *A* is sufficient for freely choosing to *A*. For I have been unable to ascertain why, for example, the crucial difference in causal determination at *t* between the actual world and any world with the same past and laws of nature in which, at *t*, Tim directly causally determines a choice to take a break is not just a matter of luck and unable, as well, to ascertain why, if this difference is just a matter of luck, Tim nevertheless freely chooses to continue working and is morally responsible for that choice. If O'Connor is legitimately to win converts to his view, he needs to lay this worry about luck to rest. The next major item of business is to determine whether Clarke succeeds where O'Connor falls short.

4. Clarke on Agent Causation

Clarke reports: "what is wanted from an account of free will is an account of an agent's *control* over which decisions he makes and which actions he performs" (2000, p. 22). He holds that not all agential control is "freedom-level" control (2000, p. 28; 2003, p. 67), and, in his view, of course, it is an account of freedom-level control that is especially wanted. Because Clarke holds that "making a decision is performing a mental action" (2000, p. 23; see 2003, p. 3), his report can be streamlined: "what is [especially] wanted from an account of free will is an account of an agent's [freedom-level] control over . . . which actions he performs." The noun "control," in the sense most directly relevant to free action, is an ability term; it denotes an ability *to control*. Clarke's idea, as I understand it, is that the power or ability to act freely is a certain kind of power or ability to control which actions one performs (including which decisions one makes). Clarke also says, "An agent's exercise of control in acting is an exercise of a positive power to determine what he does" (2002, p. 374).[8] He does not say that whenever *this* positive power is exercised in acting, the agent acts freely (more on this shortly). But the claim last quoted suggests another formulation of what I called "Clarke's idea." Here it is: the power or ability to act freely is a certain kind of power or ability to *determine* which actions one performs.[9] The word "which" here is meant to indicate that more than one course of action is open to the agent when he exercises the power or ability at issue and therefore to suggest a kind of "control *over* which . . . actions he performs" (emphasis altered).

Clarke and I agree that an agent's deciding to A is an action. On my view, as I have said, it is a momentary mental action, and it resolves uncertainty about what to do. To decide to A is to form an intention to A, "form" being understood as an action verb, and not all intentions are formed in this sense (ch. 1, sec. 3). If an action A that executes a nonactionally acquired intention to A can be free, its freedom does not derive from the freedom of a decision to A made at the time. If there are *basically* free A-ings—again, free A-ings that occur at times at which the past and the laws of nature are consistent with the agent's not A-ing then (ch. 1, sec. 1)—perhaps they include some decisions and some overt actions that execute nonactionally acquired intentions (see Clarke 2003, pp. 122–31).

On Clarke's view, deciding to A does not entail exercising an ability to control or determine which decisions one makes. For Clarke, an agent has that ability only if his world is indeterministic. As he intends the ability to be understood, an agent who decided to A exercised an ability to control or determine which decisions he makes in so doing only if "until the making of that decision [there was] a genuine chance that the agent would not make that decision. This may have been a chance that he would instead make an alternative decision . . . or it may just have been a chance that he would make no decision at all right then" (2000, p. 21).[10] I may decide at t to A in a *deterministic* world, as Clarke observes (2003, p. 8). And if agents do only what they are able to do, then given that I decided what to do, I may be said to have exercised an ability to decide what to do. But that exercise does not suffice for my having exercised an ability to control or determine *which* decisions I make, on Clarke's essentially indeterministic construal of the latter ability.

A philosopher who holds that "when a decision is freely made, . . . there remained until the making of that decision a genuine chance that the agent would not make that decision" (Clarke 2000, p. 21) may take the same view of all free actions: when any action is freely performed, there remained until its performance a genuine chance that the agent would not perform it.[11] Such claims are commonly expressed in the language of possible worlds as follows:

1. If an agent freely decided at t to A, then in a possible world with the same past until t and the same laws of nature, he did not decide at t to A.
2. If an agent freely A-ed at t, then in a possible world with the same past until t and the same laws of nature, he did not A at t.

Claim 1 takes us back to a worry of the sort sketched in my fable about the libertarian goddess in chapter 1. Claim 2 raises a related worry, to which I now turn.

Suppose that Ann freely A-ed at t in world W and that she A-ed in order to keep a promise she made—a promise to A at t. The conjunction of this supposition and claim 2 entails that in some possible world that does not diverge from W before t, Ann does not A at t. Imagine that what Ann sincerely promised was to flip, in one minute, at high noon, the coin she was holding. In so promising, she expressed an intention to flip it at noon. No unexpected substantial obstacles arose, and no excuses for not flipping the coin came to mind. Ann also had no intention not to flip it at noon, no intention to wait until later to flip it, no intention to fling it into the bushes then, and so on. Moreover, Ann was convinced, rightly, not only that she had a good reason to do what she promised but also that she had no significant reason for not tossing the coin nor for deciding to do anything other than toss it. The only thing that in any sense spoke in favor of her not flipping the coin was a very weak desire to discover what it would feel like to break a promise for no good reason. Ann occasionally has what she regards as silly desires, and she saw this as one of them. The intention expressed in Ann's promise persisted until she tossed the coin, at noon.

Now, it seemingly is conceptually impossible that, for example, Ann *intentionally* holds on to the coin at noon—or intentionally drops it, or intentionally hurls it into the bushes—in the absence of any pertinent *intention*. This leaves it open that in some possible world that does not diverge from W before noon Ann *accidentally* fails to flip the coin. For example, the coin might accidentally fall from her hand when she tries to flip it. Perhaps it is also left open that in some other possible world that does not diverge from W before noon a relevant intention appears on the scene at noon. Again, in deciding to A, one forms an intention to A. Perhaps in some possible world that does not diverge from *W* before noon Ann decides at noon—just as she is beginning to flip the coin—to continue holding it and does not flip it. This may happen provided that, in *W*, Ann's beginning to toss the coin precedes the coin's leaving her hand by enough milliseconds to permit the possibility of her holding on to it. If, for example, overt actions begin in the brain just after relevant proximal intentions are acquired (Adams and Mele 1992; Brand 1984, p. 20), there is time enough for this.

As shorthand for the expression "Ann performed a noontime coin flip," I use the expression "Ann *C*-ed." It is useful to have a label for possible worlds with the following two features: they do not diverge from *W* before noon, and in them Ann does not *C*. I call them *N-worlds*. I have mentioned two kinds of *N*-world. In one kind, in the absence of any supporting intention, Ann does not *C*, and it is an accident that she does not. I dub *N*-worlds of this kind *accident N-worlds*. In the other kind, a new, relevant intention emerges at noon. They are *new intention N-worlds*.[12] Imagine that, owing to undisclosed details of Ann's case, the only *N*-worlds are accident *N*-worlds. Would Clarke regard that as consistent with Ann's exercising at noon in *W* freedom-level control over whether she *C*-s? I doubt it. As Kane observes, the possibility of accidentally doing otherwise falls well short of "the power to do otherwise that people usually have in mind when they think about free and responsible actions" (1996, p. 112; see 2002, p. 411). Kane's claim is true not only of lay folk but also of philosophers, and a parallel claim about the power not to *A*—where not *A*-ing is distinguished from *doing* otherwise than *A*—is no less plausible.

I turn to the new intention *N*-worlds and to decisions, which brings me back to a version of the worry developed in chapter 1's fable.[13] Pick an *N*-world *Na* in which Ann decides at noon to hold the coin for another minute and continues holding it. Her making that decision at noon rather than *C*-ing, as she does in *W*—that difference—seemingly is not accounted for by anything. *Na*'s divergence from *W* begins with Ann's deciding at noon to hold the coin. So there is no difference between *W* and *Na* to account for the difference at issue. From this, it follows that there is nothing to account for that difference, unless it can truly be said that the agent, Ann, accounts for it. (The reader should be thinking "agent causation.") But given that there is no difference in Ann in the two worlds before the moment of divergence, it is not easy to see how this can be. If nothing accounts for the difference, the difference is just a matter of luck. Also, insofar as it is better, other things being equal, to keep one's promises than to break them, Ann can be said to have *better* luck in *W* than in *Na*. Now, if the difference is just a matter of luck, Ann seems not to be morally responsible for deciding at noon to hold on to the coin. After all, given exactly the same laws of nature and antecedent conditions, in a world in which she has better luck at noon, she instead *C*-s, as promised. Knowing this, one is disinclined to blame Ann for breaking her promise, and that is evidence of an inclination to believe that Ann is not morally responsible for deciding to hold on to the coin. That Ann is not morally responsible for this in turn suggests that, in *Na*, she did not freely decide at noon to hold on to the coin and did not freely break her promise. One worries that if, on these grounds, it is false that Ann decided freely at noon in *Na*, it also is false that she freely *C*-ed in *W*. After all, if Ann had not had the good fortune of lacking the bad luck she had in *Na*, she would not have *C*-ed.

The inclination to let Ann off the hook for breaking her promise gains considerable support from the fact that the only thing that in any sense speaks in favor of her not tossing the coin at noon and her deciding not to toss it then is a very weak desire to discover what it would feel like to break a promise for no good reason—a desire she regards as silly. In *Na*, at noon, under the conditions identified, Ann abandons the intention expressed in her promise and decides not to toss the coin. Her decision is not only irrational but also downright strange.

Paradigmatic akratic decisions—roughly, free decisions to *A* made at a time at which the agent rationally and consciously believes, from the perspective of his own values, principles, and the like, that a better option than *A* is open to him—are typically deemed irrational. In virtue of their clashing with the agent's rational evaluative belief, such decisions are subjectively irrational (to some degree, if not without qualification). There is a failure of coherence in the agent of a kind directly relevant to assessments of the agent's rationality. Now, in the paradigmatic cases, the agents' decisions are motivated by substantial desires. It is not especially surprising that someone with a strong desire for a cigarette or a shot of whiskey would decide accordingly, despite believing that it would be better to abstain. But it is very surprising that an agent who takes promise making seriously, as Ann does, would decide to break a promise when the only thing that speaks in favor of breaking it and of deciding to break it is a weak desire that the agent regards as silly. Ann's decision in the present scenario is plausibly viewed as a manifestation of a breakdown of agency that goes beyond the irrationality of paradigmatic akratic decisions. Ann is so constituted as an agent that she is subject to breakdowns of this kind, and she suffers such a breakdown in *Na*. If she is not responsible for this defect in her constitution as an agent, she seems not to be responsible for this manifestation of it. To make the case for pity stronger, it may be supposed that Ann is aware of her defect and does everything in her power to minimize the chance of its being manifested on this occasion.

The discovery of this agential defect in Ann also is relevant in cases in which Ann is seriously tempted to do something that she believes it best on the whole not to do. In some worlds in which, in a case of serious temptation, she decides contrary to her better judgment, the decision is due to the defect. A libertarian may grant this and claim that in other worlds in which, in a case of this kind, Ann decides contrary to her better judgment, her decision is not due to the defect and is a genuine akratic decision—hence, a free decision. Such a libertarian should explain how the etiology of the akratic decision differs from that of defective decisions like Ann's in *Na*.[14]

It may be suggested that if earlier decisions Ann freely made—decisions to break various promises, for example—increased her chance of having bad luck in the case at hand (by causing her to have an irresolute character), then we should be strongly inclined to claim that Ann is morally responsible for breaking her promise in *Na* and for her decision about the coin. However, the worry I sketched arises about all allegedly free earlier decisions Ann makes and all of her other allegedly free past actions. The critic's retreat to the past merely moves the worry back in time.

5. Persisting Intentions and Control

I have two questions about the worry I presented. Does Clarke's work on control in Clarke 2000, 2002, 2003, or 2005a lay it to rest? And, in light of the worry, would Diana, the libertarian goddess (ch. 1, sec. 1), do well to build into her agents, as best she can, an approximation of a deterministic connection between decision making and the persistence of the intentions formed in making decisions? The latter question is the topic of the present section. Discussion of the former question is reserved for section 6.

Diana's aim, again, is to build rational, free human beings who are capable of being very efficient agents. Suppose that, for what an agent takes to be good reasons, he decides at t to A at $t + n$. When he so decides, he has certain expectations about how things will be at $t + n$.

Other things being equal, if at $t+n$ things are as he expected and he rationally believes that it would be best to A, it would not be rational of him at $t+n$ to abandon his intention to A. Because Diana recognizes this, she builds into her agents a mechanism that ensures the following: (1) in the absence of biological damage, an agent with expectations about how things will be at $t+n$ who decides at t to A at $t+n$ retains through $t+n$ his intention to A, if (2) there is no point at which these expectations change, no point at which he believes he should reconsider his decision, and no point (from t to $t + n$) at which he believes that some alternative to A-ing at $t+n$ is at least as good as A-ing at $t + n$.

I suggest that the following is true:

> T. Other things being equal, a decision-making agent with this mechanism can exercise more control at earlier times over what he does at later times than can a decision-making agent in the same indeterministic world who lacks such a mechanism.

Agents of both kinds who decide at t to A at $t+n$ and satisfy condition 2 may lose their intention by $t + n$. For example, they may suffer random brain damage that eliminates the intention. But, other things being equal, agents who lack a mechanism of the kind at issue have an extra indeterministic way of losing it. In a wide range of cases, agents in indeterministic worlds who decide at a time to do something later—whatever it is that they decide to do—thereby raise the probability that they will do it. Other things being equal, agents in such worlds who have the mechanism at issue raise that probability higher by deciding than do those who lack such a mechanism. This indicates that, other things being equal, at the times at which they make their decisions, the former exercise more control than the latter over what they will subsequently do.

This is not to say that agents who lack the mechanism are unfree, nor that agents who have it can be free. As I observed elsewhere (Mele 1995, p. 202), it is open to some libertarians to hold that they must make some sacrifices in control to make room for free action. My question now is whether Clarke's work on control in Clarke 2000, 2002, 2003, or 2005a undermines T. My answer is *no*. It cannot undermine T because this work is about agents' control at a time over what they do at that time (synchronic control), not about their control at a time over what they do at later times (diachronic control).

I asked whether Diana would do well to build into her agents, as best she can, an approximation of a deterministic connection between decision making and the persistence of the intentions formed in making decisions.

Insofar as one of her concerns is to maximize the control free agents can exercise at times over what they will do at later times, the answer seems to be *yes*—provided that achieving this aim does not thwart other important aims she has for free agents. (Obviously, I am not suggesting that just any approximation of a deterministic connection here would be desirable, and I have described a particular connection that looks useful.)

6. Luck Remains a Problem

The topic of this section, as I have said, is whether a worry about luck and control voiced in section 4 is silenced by Clarke 2000, 2002, 2003, or 2005a. In Ann's case, the worry's source is the following thought:

> *A1.* The difference at noon between world *W*, in which Ann performs a noontime coin flip, as she promised, and any world, *Wn*, with the same past and laws of nature in which Ann does not so act and instead decides at noon not to toss the coin then is just a matter of luck.

Here are the subsequent worrisome thoughts; each is suggested by a predecessor:

> *A2.* Ann is not morally responsible in *Wn* for deciding at noon to hold on to the coin and for not doing what she promised. (After all, given exactly the same laws of nature and exactly the same past, in some worlds in which she has better luck at noon she instead performs a noontime coin flip, as promised.)
>
> *A3.* In *Wn*, Ann does not freely decide at noon to hold on to the coin and does not freely break her promise. (That she does not freely do these things explains why she is not morally responsible for doing them.)
>
> *A4.* In *W*, Ann does not freely perform a noontime coin flip. (Just as Ann's bad luck at noon in *Wn* blocks moral responsibility, so does her good luck at noon in *W*. After all, given exactly the same laws of nature and exactly the same past, in some worlds in which she has worse luck at noon than she does in *W*, she decides at noon not to flip the coin and breaks her promise. And that Ann's noontime coin flip is not freely performed explains why she is not morally responsible for it.)

I am not claiming that any of these propositions *entails* any subsequent proposition. Nor am I claiming that I have shown that any of these propositions or parenthetical explanatory remarks is true. My aim in setting out the sequence of thoughts that constitutes the worry under investigation is to facilitate evaluation of Clarke's resources for responding to worries of this kind. Recall that, for Clarke, the power or ability to act freely—what I now dub the *F-ability*—is a certain kind of power or ability to control or determine which actions one performs and cannot be possessed in deterministic worlds. The exercise of this latter power or ability—the *C-ability*—involves a combination of agent causation and indeterministic event causation (2003, chs. 8 and 9). Clarke's "integrated agent-causal account takes the exercise of freedom-level active control to consist in causation of an action by mental events and by the agent" (p. 178). In light of the worries I have expressed about luck, what should Clarke's readers believe about the relationship between the *C-ability*—that is, the ability to *C-control* which actions one performs—and the *F-ability*?

Suppose that Clarke were to reject *A1* on the grounds (*C1*) that the difference between *W* and *Wn* at noon is a difference in Ann's exercises of *C*-control then. If the latter difference is itself just a matter of luck, then *C1* is compatible with *A1* and this appeal to *C1* is unsuccessful. I return to this issue soon.

Clarke may reject *A2* and claim (*C2*) that even if the difference between *W* and *Wn* at noon is just a matter of luck, Ann is morally responsible in *Wn* for deciding at noon to hold on to the coin and for not doing what she promised, owing (in large part) to that decision's being an exercise of *C*-control. A successful defense of *C2* would lay to rest the worry under consideration. I return to *C2* shortly.

Now for *A3*. One might claim (*C3*) that even if *A2* is true, Ann freely decides at noon to hold on to the coin and freely breaks her promise, owing (primarily) to that decision's being an exercise of *C*-control. Theorists have distinguished among weaker and stronger kinds of freedom or senses of "freedom."[15] *C3* may be true of some kinds of freedom that are too weak to ground moral responsibility. But libertarians are especially concerned with a stronger kind of freedom—a kind such that if Ann's decision is free in that way, then (given the details of the case) she is morally responsible for her decision. I have made the project of this book manageable by limiting my discussion of freedom to freedom of that kind.

Regarding *A4*, it might be claimed (*C4*) that although Ann does not freely decide at noon to hold on to the coin in *Wn* and does not freely break her promise in *Wn*, she freely performs a noontime coin flip in *W*. To make this plausible, the asymmetry in the ascriptions of freedom would need to be defended, and libertarians are not fond of asymmetry in this connection.[16]

Libertarians would do well to shut down the worry about luck at or near its source. Some of Clarke's claims about control may seem to do that, because control and luck seem to oppose each other (Kane 2002, p. 421). However, the kind of control Clarke focuses on—what he calls "active control" in Clarke 2002 and "direct active control" in Clarke 2003—"is exercised in action" at the time of action (2002, p. 367). "Direct active control is exercised in acting, not before" (2003, p. 166). To the extent to which the difference between *W* and *Wn* in Ann's noontime actions is a matter of luck, so is the difference in her exercises of direct active control at the time. It is not as though the luck involved in the former difference is independent of luck involved in the latter.[17] That Ann is exercising something called *control* does nothing to alter that fact.

Clarke reports that if someone who raises the luck objection about a scenario featuring a "nondeterministically caused" decision is claiming "that nothing about the agent prior to the decision *makes it the case* that one rather than the other decision is made, where this just means that the decision is not causally determined (and what else could it mean), then this will of course be granted" (2002, p. 368; see 2003, p. 81). He immediately points out that the objector's claim includes no "argument that the feature remarked upon constitutes any diminution of active control." My response is that undiminished exercises of active control seemingly are entirely compatible with the luck that worries me. As far as I can see, even if Ann's exercise of direct active control in *W* in tossing the coin is a *full-blown*—that is, undiminished and un-reduced (see Clarke 2003, p. 81)—exercise of such control and the same is true of her exercise of direct active control in *Wn* in deciding not to toss it, the difference between *W* and *Wn* in exercises of direct active control at noon is just a matter of luck. Someone might say that that difference is accounted for by the conjunction of Ann's exercising her agent-causal power in tossing the coin at noon in *W* and her exercising her agent-causal power in deciding at noon to hold on to the coin in *Wn*. But this conjunction *is* the difference at issue; it does not account for the difference.

Even if the worry about luck cannot be canceled at its source, *C2* is in the running. *C2* is a reply to a claim *near* the source of the worry, and I said I would return to it. Assume that the difference at noon between *W* and *Wn* is just a matter of luck—that is, assume that *A1* is true. Why should we believe that, even so, Ann is morally responsible in *Wn* for deciding at noon to hold on to the coin and for not doing what she promised? *C2* asserts that her decision's being an exercise of *C*-control provides at least a significant part of the answer. It may be claimed that the ability to *C*-control one's actions is an ability to act freely in a sense of "freely" strong enough to ground moral responsibility, despite the luck involved in how one exercises one's *C*-control at a time. An agent causationist who makes this claim takes on the burden of explaining what it is about *C*-control in virtue of which it is related in the alleged way to free action and moral responsibility.

Libertarians may complain that their opponents are begging the question by insisting that anything less than ordinary deterministic causation of an action suffices for responsibility-undermining luck. Now, even if they were to insist on this, they would not thereby be begging the question against *incompatibilism*. A modest libertarianism (see ch. 1, sec. 2), according to which there can be free actions in worlds in which there are no *basically free actions*—no free *A*-ings that occur at times at which the past and the laws of nature are consistent with the agent's not *A*-ing then—is a theoretical option, and an opponent can criticize conventional libertarianism from a modest libertarian perspective. According to a modest libertarian view of the sort I have in mind, even if the proximal cause of a free action deterministically causes it, that action depends for its freedom on the absence of deterministic causation a bit further back in the causal chain. For example, a free decision to *A* might have been directly deterministically caused by something that includes the agent's acquiring, on the basis of deliberation, a belief that it would be best to *A* at once, and that event of belief acquisition may have been nondeterministically caused. A philosopher may find a position of this kind attractive partly because he or she worries about the implications of luck at the very time of action—*present luck*.[18] A successful defense of *C2* would make some philosophers more comfortable about a bolder libertarianism. Until such a defense is produced, bold libertarians need to worry about present luck.

The libertarian complaint about question begging misses its mark on other grounds as well. If conclusive arguments for incompatibilism or for the possibility of basically free actions were in circulation, certain debates that have heated up would have cooled down instead. It is still up for grabs whether incompatibilism is true and whether basically free actions are possible. People in search of the truth about free will are right to look for strengths and weaknesses in the various proposals on offer. And one apparent weakness of conventional libertarian proposals is exposed by attention to luck. It is understandable that some philosophers would regard that weakness as less tolerable than, for example, apparent weaknesses of their favorite compatibilist account of free will. Such philosophers can fairly argue with libertarian opponents about whose view is more credible without insisting that indeterministic causation of action and agent causation of action (integrated or otherwise) *entail* responsibility-undermining luck. And people in search of a view to embrace can fairly ask to be persuaded that the entailment thesis is false.

An agent-causal libertarian may claim that because a crucial part of this conventional libertarian view is that, necessarily, if A is a basically free action, it is performed at a time at which the combination of the past and the laws of nature is compatible with the agent's not A-ing then, and because this requirement itself seems to provide the basis of the worry about luck, the worry misses the point of agent-causal libertarianism. However, what, in the end, those who worry about luck in this connection find troublesome is the claim that an agent who A-s at t can be morally responsible for his A-ing, even though in another possible world with the same past and laws of nature, he does not A at t. The worriers are not missing the point; some are rejecting it, and others are asking to be persuaded that they should accept it despite the appearance of responsibility-undermining luck.

It may be suggested that agent-causal libertarianism can handle luck better than event-causal libertarianism can. Derk Pereboom contends that although the latter view may, unlike compatibilism, "provide leeway for decision and action," it does not provide "enhanced control" (2001, p. 55; also see Clarke 1997, pp. 45–46, Clarke 2003, p. 133; Watson 1987, p. 165). On event-causal libertarian views, Pereboom argues, alleged free choices are "partially random" events (p. 54) in the sense that "factors beyond the agent's control [nondeterministically] contribute to their production . . . [and] there is nothing that supplements the contribution of these factors to produce the events" (p. 48). What Pereboom calls "enhanced control" is provided by supplementation of this contribution, and agent causationists can claim that *agents* supplement it in producing their free choices. A certain kind of agent causationism "posits, as a primitive feature of agents, the causal power to choose without being determined by events beyond the agent's control, and without the choice being a truly random [i.e., uncaused] or partially random event. . . . In the best version of this position, free choices are identical to activations of this causal power" (p. 55).[19] Voila!

Assume that agent-causal libertarianism provides agents with a species of control that is not available in compatibilist and event-causal libertarian theories. Even then, it seems to be just a matter of luck that an agent exercised his agent-causal power at *t* in deciding to *A* rather than exercising it at *t* in any of the alternative ways he does in other possible worlds with the same past and laws of nature. In light of this, one is entitled to worry that free choices are *not* identical to activations of the causal power that Pereboom describes—one that includes "enhanced control." The "enhanced control" that he identifies leaves the worry intact.

Suppose, for the sake of argument, that there is an agent-causal power and that it is different from all event-causal powers that agents can have. Suppose also that because it is a different power and has something to do with controlling one's actions, mixing it with agents' event-causal powers provides "enhanced control." Even with these suppositions in place, the difference identified in the preceding paragraph seems to be just a matter of luck. One can enhance a collection of powers that is not up to the task of securing a capacity for free and morally responsible action and get an enhanced collection that also is not up to that task.

Comparing an agent whose decision is indeterministically caused by events alone with a counterpart agent whose decision is "brought about as characterized by an integrated agent-causal account" (2003, p. 159), Clarke contends that the latter agent:

> exercised greater active control; he exercised a further power to causally influence which of the open alternatives would come about. In so doing, he was literally an originator of his decision, and neither the decision nor his initiating the decision was causally determined by events. This is why [he] is responsible for his decision, and why it was performed with sufficient active control to have been directly free. If this explanation is correct, then . . . the concept of agent causation is crucially relevant to the problem of free will. (p. 160)

The central point made in the preceding paragraph applies here as well. Are we to believe that the pertinent cross-world difference is not just a matter of luck? If so, why? Are we to believe that although that difference is a matter of luck, the agent is morally responsible for his decision and makes it freely? If so, why? Why should we not believe that the difference is just a matter of luck and that, because it is, the agent is not morally responsible for his decision and does not make it freely, despite exercising "the further power" Clarke cites? I may try to lift a weight by using the power of my right arm alone and fail. I may try again, this time using in addition the further power of my left arm, and I may fail again, the combined powers not being up to the task. If the weight is a ton, the combined powers are not enough to give me even a ghost of a chance of lifting it. For all I have been able to ascertain, the combination of agent causation with indeterministic event causation is similarly inadequate.

A possible objection to my procedure in this section merits attention. It may be claimed that although I have been giving the impression that I am leaving it open how the ability to *C*-control which actions one performs (*C*-ability) is related to the ability to act freely (*F*-ability), I am not leaving this open. A critic may argue as follows for this claim. Perhaps *C*-ability is identical with *F*-ability. Suppose that it is and that Ann appropriately exercises *C*-ability at the relevant time in *W* and *Wn*. Then Ann appropriately exercises *F*-ability at that time in these worlds and therefore acts freely then in them. Now, I remarked on the apparent possibility that the difference between *W* and *Wn* in exercises of *C*-control at noon is just a matter of luck. The conjunction of this possibility and the current supposition entails the possibility that the difference in how Ann acts *freely* in these worlds is just a matter of luck, which (the critic contends) is absurd.

Two observations are in order. First, among the things that I do not know is that *C*-ability is identical with (or conceptually sufficient for) *F*-ability—partly because I am uncertain exactly how *C*-control is supposed to bear on the problem of present luck. So, as far as I know, what I identified as an apparent possibility—that the difference between *W* and *Wn* in exercises of *C*-control at noon is just a matter of luck—is a real possibility, even if differences in how an agent exercises *F*-ability at *t* across worlds of the relevant kind cannot be a matter of luck. Second, it is not clear that what the imaginary critic says is absurd is, in fact, absurd. Perhaps some libertarians are committed to holding that, in cases of basically free action, the difference in how an agent acts freely in relevant worlds is just a matter of luck, and perhaps they can explain why this commitment should be accepted. (On this, see ch. 5.)

"*C*-control," again, is my name for the power (or ability) Clarke has in mind in his work on a certain power (or ability) to control or determine which actions one performs that cannot be possessed in deterministic worlds. Of course, one may say that he has in mind the power to act freely and morally responsibly. If so, what I want to know is what it is about this power in virtue of which it is a power to do this. Suppose it is said that *C*-control includes the power to act in such a way that the differences in an agent's exercises of *C*-control at a time across worlds with the same past and laws of nature are not just a matter of luck, or that it includes the power to act in such a way that even though these differences *are* just a matter of luck, one nevertheless acts freely and morally responsibly when properly exercising that power. Then what I want to know is what it is about *C*-control in virtue of which these claims are supposed to be true.

It may be replied that it is my job to show that these claims are false. I disagree. First, I am not asserting that they are false. I do not see how I can confidently do so before it has been made clear what it is about *C*-control in virtue of which these claims are supposed to be true. Second, my aim in developing this chapter's central problem for agent causationists and other conventional libertarians is to present it sufficiently forcefully to motivate them to work out solutions to it—proposed solutions that I and others can then assess. That is the way of progress.

I have been operating with an informal, intuitive notion of luck. A common defensive tactic is to question the meaning of a troublesome objection's key terms. What, I will be asked, is luck? Well, if the question why an agent exercised his agent-causal power at *t* in deciding to *A* rather than exercising it at *t* in any of the alternative ways he does in other possible worlds with the same past and laws of nature is, in principle, unanswerable—unanswerable because there is no fact or truth to be reported in a correct answer, not because of any limitations in those to whom the question is asked or in their audience—and his exercising it at *t* so deciding has an effect on how his life goes, I count that as luck for the agent—good luck or bad, depending on the goodness or badness of the effect the particular exercise of agent-causal power has. If "luck" is not the best short label for this sort of thing, I am open to correction. Whatever it is called, agent causationists should try to persuade people who have the worry I have described that this worry should not stand in the way of their accepting agent-causal libertarianism.[20]

Two possible responses to the preceding paragraph merit discussion. One directly concerns luck and the other contrastive explanation. Replying to an article from which much of this chapter derives (Mele 2005b), Clarke asserts that if an agent's "actual decision [to *A*] is free, and if the alternative decision [to *B*], had it been made, would have been free," then it is false that "the difference between the actual world, where [he] decides to [A], and world W, where he decides to [B], is just a matter of luck" and false that "the difference between the actual world, where [he] causes a decision to [A], and world W, where he causes a decision to [B], is just a matter of luck" (2005a, p. 416). His claim, in short, is that the agent's deciding freely at *t* in both worlds suffices for its being false that the featured cross-world differences at *t* are just a matter of luck. Clarke contends that "what would be true" is that these differences between the actual world and W are a matter of the agent's "exercising his free will one way in the actual world and another way in W." An alternative view is that the difference between the ways in which the agent exercises his "will" at *t* in the two worlds is just a matter of luck, and an important question is whether, even so, he exercised his will *freely* in these worlds at the time and exercised it in making *free* decisions. Clarke asserts that the agent exercises his *free* will. Critics will ask how that can be so, given that the cross-world difference in the agent's exercises of his will at *t* seems to be just a matter of luck.

Clarke introduces a character named Leo to answer his critics. When asked whether he is morally responsible for a decision he made, Leo replies as follows:

> I once witnessed someone who had done something rather despicable try to get off the hook using an argument like the one that worries you. He explained how his action had been caused—the same way as my decision. And he pleaded: "I did this awful deed, I did it for reasons, and I did it knowing full well what I was doing. No one forced me to do it; I didn't have to do it; it was open to me not to do it. I determined that I do this. When I did, I was an ultimate source of my foul behavior; I originated it. But I'm not to blame. In another world with the same laws and the same history up until the time of my action, I determined and originated a decent action. The difference is just a matter of luck." (2005a, p. 418)

Leo apparently regards this person's plea for nonresponsibility as preposterous, as would normal jurors in a normal court of law and neighbors of mine who witnessed what Leo witnessed. But event-causal libertarians would take a similarly dim view of a plea for nonresponsibility that replaces the agent-causal elements Leo mentions with their preferred event-causal elements, and compatibilists would reject pleas for nonresponsibility that grant the satisfaction of their preferred sufficient conditions for morally responsible action. My neighbors and normal jurors in a normal court of law would share these attitudes with these theorists. In real life, people are rarely let off the hook for awful deeds on metaphysical grounds. The strategy of attempting to shape intuitions by placing one's proposed set of conceptually sufficient conditions for morally responsible action in a context in which an acquaintance is appealing solely to metaphysical considerations in making a case that he should be excused for a serious offense can be used to the same effect by theorists of each of these three kinds. This suggests that the strategy pumps intuitions in a way that generates more heat than light. Alternatively, if intuitions generated by this strategy not only accord with conceptually sufficient conditions of these three different kinds—agent-causal libertarian, event-causal libertarian, and compatibilist—for morally responsible action but also *reveal the truth*, then moral responsibility is compatible both with determinism and with indeterminism, which is very good news for my project in this book.

Most philosophers are sufficiently in touch with the real world to have a pretty good sense of what kinds of excuses for serious offenses are likely to be accepted by jurors and neighbors. If jurors and neighbors do not accept metaphysical excuses, and if it is to be inferred from this that metaphysical considerations are irrelevant to moral responsibility, then much of the literature on moral responsibility is irrelevant. If metaphysical considerations are relevant, the problem of present luck cannot easily be brushed aside.

On the topic of deciding freely, Leo is more concise: "I made the decision, I made it for reasons, and I could have done otherwise. It was up to me what to do. A plurality of alternatives was open to me, and I determined which I would pursue—I made it happen that I decide to tell the truth. When I did, I originated my decision. If this isn't acting freely, I don't know what is" (Clarke 2005a, p. 417). Here, again, the question arises how the addition of agent causation to indeterministic event-causation is supposed to solve the problem of present luck. Leo's answer, evidently, is (1) that the addition adds all that needs to be added to yield free decisions and (2) that because the pertinent decisions are free, the pertinent cross-world differences in decisions are not just a matter of luck. But no argument is offered for 2, and no support is offered for 1 beyond what has already been considered in this chapter.

I turn now to a foreseeable criticism about contrastive explanation. A critic may contend that I am falsely assuming that indeterministic contrastive explanations are impossible. However, I am not assuming that. Christopher Hitchcock ably defends the possibility of indeterministic contrastive explanations in an article that pays instructive attention to various kinds of presupposition that someone who asks why one thing happened rather than another may be making and to the bearing of presuppositions on the relevance of answers that may be offered to the questioner (1999). One observation Hitchcock makes is especially germane to the present issue: "it cannot be the case that one who asks 'why *P* rather than *Q*' is always presupposing everything that is explanatorily relevant to *P*, or else contrastive explanation would never be possible" (p. 601). Notice that in my formulation of the worry about luck, everything that is explanatorily relevant to, for example, an agent's exercising his agent-causal power at *t* in deciding to *A* *is* presupposed, for the entire history of the world up to *t* and the world's laws of nature are presupposed. (And why does my formulation presuppose all that? Because conventional libertarians hold that being a free agent entails performing basically free actions and, at least, that an agent performs a basically free action *A* at *t* only if in a possible world with the same past until *t* and the same laws of nature he does not *A* at *t*.)

Clarke contends that when the topic is deciding freely, "It is how a decision such as Leo's is caused that is the crucial matter. Requests for explanation can introduce pragmatic considerations that are extraneous to the causal story, and thus extraneous to the question of a decision's freedom. The debate over free will—including debate over the contrast argument—is not hostage to the debate over contrastive explanation" (2005a, p. 416).[21] These are sensible remarks. However, it is not debatable that if worlds *W1* and *W2* do not diverge until *t*, there is no difference between the world segments those worlds share to account for or explain the difference at *t*. No claim about contrastive explanation that is not entailed by this one—and therefore no debatable claim about it—needs to be made for the purposes of posing the problem of present luck for conventional libertarianism.

I close this section with a reaction to a potential objection to my story about Ann. It may be claimed that all basic instances of free and morally responsible action essentially involve an internal struggle about what to do at the time. And it may be argued, accordingly, that because there is no such struggle in Ann's story, whatever sort of control is such that its appropriate exercise in a moral context suffices for basically free and morally responsible action cannot be exercised in that story. Clarke and O'Connor do not advocate the premise of this objection, but that premise is available to agent-causal libertarians.

So I will tell another tale. Bob lives in a town in which people bet not only on football games but also on such things as whether the opening coin toss will occur on time. After Bob agreed to toss a coin at noon to start a high school football game, Carl, a notorious gambler, offered him $50 to wait until 12:02 to toss it. Bob, who was uncertain about what to do, continued struggling with his dilemma as noon approached. He was tempted by the $50, but he also had moral qualms about helping Carl cheat people out of their money. He judged it best on the whole to do what he agreed to do. Even so, at noon, he decided to toss the coin at 12:02 and to pretend to be searching for it in his pockets in the meantime. In a possible world that does not diverge from the actual world before noon, Bob decides at noon to toss the coin straightaway and acts accordingly.

Does Bob's internal struggle help to answer the worry that the pertinent difference between these two worlds at noon is just a matter of luck? It may be argued that it does, if the struggle is made possible by certain aspects of Bob's character that are partly explained by past basically free actions of his. One might claim that when we take Bob's past into account, we may see that the noontime difference between these two Bob-worlds is not just a matter of luck, because the practical accessibility itself of these worlds to Bob at the time is partly explained by basically free actions he performed at earlier times. For example, it may be claimed that if, in certain past situations, Bob had performed— as he could have—better free actions than he in fact performed, the cheating worlds would not have been practically accessible to him at noon.

There is an obvious problem with this line of reasoning. The worry about luck that I have developed is a worry about whether there are any basically free actions at all. So it directly applies to the alleged past actions to which the reasoning appeals. One cannot undermine the worry by ignoring it.

Does Bob's struggle suggest that the difference between the relevant worlds at noon is not just a matter of luck or that even though the difference is just a matter of luck, his decision at noon in the actual world is a basic instance of free and morally responsible action? That an agent is engaged in an internal struggle about what to do at the time of decision indicates that he takes himself to have some live options. A suitable description of the struggle sheds light on the motivation he has to pursue these options. Our knowledge of his motivation gives us a sense of why he chooses whichever live option he chooses. But none of this suggests that the difference at the time of choice or decision between the actual world and any world in which he instead decides in favor of another live option is not just a matter of luck. If it does suggest that even if the difference is just a matter of luck, Bob's actual decision is a free and morally responsible action, someone should explain how it does so.

7. Some Recent History

A very brief review of a portion of the recent history of the luck problem will prove instructive. Bruce Waller (1988, p. 151) raises an interesting worry about luck in criticizing the view of free will and moral responsibility advocated in Kane 1985. Kane summarizes the objection as follows:

> "Suppose two persons had exactly the same pasts and made exactly the same efforts of will," says Waller, but one does the moral or prudential thing while the other does not. Given that their pasts were exactly the same up to the moment of choice, as indeterminism requires, wouldn't that mean that the outcome was a matter of luck? One of them got lucky and succeeded in overcoming temptation, the other failed. Would there then "be any grounds for distinguishing between [them], for saying that one deserves censure for a selfish decision and the other deserves praise for generosity? If they are really identical, and the difference in their acts results from chance, then it seems irrational to consider one more praiseworthy (or more blameworthy) than the other should be." (1996, p. 171)

Kane argues in response that efforts to resist temptation in free agents are *indeterminate*, and because that is so, we cannot "imagine the same agent in two possible worlds with exactly the same pasts making exactly the same effort and getting lucky in one world and not the other. Exact sameness or difference of possible worlds is not defined if the possible world contains indeterminate efforts or indeterminate events of any kinds" (p. 172).

In Mele 1999b, I argued that this appeal to indeterminacy does not help, even if it is granted that exact sameness and difference are not defined:

> Kane's appeal to the indeterminacy of an effort makes it more difficult to formulate crisply the "objection from luck" to libertarianism. But the spirit of the objection survives. If John's effort to resist temptation fails where John₂'s effort succeeds, and there is nothing about the agents' powers, capacities, states of mind, moral character, and the like that

explains this difference in outcome, then the difference really is just a matter of luck. That their efforts are indeterminate explains why the outcomes of the efforts might not be the same, but this obviously does not explain (even nondeterministically or probabilistically) why John failed whereas John$_2$ succeeded. (p. 280; also see Mele 1999a and Haji 1999)

Kane replies (1999b) by modifying his view to include the doubled effort maneuver criticized in section 2.

It is obvious that Kane, a leading event-causal libertarian, takes the luck problem seriously. If he were to deem the worry about luck fundamentally misguided, he would not keep revising his view in an effort to lay the worry to rest. O'Connor also takes the problem seriously—at least as a problem for Kane, as I observed in section 2. Part of what I have been arguing here is that it is a problem for agent-causal libertarians, too, including O'Connor.

8. Conclusion

I identified the aim of this chapter as the clarification of issues about control central to the debate between conventional libertarians and their critics. Suppose, with John Fischer, that "there are at least two sorts of conditions relevant to moral responsibility: epistemic conditions and freedom-relevant conditions" (1994, p. 238, n. 4). And suppose that someone claims that exercises of agent causation are exercises of a kind, *K*, of control such that to exercise control of that kind is to satisfy all freedom-relevant conditions for basic moral responsibility; in short, it is to exercise *MR freedom-level control*. Then it should be asked what it is about control of kind *K* in virtue of which this is true. As far as I can see, what is said about control in Clarke 2000, 2002, 2003, and 2005a and in O'Connor 2000 leaves intact the worry I sketched about present luck. As I explained, the difference in an agent's exercises of *C*-control or "active power" at a time in possible worlds with the same past and laws of nature—*difference D*, for short—seems to be just a matter of luck; and neither Clarke nor O'Connor argues that *D*'s being just a matter of luck is consistent with the agent's freely performing the pertinent actions. However, even if appearance matches reality here, agent-causal libertarians may have room to maneuver. They can try to explain why although *D* is just a matter of luck, people who agent-cause an action can exercise *MR* freedom-level control at the time and be basically morally responsible for what they do then. Agent causationists would significantly advance their cause if they were to show that D is not just a matter of luck or explain why, despite D's being just a matter of luck, in agent-causing an action an agent exercises MR freedom-level control.[22]

These issues about control are instances of more general issues for all traditional libertarians, including those who have no use for agent causation. Whatever positive account a traditional libertarian gives of what may be termed "basic moral-responsibility-level free action," there is the question whether the pertinent cross-world actional differences are just a matter of luck and the question why, if they are, agents who instantiate the account a libertarian offers of the production of basically free actions should be believed to exercise MR freedom-level control at the time and to be basically morally responsible for what they do. In the absence of convincing answers to these questions, it is epistemically open that something along the lines of the nontraditional, modest libertarian proposal that I described in chapter 1 (sec. 2) is the best a libertarian can do. Of course, as I observed in chapter 1, even if that is the best libertarian option, it does not follow that everyone who believes that there are free and morally responsible agents should gravitate toward it—as long as compatibilism is still a live option.

Compatibilism also is challenged by a kind of luck. Incompatibilists want to know how agents can be morally responsible for actions of theirs or perform them freely, if, relative to their own powers of control, it is just a matter of luck that long before their birth their universe was such as to ensure that they would perform those actions.[23] How, they want to know, is agents' *remote deterministic luck* compatible with their exercising MR freedom-level control in acting?

Consider the following propositions:

P1. If at t an agent exercises MR freedom-level control in deciding to A, then there is another possible world with the same past and laws of nature in which, at t, he does not decide to A.

P2. If at t an agent decides to A and there is another possible world with the same past and laws of nature in which, at t, he does not decide to A, then at t he does not exercise MR freedom-level control in deciding to A.

P1, a typical libertarian claim, is motivated partly by worries about remote deterministic luck. P2, an antilibertarian claim, is motivated by worries about present luck. Putting them together, we get the result that if at t an agent exercises MR freedom-level control in deciding to A, then at t he does *not* exercise MR freedom-level control in deciding to *A*. Readers who are pleased to deny that there are free agents undoubtedly are pleased by the result. Compatibilists, traditional libertarians, and modest libertarians all face opposing claims about agential control that derive at least partly from considerations of luck. Modest libertarians do not face the challenge to compatibilists about remote deterministic luck nor the challenge to traditional libertarians about present luck. But, of course, if it is plausible that *MR* freedom-level control presupposes or entails present luck, modest libertarians have a problem. They also have the burden of explaining why the luck they countenance in certain action-producing processes they describe does not block *MR* freedom-level control over the actions produced, an issue I take up in chapter 5. Luck and control are at the heart of important unfinished business for all believers in free, morally responsible agency.

NOTES

1. For references to Clarke's earlier work defending agent-causal libertarianism, see Clarke 2003.

2. I say "conventional" libertarians because I and others have floated some unconventional positive libertarian accounts of free and morally responsible action designed to avoid certain problems that conventional libertarians apparently have with luck (Dennett 1978; Ekstrom 2000; Fischer 1995; Mele 1995, ch. 12; 1996; 1999b). I say "floated" because Dennett, Fischer, and I are not incompatibilists. They are compatibilists, and I am officially agnostic about the truth of compatibilism (Mele 1995). Ekstrom is an incompatibilist.

3. For a recent critique of noncausal libertarian accounts of free action, see Clarke 2003, ch. 2.

4. Also see Kane 1999a, 2000, and 2002. Readers who balk at the thought that an agent may *try to choose to A* (Kane 1999b, pp. 231, 233–34) may prefer to think in terms of an agent's trying to bring it about that he chooses to *A*.

5. Kane writes: "The core meaning of 'He got lucky,' which *is* implied by indeterminism, I suggest, is that 'He succeeded *despite the probability or chance of failure*'; and this core meaning does not imply lack of responsibility, if he succeeds" (1999b, p. 233).

6. Kane suggested this in a question-and-answer session following his presentation of "Three Freedoms and What They Tell Us about Agency, Responsibility, and Free Will" (University of Florida, February 2005). Neil Levy made the same suggestion in correspondence.

7. As I understand O'Connor, to exercise the *F*-power is freely to exercise the *D*-power. I do not see how exercising the *D*-power in choosing can itself be sufficient for choosing freely, in a sense of "freely" closely associated with moral responsibility. If there is such a thing as the power of an agent directly to causally

determine his choices, insane agents can have that power, and they can exercise it in making unfree, insane choices for which they are not morally responsible.

8. Clarke holds that "an agent's exercise of direct active control is not itself an action" (2003, p. 138). Incidentally, O'Connor asserts, "Agent-causal events are intrinsically actions—the exercising of control over one's behavior" (2000, pp. 58–59).

9. One can only speculate about whether Clarke would take this ability to be, for example, an *I*-ability or something more demanding.

10. The quoted passage is about freely made decisions, but I take it that, for Clarke, even if not all exercises of the ability to determine which decisions one makes are free, all exercises of this ability, owing to the nature of the ability, do require the chanciness he describes here.

11. An alternative view is that this is true, more specifically, of all *basically free* actions. Because the following discussion applies straightforwardly to all such actions, I will not discuss the two views separately.

12. I am not claiming that these two kinds of *N*-world are the only kinds. For example, I have said nothing about worlds in which, owing to something's distracting her at noon, Ann continues holding the coin for another minute. Perhaps in some such worlds it is not plausibly said to be an *accident* that Ann does not *C*.

13. In one kind of new intention *N*-world, there is a relevant decision to *A* (e.g., to hold the coin for another minute) at the pertinent time, and in another there is, instead, a nonactionally acquired intention to *A*. The problem I am about to raise features worlds of the first kind. A parallel problem featuring worlds of the second kind is at least as worrisome.

14. For more on akratic decisions and defective decisions, see ch. 5, sec. 5.

15. For discussion and references, see Kane 1996, pp. 14–17.

16. Suppose that among the worlds with the same past and laws, *Wn* is very remote. It might be claimed that in this world Ann suffers a breakdown and therefore decides unfreely. So what is important about there being a world like *Wn*? Perhaps simply that it entails the falsity of determinism. And what is important about determinism's being false? For one answer, see ch. 4, sec. 3.

17. This is not to say that, holding the past and the laws of nature fixed, all cross-world differences in an agent's actions at a time depend on an intrinsic difference in her exercises of active control at the time. Consider two worlds, *W1* and *W2*, in which Ann performs a noontime coin flip. The worlds do not diverge before the coin leaves her hand. In *W1* it lands heads, and in *W2* it lands tails; Ann tosses heads in the former world and tails in the latter. According to one possible view, in *W1* Ann performs the action of tossing heads, that action ends when the coin lands heads up, and her pertinent exercise of active control is over by the time the coin leaves her hand and is part of her action of tossing heads. On this view, that exercise does not differ intrinsically from Ann's pertinent exercise of active control in *W2* at noon. (Bear in mind that the worlds diverge only after these

exercises of active control have ended.) However, presumably, the same sort of view cannot plausibly be taken about the relationship between Ann's exercise of active control in flipping the coin in *W* and her exercise of active control in deciding not to flip the coin then in *Wn*. Presumably, active control is exercised very differently in coin flipping and in decision making.

18. Dennett (1978) sketches a view of this kind (without endorsing it). The view does not include the thesis that there are no basically free actions. Its focus is the production of free actions that are deterministically caused by the agent's indeterministically produced "assessment of the best available course of action" (p. 295). The view says nothing about akratic actions, for example. But a variant of this view that makes all free actions directly deterministically caused and indirectly indeterministically caused is conceivable.

19. If the primitive feature Pereboom describes here can be a feature of agents, it can be a feature of insane agents, and they can exercise the power he characterizes in making unfree, insane choices for which they are not morally responsible. So I do not see how all "activations of this causal power" can be free choices, in a sense of "free" closely associated with moral responsibility. See note 7 for a similar point.

20. As Susan Hurley defines *thin luck*, it "is just the absence or negation of whatever it is that makes for responsibility" (2003, p. 107). I am not using "luck" in that sense. One option for libertarians is to argue that cross-world luck at the time of action does not preclude moral responsibility for one's action. I produce such an argument in chapter 5.

21. "The contrast argument" is Clarke's label for an argument from present luck against an integrated agent-causal account of free action.

22. An agent causationist may reply that my worry does not *prove* that libertarianism is false or that indeterministic agents exercise any less proximal control than well-functioning deterministic agents, as Clarke, in effect, does (2002, pp. 368–69). However, a positive move called for in the sentence to which this note is appended would improve our understanding of agent-causal libertarianism and facilitate our assessment of it.

23. In Beebee and Mele 2002, it is argued that if the standard assumption of necessitarianism about laws of nature in the contemporary free will literature is set aside and replaced by a Humean view of laws, there is no such ensuring even in deterministic universes. However, it also is argued there that Humean compatibilists face a problem about luck much like the one typical libertarians face. Because necessitarianism about laws of nature is far more popular than Humeanism, and because Beebee and I have done our best to situate Humean compatibilism in the debate about free will and moral responsibility, my discussion of compatibilism in this book presupposes necessitarianism about laws.

$\cdot \cdot \cdot$

Frankfurt-style Cases, Luck, and Soft Libertarianism

In the preceding chapter, I argued that present luck raises an as yet unresolved problem for traditional libertarians about basically free actions—free A-ings occurring at times at which the past and the laws of nature are consistent with the agent's not A-ing then. In the absence of a successful resolution of the problem, skepticism about basically free actions is a live option. However, a philosopher can deny that there are basically free actions and consistently assert that there are free actions. Such a philosopher would accept the view, V, that all free A-ings occur at times at which the past—perhaps just the immediate past—and the laws of nature are incompatible with the agent's not A-ing then. Many versions of V are conceivable. According to one, free action requires determinism. According to another, although free action does not require determinism, it does require that the internal workings of agents—or at least everything in agents involved in the production of free actions—be deterministic. Yet another is incompatibilist about free action but not about the proximate causes of free actions. Reflection on present luck may contribute to a philosopher's moving toward a version of V.

If the following libertarian thesis is true, V is false:

> LT. No possible agent ever acts freely unless he sometimes freely A-s at times at which the combination of the past up to those times and the laws of nature is consistent with his not A-ing then. (That is, no possible agent ever acts freely unless he performs some *basically* free actions.)

But is LT true? On a straightforward interpretation of LT, some Frankfurt-style cases speak against it, as I explain in section 2. If they falsify *LT*, they remove an obstacle to the acceptance of *V*. I say this not because I wish to defend *V*, but rather as an illustration of the point that a combination of reflection on luck and reflection on Frankfurt-style cases can motivate alternatives to traditional libertarianism. Present luck raises a problem for standard libertarian requirements on free action— for example, *LT* and theses that entail *LT*—and Frankfurt-style cases are designed to show, among other things, that some of those theses are false. In the present chapter, I explore what can be learned from combining Frankfurt-style cases with the central theme of chapter 3.

1. Introducing Frankfurt-style Cases and Clarifying PAP

Although compatibilists and incompatibilists disagree about much, both sides agreed for many years that having been able to do otherwise than one did is required both for free action and for moral responsibility. Incompatibilists argued, of course, that in any deterministic world, no one could ever have done otherwise than he did. Compatibilists argued against this claim, and some offered compatibilist accounts of the sort of ability to do otherwise that they regarded as appropriate for free action and moral responsibility (see, e.g., Moore 1912, ch. 6). Harry Frankfurt attacked the point of agreement in an article that played an important role in changing the shape of the debate about moral responsibility and freedom (1969). More specifically, he sought to falsify what he called "the principle of alternate possibilities":

> PAP. A person is morally responsible for what he has done only if he could have done otherwise. (1969, p. 829)

Here is Frankfurt's main story:

> Black . . . wants Jones to perform a certain action [*A*]. Black is prepared to go to considerable lengths to get his way, but he prefers to avoid showing his hand unnecessarily. So he waits until Jones is about to make up his mind what to do, and he does nothing unless it is clear to him (Black is an excellent judge of such things) that Jones is going to decide to do something other than what he wants him to do. If it does become clear that Jones is going to decide to do something else, Black takes effective steps to ensure that Jones decides to do, and that he does do, what he wants him to do. Whatever Jones's initial preferences and

inclinations, then, Black will have his way.... [However] Black never has to show his hand because Jones, for reasons of his own, decides to perform and does perform the very action Black wants him to perform. (1969, pp. 835–36)[1]

Frankfurt claims that although Jones could not have done otherwise than decide to *A* and *A*, he is morally responsible for deciding and acting as he did. For reasons articulated in section 2, the Frankfurt-style story I explore is significantly different in structure.

Frankfurt's objection to PAP has played a major role in subsequent literature on responsibility and freedom. Many contributors to that literature regard the objection as successful. Some compatibilists use it in criticizing incompatibilism about moral responsibility and about the kind of freedom most closely associated with such responsibility (Fischer 1994, ch. 7), and some libertarians attempt to accommodate Frankfurt's moral in refined libertarian views (Stump 1990, Stump and Kretzmann 1991, Zagzebski 1991). Several philosophers argue that Frankfurt's story and stories like it are fundamentally flawed (Ginet 1996; 2003, pp. 597–604; Kane 1996, pp. 142–43, 191–92; 2000, pp. 161–63; 2003; Lamb 1993; O'Connor 2000, pp. 81–84; Widerker 1995, 2000, 2003; Wyma 1997). However, David Robb and I have developed a way of constructing Frankfurt-style cases that, we argue, circumvents any genuine problems that these philosophers have identified and falsifies PAP on a standard libertarian reading of that principle (Mele and Robb 1998, 2003).

I discuss the merits and implications of Frankfurt-style cases in the following sections. Three issues require prior attention. First, Frankfurt's thought experiment is designed to undermine PAP whether its being true that someone "could have done otherwise" is understood as being incompatible or compatible with determinism. However, my concern in this chapter is with libertarianism, and I focus accordingly on libertarian interpretations of PAP and more precise variants of that principle. The variants are formulated in terms of ability to do otherwise rather than "could have done otherwise," and libertarians standardly hold that its being true that one was able to do otherwise than one did— like its being true that one could have done otherwise than one did—is incompatible with determinism. In terms of possible worlds, they hold that an agent who *A*-ed at *t* in world *W* was able at *t* to do otherwise at *t* only if there is a possible world with the same laws of nature as *W* and the same past up to *t* in which the agent does otherwise at *t*.

Theorists do not always distinguish between being able at t to do otherwise at t—*synchronic* ability to do otherwise—and being able at some earlier time $t - n$ to do otherwise at a nonoverlapping time t—*diachronic* ability to do otherwise. I comment on the latter shortly. To indicate that "able" is to be read in a libertarian way in the variants of PAP that I discuss in this chapter, I place an l—for libertarian—immediately after "PAP" in my names for these principles. The l is meant to signal that the thesis as stated is to be conjoined with a libertarian understanding of "able to do otherwise." (There are additional single-letter abbreviations in the names: for example, f for variants of PAP that are specifically about free action, m for variants that are specifically about moral responsibility, and h for history-sensitive versions.)

Second, a reminder about the expression "A-ed at t" is in order (see ch. 1, sec. 3). Except in the case of momentary A-ings, "t" in "S A-ed at t" is a placeholder for a stretch of time longer than a moment. So such expressions as "same past up to t," where t is the time of an A-ing, are potentially misleading. An agent's having an incompatibilist synchronic ability to do otherwise than A at t, where A is what he did in world $W1$ at t, is secured only by there being a possible world $W2$ with the same laws of nature as $W1$ and the same past as $W1$ up to a moment at which what happens first diverges from the agent's A-ing. In the case of nonmomentary A-ings, this initial divergence can happen at a moment at which the agent is A-ing in $W1$ or at the moment at which his A-ing begins in $W1$. Traditionally, it is said that $W2$ has the same past as $W1$ "up to t," but this is shorthand for the assertion that it has the same past as $W1$ up to the moment of initial divergence—a moment t in the case of a momentary A-ing, and some moment during t (including the moment at which the A-ing begins) in the case of nonmomentary A-ings.

The third issue is the interpretation of PAP. The principle is unspecific in ways that need to be identified. "Could have done otherwise" in PAP is typically given a synchronic reading. That is, PAP is typically understood to assert that a person is morally responsible for what he did at t only if, at t, he could have done otherwise then. However, when PAP is read that way, it is counterintuitive for mundane reasons. It is very plausible that in a typical case in which a drunk driver who, owing to his being drunk, runs over and kills a pedestrian he does not see, the driver is morally responsible for killing the pedestrian. But in many such cases, as t draws very near, it is simply too late for the driver to do otherwise at t than hit and kill the pedestrian.

It also is plausible that the driver's moral responsibility for the killing in cases of this kind derives partly from his being morally responsible for some relevant intentional actions. In a typical case, the driver knows that he is impaired and drives even so: he intentionally drives-while-impaired. Suppose that, after a time, owing partly to his drunkenness, he ceases to realize that he is impaired and his driving-while-impaired is no longer properly said to be intentional. Even so, he would typically be deemed responsible for intentional actions that put him in this position: for example, his decision to drive even though he knew he was impaired and the intentional driving-while-impaired to which it led. Suppose now that the man was so drunk that he did not realize he was impaired even when he started his car. In a normal case of this kind (e.g., the man was not force-fed alcohol against his will), we say that the man was morally responsible for the killing, and we see that responsibility as inherited partly from his moral responsibility for his drinking.

One way to solve the problem that cases of this kind pose for PAP as standardly interpreted is with adjusted temporal indices, as follows:

> PAPlmh. A person is morally responsible for what he did at t only if he was able (more specifically, S-able), either before t or at t, to do otherwise at t.[2]

In an ordinary case of the kind under consideration, the agent was S-able at a time significantly earlier than t to do otherwise at t than kill the pedestrian then. For example, he might have been at least S-able a half hour before t to climb into a taxi for a ride home, in which case he might have been brushing his teeth at t, miles away from the pedestrian. On a libertarian view of ability to do otherwise, being S-able at a time $t - n$ to do otherwise than one actually did at a significantly later time t may be understood as a matter of being S-able at $t - n$ to do something then or to do something at some time between then and t such that, if one were to do it, then at t one might do otherwise than one actually did at t. In terms of possible worlds, the idea is that an agent is S-able at $t - n$ to do otherwise than he did at t in W if and only if there is a possible world with the same laws of nature as W and the same past up to $t - n$ in which, at $t - n$ or at some time between then and t, he does otherwise than he does at that time in W and, as a partial consequence, he also does otherwise at t. Because my concern is with the falsification of PAPlmh and related principles, I focus on cautious readings of these alleged necessary conditions of morally responsible—and later, free—actions. When ability is at issue, the most cautious readings are in terms of S-ability.[3]

Another way to solve the problem is to rewrite PAP as a principle about what may be termed *direct moral responsibility*—moral responsibility that is not inherited from the agent's moral responsibility for other actions:

> PAPlmd. A person is directly morally responsible for what he did at *t* only if at *t* he was able (more specifically, S-able) to do otherwise at *t*.

In the typical scenario, the drunk driver is morally responsible for killing the pedestrian because he is morally responsible for driving drunk and because he kills the pedestrian. It is in virtue of the combination of his being morally responsible for driving drunk and of his killing the pedestrian he does not see while so driving that he is morally responsible for the killing. I mark the existence of an in-virtue-of relation of this sort between an agent's *X*-ing and his *Y*-ing by saying that his moral responsibility for *Y*-ing is *inherited from* his moral responsibility for *X*-ing. Moral responsibility that is not inherited is *direct*.[4]

The following three principles about free action are analogues, respectively, of PAP, PAPlmh, and PAPlmd:

> PAPf. A person freely did what he did only if he could have done otherwise.

> PAPlfh. A person freely did what he did at *t* only if he was able (more specifically, S-able), either before *t* or at *t*, to do otherwise at *t*.

> PAPlfd. What a person did at *t* was directly freely done only if at *t* he was able (more specifically, S-able) to do otherwise at *t*.

I comment briefly on each, starting with a pair of observations about PAPf, which, like PAP, I treat as not specifically incompatibilist. First, although, as I explained, PAP seemingly is falsified by a mundane counterexample when "could have done otherwise" is given a synchronic reading, that style of counterexample does not work against PAP's freedom analogue, PAPf, on the same reading of "could have done otherwise." It would typically be denied that the drunk driver who did not even see the pedestrian freely killed him. This is a noteworthy observation for anyone who had been inclined to believe that a person is morally responsible for *A*-ing only if he freely *A*-s. Second, PAPf is unspecific in at least two ways, as is PAP. On the most natural reading of "could have done otherwise," the principle requires that the agent have been able to *act* otherwise. However, a proponent of PAPf need not require this. We say such things as that someone did nothing when he should have taken action, and it is open to proponents of PAPf to say that on their preferred reading of the principle, one way of doing otherwise than what one did is doing nothing at all (provided, of course, that what one did was not nothing). Also, is "could have done otherwise" to be given a synchronic reading or not? PAPlfh is a non-synchronic version of PAPf. The following is a synchronic version:

> PAPlfs. A person freely did what he did at t only if, at t, he was able (more specifically, S-able) to do otherwise at t.

PAPlfh, PAPlfs, and PAPlfd, like PAPf, are not specific about doing otherwise. Does doing otherwise mean *acting* otherwise or not? Precision on this matter can be secured by replacing each principle by a pair of principles, with one member requiring *acting* otherwise and the other being more relaxed.

How is "directly" in PAPlfd to be understood? I suggest the following: by definition, an agent directly freely A-s if and only if he freely A-s and that is so not even partly in virtue of his having freely done something earlier.[5] As shorthand for "S directly freely A-ed," I use "S freely$_d$ A-ed."

2. A Frankfurt-style Story and Alternative Possibilities

In Frankfurt's attempted counterexample to PAP, the agent, Jones, A-s "on his own," and it is claimed that he is morally responsible for A-ing even though, owing to the presence of a potential controller, Black, he could not have done otherwise at the time than A (1969, pp. 835–36). Black does not interfere, but he would have if he had needed to.[6] A problem with Frankfurt's story may be formulated as a dilemma (Kane 1996; Widerker 1995).[7] Assume a story featuring *deciding* to A. On the one hand, if a deterministic setting is assumed, the story cannot persuade traditional incompatibilists: the truth of determinism itself, they will say, ensures that Jones could not have done otherwise than decide to A and therefore ensures that he did not decide morally responsibly and freely. That Jones also could not have done otherwise for an additional reason certainly does not improve things. On the other hand, if the setting is indeterministic and Jones's decision is not deterministically caused, Black cannot be certain what Jones will decide on his own, in which case Jones could have decided otherwise than he did. Black can be mistaken about what Jones will decide on his own and refrain from intervening; in some such scenarios, Jones decides otherwise than Black wants him to.

In Mele and Robb 1998, a Frankfurt-style case designed to avoid this line of objection is constructed. In a slightly modified version of the story's core (pp. 101–2), Black initiates a certain internally deterministic process P in Bob's brain at $t1$ with the intention of thereby causing Bob to decide at $t2$ (an hour later, say) to steal Ann's car. The process, which is screened off from Bob's consciousness, will culminate in Bob's deciding at $t2$ to steal Ann's car unless he decides on his own at $t2$ to steal it or is incapable at $t2$ of making a decision (because, for example, he is dead by $t2$). The process is in no way sensitive to any "sign" of what Bob will decide. As it happens, at $t2$ Bob decides on his own to steal the car, on the basis of his own indeterministic deliberation about whether to steal it, and his decision is not deterministically caused. But if he had not just then decided on his own to steal it, P would have issued, at $t2$, in his deciding to steal it.[8] Rest assured that P in no way influences the indeterministic decision-making process that actually issues in Bob's decision.

Given further details (including, e.g., that Bob is sane), Bob, in the actual world, W, would appear to be morally responsible for deciding at $t2$ to steal Ann's car, even by libertarian standards.[9] Event-causal and agent-causal libertarians should suppose that Bob satisfies both their positive and their negative causal requirements for moral responsibility. I start with the positive causal requirements. Event-causal libertarians should suppose that Bob's decision was indeterministically caused in their preferred way. Agent causationists who hold that agents agent-cause their free decisions should suppose that Bob agent-caused his decision to steal the car. And agent causationists who hold that what an agent who freely decides to A agent-causes is an intention to A rather than a decision to A (O'Connor 2000, p. 72) should suppose that Bob agent-caused his intention to steal the car.

The negative causal requirement at issue is that Bob's decision and intention not be deterministically caused. On the supposition that an event-causal process, x, issues in Bob's decision, that x does not deterministically cause the decision is clear: even though x actually causes Bob's deciding to steal Ann's car, which decision is made at $t2$, there are possible worlds with the same laws of nature as W and the same past up to $t2$ in which Bob is capable at $t2$ of making a decision, x is not preempted or disturbed in any way by anything external to it, and, even so, x does not cause Bob's deciding at $t2$ to steal Ann's car. (In those worlds, P causes Bob's deciding to do that, which decision is made at $t2$.) The supposition that, at $t2$, Bob agent-caused his decision or intention to steal the car complicates matters, owing to certain disagreements among agent causationists. Obviously, if agents cannot be caused to agent-cause things (O'Connor 2000, pp. 52–53), then Bob was not deterministically caused to agent-cause his decision or intention. But suppose that agents can be caused to agent-cause their decisions or intentions (Taylor 1966, pp. 114–16) in cases of free action. Then two opposing theses are relevant: (1) agents like Bob who have the agent-causal power when they act can act without exercising it; (2) such agents cannot act without exercising their agent-causal power (Clarke 2003, p. 145). If Bob was caused to agent-cause his decision or intention to steal the car in W and 1 is true, then (other things being equal) there are possible worlds with the same laws of nature as W and the same past up to $t2$ in which, at $t2$, Bob is capable of making a decision then and he does not agent-cause a decision or intention to steal the car. (In those worlds, P causes Bob's decision or intention to steal the car.) So Bob was not deterministically caused to agent-cause his decision or intention to steal the car. Finally, if Bob was caused to agent-cause his decision or intention to steal the car in W and 2 is true, then what caused Bob—call it C—to agent-cause that in W did not deterministically cause him to agent-cause that, for there are possible worlds with the same laws of nature as W and the same past up to $t2$ in which, at $t2$, Bob is capable of making a decision then, and P, rather than C, causes Bob to agent-cause his decision or intention to steal the car.

Two further points about the part of Bob's story that I have told merit emphasis. First, P, the internally deterministic process in Bob's brain, makes it impossible for Bob to avoid deciding at $t2$ to steal Ann's car, given that he is capable of making a decision then. P's internal operations are deterministic, and unless P is preempted by some event or process external to it, it will cause Bob to decide at $t2$ to steal Ann's car. Given that Bob is capable of making a decision at the time, the only thing that can preempt P is Bob's deciding on his own at $t2$ to steal Ann's car. Thus, all worlds with the same laws of nature as W and the same past up to $t2$ are worlds in which Bob decides at $t2$ to steal Ann's car. P makes it inevitable that Bob will decide at $t2$ to steal the car, if he is capable of making a decision at $t2$, but because P does not actually cause Bob's deciding to do that, it does not deterministically cause it.

Second, in the actual scenario, P is preempted at $t2$. P is not sensitive to a prior sign of Bob's decision. At every moment up to $t2$, P is poised to cause Bob to decide at $t2$ to steal Ann's car. P is preempted only at the very moment that Bob decides to steal the car.

There is more to the story, including details of Bob's constitution as an agent offered to help readers see how direct preemption of the featured kind is possible in Bob (Mele and Robb 1998, 2003). Because Robb and I have defended the coherence of our story elsewhere (see especially Mele and Robb 2003), I will not defend it again here.

If the story about Bob is coherent, what are the consequences for the libertarian principles about moral responsibility and freedom identified in the preceding section? Recall PAPlmh: a person is morally responsible for what he did at t only if he was able (more specifically, S-able), either before t or at t, to do otherwise at t. In the Mele-Robb story, process P is initiated an hour before $t2$. To avoid an unnecessary, technical discussion of the nature of diachronic ability, I now suppose that P was initiated at Bob's birth, many years before $t2$, and that any subsequent tinkering with it would have immediately resulted in Bob's death. Given this supposition and assuming the truth of a standard libertarian view of ability to do otherwise (see sec. 1), there is no time at which Bob was able to do otherwise at $t2$ than decide to steal Ann's car, given that he is capable at $t2$ of making a decision then. Because Bob's world is indeterministic, some readers will worry that he might never have encountered Ann's car and never have been in a position to decide to steal it. Here is an addition to the story: Black, a being of enormous power, was prepared to acquaint Bob with Ann's car (and even to render him capable at $t2$ of making a decision) if necessary, but he had no need to.

Consider a variant of Bob's story from which Black (along with P, of course) is removed. Event-causal and agent-causal libertarians should hold that Bob is morally responsible in it for deciding to steal Ann's car, for, by hypothesis, that decision is produced in whatever way they say decisions for which agents are morally responsible are produced and Bob is a sane, rational agent. Return now to the story about Bob and Black. Aside from initiating P, Black does not interfere, and Bob's decision is produced in the same way as in the Blackless version of the story. So, again, event-causal and agent-causal libertarians should hold that Bob is morally responsible for deciding to steal Ann's car. However, on any standard libertarian construal of the ability to do otherwise, Bob was not even S-able before $t2$ or at $t2$ to do otherwise at $t2$ than decide then to steal Ann's car. (Recall that Black would have rendered Bob capable at *t* of making a decision then if Bob had lacked that capacity then.) So libertarians of these kinds should reject PAPlmh.[10]

The same line of reasoning applies to PAPlmd: a person is directly morally responsible for what he did at *t* only if at *t* he was able (more specifically, *S*-able) to do otherwise at *t*. Stories without Black can be told about Bob in which Bob's decision at *t2* to steal the car is produced in ways that event-causal and agent-causal libertarians deem appropriate for direct moral responsibility, and then Black can be imported into variants of those stories in which, aside from initiating *P* (which does not interfere with Bob's production of his decision), he does not intervene. The same strategy can also be used against event-causal and agent-causal libertarian endorsements of PAPlfh, PAPlfd, and PAPlfs.

Am I claiming that Bob has no alternative possibilities at all at *t2*? No. In *W*, he decides on his own at *t2* to steal the car, and in some other possible worlds with the same past up to *t2* and the same laws of nature, *P* causes him to decide at *t2* to steal the car. Doing otherwise than deciding at *t2* to steal the car is not open to Bob at the time, but doing otherwise than deciding on his own at *t2* to steal it is open to him at the time, in the sense that it is compatible with the combination of *W*'s past up to *t2* and its laws of nature.

What use, if any, might a libertarian reasonably make of this alternative possibility? Now, if although Bob was unable before *t2* and at *t2* to do otherwise at *t2* than decide to steal Ann's car, he nevertheless is directly morally responsible for deciding to steal it and freely$_d$ decides to steal it, then all the PAPl principles identified in the preceding section should be rejected by libertarians (unless they understand the expression "what he did" in these principles in a way I am about to discuss). However, there are PAPl principles that are not falsified by Bob's story. A crucial question about them is a question about their merits.

The following principle may be a case in point, depending on the transworld identity conditions for action-tokens:

> PAPlfdt. A person freely$_d$ performed an action-token he performed at *t*
> in *W* only if there is a possible world with the same laws of nature as
> *W* and the same past up to *t* in which he does not perform that action-
> token at *t*.[11]

A proponent of this principle can contend that, owing to differences in how they are produced, Bob's decision about Ann's car at *t2* in *W* is a different action-token from his decision about her car at *t2* in a world in which *P* causes the decision. This proponent can grant that, at *t2*, Bob could not have done otherwise then than decide to steal Ann's car, assert that he did not freely decide to steal it, and assert that, even so, he freely performed his action-token of deciding to steal it.[12]

This is an interesting idea. Representative alternative possibilities featured in typical libertarian discussions of free$_d$ action include the following: at *t*, the agent can do what he judges best and can instead succumb to temptation to do otherwise; at *t*, the agent can decide to accept a job offer and can instead decide to reject it or continue deliberating about it. What PAPlfdt suggests is crucial for free$_d$ action is not alternative possibilities such as these but rather some kind of indeterministic agency. I will explore that idea after providing some background.

It will be useful to have labels for two species of incompatibilist alternative possibilities. A distinction between two kinds of action-description facilitates matters (Mele 1996, pp. 126–27). Examples of what I dub *fancy action-descriptions* are "Bob's deciding on his own to steal the car" and "Bob's deciding otherwise than on his own to steal the car." What I call *normal action-descriptions* make no reference to whether the agent acted on his own or otherwise than on his own. A similar distinction can be made regarding intentional refrainings, if not all intentional refrainings are actions.

What I term *robust alternative possibilities* for a person *S* to an actual item *x* are limited to possibilities of action and possibilities of intentional refraining and, more specifically, to such possibilities in virtue of which it is true, on an incompatibilist reading, that "*S* could have done otherwise than —," when the blank is filled in by some correct normal action-description or refraining-description of *x* (or a version of such a description appropriately modified for the grammatical context).[13] So, for example, even if someone who was not inclined to *A* could have been inclined to *A*, this alternative possibility is not a robust one, for inclinations are neither actions nor refrainings. Additionally, its being true that someone could have acted otherwise than he did does not suffice for his having a robust alternative possibility, in my sense. Suppose that at *t* Barney decided to steal a car and he decided that on his own. Assuming an incompatibilist reading of "could have done otherwise," its being true that he could have done otherwise at *t* than *decide to steal the car* (notice the normal action-description) suffices for his having a robust alternative possibility at *t*, but its being true that he could have done otherwise at *t* than decide *on his own* to steal the car does not. If Barney's action of deciding on his own to steal the car cannot properly be given any normal action-description d (e.g., "Barney's deciding to steal the car") such that "Barney could have done otherwise than d_{mod} (e.g., decide to steal the car)" is true, then Barney has no robust alternative possibility, in my sense, to deciding on his own to steal the car.[14] An alternative possibility to deciding on one's own to steal a car that consists merely in the possibility of deciding otherwise than on one's own to steal it is a nonrobust alternative possibility.[15]

Bob decides *on his own* at *t2* to steal Ann's car. John Fischer includes such an alternative possibility as Bob's deciding at *t2* to steal it because some sort of alien intervention made him so decide in the category of "flickers of freedom" (1994, pp. 139–40). He argues that the flickers "are simply not sufficiently robust to ground our ascriptions of moral responsibility," and he concludes that moral responsibility does not require a kind of control that depends on there being alternative possibilities (p. 147). On Fischer's view, the alternative possibilities left open in Frankfurt-style cases are "essentially irrelevant" to moral responsibility (p. 159). The libertarian, he says, "must claim that the addition of the sort of alternative possibility he has identified would transform a case of lack of responsibility into one of responsibility" (p. 141). Of course, the libertarian can agree that, with this addition, some cases of nonresponsibility would become cases of responsibility. But, Fischer contends, "this seems mysterious in the extreme: how can adding an alternative scenario (or perhaps a set of them) in which [an agent] does not *freely* [A] make it true that he actually possesses the sort of control required for him to be morally responsible for his [A-ing]? This might appear to involve a kind of alchemy, and it is just as incredible" (p. 141).

In Mele 1996, I argued that a typical libertarian might not find this at all mysterious or incredible. Suppose that some agent in a deterministic world who A-s on the basis of careful deliberation satisfies the most robust and plausible set of sufficient conditions for having A-ed freely and for being morally responsible for A-ing that a compatibilist can offer. Libertarians would, of course, deny that the agent A-ed freely and is morally responsible for A-ing. But it is open to some libertarians to hold that a compatibilist account of free action and moral responsibility can take us part of the way toward the truth and that what is needed to take us the rest of the way is the requirement that the agent be a suitably indeterministic initiator of his action. Some libertarians who thought, before reflecting on Frankfurt-style cases, that the problem with determinism was simply that it entails, for example, that no one who decides to steal a car could have done otherwise than decide to do that (on some preferred incompatibilist reading of "could have done otherwise") might have misidentified what actually bothered them about determinism. What bothered them might have been the entailment at issue in conjunction with the entailment that the causal sequence or sequences that actually issue in the agent's decision (as opposed to an unrealized, Frankfurt-style sequence) are such that he could not have done otherwise (see Fischer 1982). A libertarian may see an agent's indeterministically initiating some actions of his as crucial to his being a free, morally responsible agent, and although determinism precludes indeterministic initiation, *Frankfurt-style cases do not.*[16]

A more pressing problem for a libertarian view of this kind about free$_d$ action is the problem of present luck. In chapter 3, I argued that indeterminism at the moment of action poses a serious problem for libertarians. Even if libertarians may be excused for not regarding Fischer's alleged mystery as mysterious, they seem to be stuck with a mystery unless and until they lay the problem of present luck to rest. The basic question is this: Why doesn't indeterminism at the time of action *block* responsibility and freedom?

In the following section and in chapter 5, I explore some libertarian ways of trying to avoid the problem. One last libertarian principle requires prior attention, the first one stated in this chapter:

> LT. No possible agent ever acts freely unless he sometimes freely A-s at times at which the conjunction of the past up to those times and the laws of nature is consistent with his not A-ing then.

One way to read this is as an "action-token" principle of PAPlfdt's ilk. If it is read that way, it is too similar to PAPlfdt to merit separate discussion. I read it first in a way that assumes that what I have called fancy action-descriptions are irrelevant to it and then in a less restrictive way. Now, if Frankfurt-style cases like mine are coherent, so are global variants of them. In global Frankfurt-style cases of this kind, none of the agent's actions (including decisions) are produced by processes like *P*, but, *whenever* the agent acts, such processes would have caused relevant actions if the agent had not, at just the right time, performed actions of the pertinent types on his own.[17] In cases of this kind, agents sometimes act freely even though they *never* have robust alternative possibilities and even though, setting aside fancy action descriptions as irrelevant, it is never the case that when an agent freely

A-s, the past up to the time of his *A*-ing and the laws of nature are consistent with his not *A*-ing then. Consider now a reading of *LT* on which fancy action-descriptions like "Bob's deciding on his own to steal Ann's car" are relevant. There are alternative possibilities to Bob's so deciding and actions of its kind in Frankfurt-style cases. And a proponent of *LT* can appeal to them in defending this principle. To support this appeal, it is not necessary to defend the claim that an agent's *A*-ing on his own at *t* is a distinct action-token from his *A*-ing otherwise than on his own at *t*. The basic difference is in the way the *A*-ing is produced, and the basic appeal is to some kind of indeterministic agency, either agent causation—recall that agent-causings are not deterministically caused—or some kind of indeterministic event-causation of actions.

Why should it be thought that moral responsibility and freedom depend on indeterministic agency? *Not* because such agency ensures robust alternative possibilities. If some Frankfurt-style cases hit their mark, an indeterministic agent who never has robust alternative possibilities may nevertheless act freely and morally responsibly. So why? I begin developing an answer to a related question in the following section: What contribution can indeterministic agency make to moral responsibility and freedom?

3. Soft Libertarianism and Frankfurt-style Cases

In Mele 1996, I present a kind of libertarianism—soft libertarianism— that provides a perspective on moral responsibility and freedom from which compatibilists may find it less difficult than usual to see why someone might reasonably value indeterministic agency as a contributor to moral responsibility and freedom. A summary of it will prove useful here. Traditional libertarians are hard-line incompatibilists. They claim that free action and moral responsibility are incompatible with determinism. I call them *hard libertarians*. A softer line is available to theorists who have libertarian sympathies. A theorist may leave it open that free action and moral responsibility are compatible with determinism but maintain that the falsity of determinism is required for a more desirable species of free action and a more desirable brand of moral responsibility. This is a *soft libertarian* line. Soft libertarians would be disappointed to discover that determinism is true, but they would not conclude that no one has ever acted freely and that no one has ever been morally responsible for anything.[18] In principle, a soft libertarian may or may not treat the desirability at issue in a way that relativizes it to individuals. The brand of soft libertarianism that I present in Mele 1996 is relativistic: it maintains that at least some human agents are possessed of kinds of freedom and moral responsibility that are incompatible with determinism and are reasonably preferred *by at least some of these agents* to any kind of freedom or moral responsibility that is consistent with the truth of determinism.

Now, it is open to soft libertarians to maintain that the more desirable incompatibilist species of free action and moral responsibility are not present in my Frankfurt-style stories. They can contend that these more desirable species are incompatible not only with determinism but also with the absence of robust alternative possibilities. The brand of soft libertarianism presented in Mele 1996 is *not* of this kind; it does not view the mere presence of a Frankfurt-style potential controller as a bar to the more desirable species of freedom and moral responsibility.

From the perspective of a soft libertarian of the sort in question, what is undesirable about determinism, and what is undesirable about it that isn't just as undesirable about Frankfurt-style scenarios? In a deterministic world, if Wilma tries to save a baby from a burning building at *t*, then even before she has any idea that the baby is in danger (indeed, even before Wilma is born), events are in progress that will result, deterministically, in her trying to save the baby at *t*. It may also be true that in a Frankfurt-style scenario in which Wilma tries on her own to save a baby, sufficient conditions are present for her trying to save the baby at *t* even before Wilma discovers that the baby is in danger. However, if Wilma tries on her own to save the baby, then central elements of the pertinent sufficient conditions—for example, a process like *P* being up and running and a potential controller's powers and intentions—play no role in producing her attempt to save the baby. What some libertarians want may be a causal bearing on some of their actions that they would lack in any deterministic world. They may desire something that requires their being able to make a causal contribution to some of their actions, the making of which is not entailed by any true description of the laws of nature and the state of their world at some time prior to their having any sense of the apparent options but does not require their having robust alternative possibilities.

Consider two hypotheses about the universe we inhabit. (*H1*) Either the universe is deterministic, or it is indeterministic only in ways that have no significant bearing on human agency. (*H2*) The universe is indeterministic in ways that have had and will continue to have a significant bearing on human agency. Plainly, libertarians prefer the truth of *H2* to the truth of *H1*. Why?

A common incompatibilist worry about determinism is voiced in Peter van Inwagen's consequence argument: "If determinism is true, then our acts are the consequences of the laws of nature and events in the remote past. But it is not up to us what went on before we were born, and neither is it up to us what the laws of nature are. Therefore, the consequences of these things (including our present acts) are not up to us" (1983, p. 16). Unlike hard libertarians, soft libertarians leave it open that determinism is compatible with our actions' being up to us in a way conducive to freedom and moral responsibility. However, they believe that a more desirable freedom and moral responsibility require that our actions not be parts of the unfolding of deterministic chains of events that were in progress even before we were born. If soft libertarians can view themselves as making some choices or decisions that are not deterministically caused or that are deterministically caused by, for example, something that includes deliberative judgments that are not themselves deterministically caused, then they can view themselves as initiating some causal processes that are not intermediate links in a long deterministic causal chain extending back near the big bang. (The chain may branch in the backward direction: two or more causally independent sequences of events may combine to issue in a subsequent event.) And they take the power to be an initiator of this kind—an *indeterministic initiator*—to be required for a more desirable freedom and responsibility.

Thomas Nagel raises a relevant worry about the coherence of what soft libertarians want:

> Even if some [alternatives] are left open, given a complete specification of the condition of the agent and the circumstances of action, it is not clear how this would leave anything further for the agent to contribute to the outcome—anything that he could contribute as source, rather than merely as the scene of the outcome—the person whose act it is. If they are left open given everything about him, what does he have to do with the result? (1986, pp. 113–14)

Suppose that soft libertarianism were combined with the modest libertarianism sketched in chapter 1 (sec. 2). The latter view, as I explained, gives agents ample control over their deliberation. "Given a complete specification of the condition of the agent" and his circumstances at any point during deliberation, various alternatives are left open. Yet, the agent can have much to contribute to his continued deliberation and thereby to his subsequent overt actions.

Possibly, Nagel's worry is about scenarios in which right up to the time of action, it is open whether the agent will *A*, or even try to *A*, "given a complete specification of the condition of the agent and the circumstances of action." However, modest libertarians do not claim that indeterminism at the time of action is a necessary condition for free action or moral responsibility for one's action. Worries about present luck guide them away from that requirement.

Someone who prizes being an indeterministic initiator need not prize anything that is absent in representative Frankfurt-style scenarios. Being an indeterministic initiator does not require having robust alternative possibilities—either present or past. It does require that one have at least nonrobust alternative possibilities (though not necessarily at the time of action), but only because the possession of such possibilities is necessary if any action-influencing internal events are not to be intermediate links in a deterministic causal chain. Having alternative possibilities is not intrinsically valuable from a soft libertarian point of view; it is valuable as a logically necessary condition of one's being an indeterministic initiator.

The soft libertarian need not claim that everyone—or every reasonable person—values being an indeterministic initiator. Some people may take comfort in the thought that their world is deterministic, or indeterministic only in ways that have no significant bearing on their agency, and they may have no desire to be an indeterministic initiator; others evidently view determinism as uncomfortably limiting. Ultimately, in some cases, the difference might be a difference in taste. Faced with a choice between $500 and a 0.5 chance at $1,000, some people prefer the former and others the latter, even when they do not differ from one another in the value they place on $500 and $1,000, respectively. Neither preference is irrational. Some people find gambling pleasantly exciting; others do not. For those who do, the second option has a special attraction. Similarly, some people may prefer *H1* to *H2*, whereas others prefer *H2* to *H1* without either preference being irrational. Soft libertarians can grant that, from the perspective of some people, species of freedom and responsibility associated with indeterministic initiation are no more desirable than compatibilist freedom and responsibility, and perhaps even less desirable. And they can grant that not all such perspectives are irrational. What soft libertarians insist on is that, from their own perspective, certain incompatibilist species of freedom and responsibility are more desirable than any compatibilist species, and that their own perspective is not irrational. They value these incompatibilist species of freedom and responsibility more than they value any compatibilist species, and they see nothing irrational in this.

It might be difficult, indeed, to convert to soft libertarianism someone who does not value being an indeterministic initiator. Soft libertarians are not saddled with this burden, but just as a gambler might lead a risk-averse person to understand, in some measure, what the former finds attractive about gambling, a person who values being an indeterministic initiator might be in a position to explain to someone who does not share this value what he finds attractive about being such an initiator. At least part of what attracts a soft libertarian to indeterministic initiation, it is safely said, is that being such an initiator opens the door to robust alternative future possibilities. But even if that door is closed by a Frankfurt-style counterfactual controller, a soft libertarian may value being the kind of agent of whom it is false that his every thought and action is part of a deterministic causal chain stretching back to the vicinity of the big bang. He may value the ability to make contributions to the world that are not part of such a chain. And *why* might he value that ability? Here, it is best to let a libertarian speak for himself. Robert Kane writes: "What determinism takes away is a certain sense of the importance of oneself as an individual. If I am ultimately responsible for certain occurrences in the universe... then my choices and my life take on an importance that is missing if I do not have such responsibility" (1985, p. 178). (Notice that Kane uses "I" in the second sentence. At least one kind of libertarian would favor a relativistic version of the first sentence, too, wanting to leave it open that the claim there is not true of everyone.)

Now, Kane in fact requires robust alternative possibilities (at some point in time) for moral responsibility. But there is no mention of that requirement in this passage. Furthermore, even if some people would not regard their choices and their lives as being any less important on the hypothesis that determinism is true than on the hypothesis that determinism is false, other people evidently share Kane's sentiment. There need be no irrationality in this sentiment and no confusion at its source. People who hold the view expressed by Kane in the quoted passage might not confuse deterministic causation with compulsion or constraint, for example, and they might not conflate it with an external agency. When they carefully reflect on their values and "life-hopes," they may find that they prize possessing the power of indeterministic initiation as something that, when suitably exercised, gives their lives a greater personal significance or importance than would otherwise be the case.[19] Given their own aspirations, indeterministic initiation matters to them. People with other life-hopes might be indifferent about it, or they might disvalue it.

Soft libertarians need not claim that all reasonable, informed people would, after due reflection, value species of freedom and moral responsibility that are open to them only on the hypothesis that they are indeterministic initiators more highly than they value compatibilist freedom and moral responsibility. However, they do claim that, for themselves, some species of freedom and responsibility that encompass or require indeterministic initiation are more attractive than anything the compatibilist can offer. And, again, they contend that the attractiveness does not derive from confusion. If there is confusion here, the burden is on their opponents to uncover it.

Wilma, my spokesperson for soft libertarianism in Mele 1999b, is in partial agreement with Kane. She reports that the thought of her actions as links in a long deterministic causal chain is somewhat deflating and that the truth of determinism is inconsistent with her life's being as important and meaningful as she hopes it is. The thought that she is an indeterministic initiator of at least some of her rational, deliberative, intentional actions, however, coheres with the importance and significance she hopes her life has.[20] Wilma observes that *independence* is among the things that some people intrinsically value. Some people value independence, in some measure, from other people and from institutions. Wilma values, as well, a measure of independence from the *past*. She values, she says, a kind of independent agency that includes the power to make a special kind of contribution to some of her actions and to her world—contributions that are not themselves ultimately deterministically caused products of the state of the universe in the distant past. She values having a kind of causal bearing on her conduct that she would lack in any deterministic world. She prizes indeterministic freedom as an essential part of a life that she regards as most desirable for her. The kind of agency she hopes for, Wilma says, would render her decisions and actions personally more meaningful from the perspective of her own system of values than they would otherwise be. Although Wilma emphasizes that this kind of agency is essential to the kind of meaningful life she prizes, she says that she is not claiming that it is required for freedom or moral responsibility. Wilma is not a traditional incompatibilist; rather, she holds that determinism is incompatible with the satisfaction of some of her deepest life-hopes. Her satisfying those hopes requires that she have *ultimate* responsibility for some of her actions.[21]

Some people might value the kind of agency Wilma values because they prize a kind of *credit* for their accomplishments that they regard as weightier than compatibilist credit (see Kane 1996, p. 98). Wilma says that although she respects this attitude, she does not share it. Her personal concern is not with pluses and minuses in a cosmic ledger but with the exercises of agency to which these marks are assigned. It is not credit that interests her, she says, but independence. More fully, it is independence as manifested in rational decisions and rational intentional overt actions. Wilma acknowledges that she values compatibilist independence, but she reports that she values indeterministic independence more highly—provided that it brings with it no less *nonultimate* control than she would have should determinism be true. (She takes the problem of present luck very seriously.)

Wilma is trying, she says, to understand why some people might not share her preference for libertarian independence over a compatibilist counterpart. She reports that she is keeping an open mind, and she urges us to do the same. Wilma hopes that we can understand why, other things being equal, she would deem her life more important or meaningful if she were to discover that determinism is false than if she were to discover that it is true.

To be sure, Wilma may never know whether she has or lacks the agency she prizes, but that does not undermine her preferences. I hope that I will never know how my children's lives turned out (for then their lives would have been cut too short), but I place considerable value on their turning out well. There is nothing irrational in this. Nor need there be anything irrational in Wilma's prizing her having a kind of agency that she can never know she has.

In chapter 1, I described agnostic autonomism. It is agnostic about whether determinism is compatible with free agency and about the existence of libertarian free agency in our world, but committed to the conceptual coherence of libertarian free agency and to the thesis that the belief that there are free agents is more defensible than the belief that there are none. (If agnostic autonomists were shown that determinism is true or that our world is indeterministic only in ways that have no significant bearing on human agency, they probably would embrace compatibilism; but so, apparently, would some hard libertarians.)[22] Soft libertarianism is consistent with agnostic autonomism, but it is bolder. Soft libertarians contend that an incompatibilist species of free agency is realized in our world.

In the following chapter, I explore a pair of responses a soft libertarian may make to the problem of present luck. One is modest libertarianism. The other is more daring.

NOTES

1. In reproducing this passage, I deleted a subscript after "Jones."
2. On S-ability, see ch. 1, sec. 4.
3. In falsifying a principle that requires S-ability to do otherwise for moral responsibility or free action, I will have falsified any principle that differs from it only in requiring a stronger form of ability to do otherwise, and I want to make the falsification task harder for myself, not easier.
4. If moral responsibility comes in degrees, an agent's degree of moral responsibility for an action may involve a mixture of inherited and direct moral responsibility for it. If PAPlmd is true, then an agent's degree of direct moral responsibility for what he did at t is zero if at t he was not even S-able to do otherwise at t.
5. For a related notion of "direct freedom," see Zimmerman 1988, pp. 29–30.
6. In the remainder of this paragraph, I borrow from Mele and Robb 2003, pp. 127–28.
7. Also see Ginet 1996 and Wyma 1997. For exposition that distinguishes Kane's and Widerker's versions of this problem, see Mele and Robb 1998.
8. In Mele 2003a (ch. 2), as I have mentioned, I argued that actions (including decisions) are, essentially, events with a causal history of a certain kind. One might worry that no event that P can produce at $t2$ can be produced by P in a way consistent with the event's being a decision. The worry might, for example, derive from the thought that all decisions have beliefs and desires of the agent among their causes and that this would not be true of an alleged decision in which P issues. However, a process like P may be designed to produce relevant beliefs and desires for use in producing a decision unless it detects that such beliefs and desires are already present; and if suitable beliefs and desires are already present (as they are in Bob's case), P can use them in producing the decision.
9. This paragraph and the next two incorporate material from Mele and Robb 2003, pp. 128–29.
10. Imagine a world in which Bob dies in a car accident years before $t2$. Must Black bring him back to life in order for the thought experiment to work? No. If Bob is dead at $t2$, he cannot do anything at $t2$ and so cannot do otherwise than what he did in W then. Obviously, this is so even if doing is interpreted as including some nonactions of agents.

11. See McKenna 1997; Naylor 1984; Rowe 1991, pp. 75–93; and van Inwagen 1983, pp. 166–80.

12. It is open to a libertarian to claim that in all the PAPl principles identified in this chapter "what he did" (and "what a person did," in the case of PAPlfd) is to be understood as specifically about action-tokens. Thus, whereas most libertarians would take "Bob, who decided at *t* to steal Ann's car, is directly morally responsible for deciding to steal her car only if at *t* he was able (more specifically, S-able) to do otherwise at *t* than decide to steal her car" to be an instance of PAPlmh, a libertarian of the sort at issue now would not. Rather than discuss "action-token" versions of all these principles, I discuss PAPlfdt.

13. In this definition of *robust alternative possibilities*, I follow Mele 1996, pp. 126–27. Others have subsequently defined the expression differently (see Pereboom 2001, p. 8).

14. d_{mod} is simply *d* as appropriately modified for the grammatical context.

15. In using the notion of action-descriptions as I do here, I am not taking sides in a familiar old dispute about act-individuation. Even if Barney's stealing the car and his stealing it on his own are distinct actions (rather than the same action under two different descriptions), presumably the latter action can properly, if incompletely, be described as one of stealing the car.

16. For a similar point, see Della Rocca 1998.

17. On global Frankfurt-style cases, see Fischer 1994, p. 214; Haji 1996, p. 707; Kane 1996, pp. 42–43, 143; Mele 1995, p. 141; 1996, pp. 123–41; Mele and Robb 1998, pp. 109–10; Pereboom 2001, p. 22.

18. A soft libertarian may go beyond merely leaving compatibilism about freedom and moral responsibility open and embrace compatibilism, while also wanting more in the way of freedom and responsibility than compatibilism has to offer. In this connection, two kinds of compatibilism may be distinguished. Proponents of what may be termed *hard compatibilism* insist that there are no more desirable species of free choice, free action, and moral responsibility than compatibilist species. Hard compatibilists may maintain that freedom and responsibility *require* determinism, as some theorists have done (e.g., Ayer 1954, ch. 12; Hobart 1934; Nowell-Smith 1948; Smart 1961), or they may simply contend that indeterminism cannot help. *Soft compatibilism* leaves soft libertarianism open but is not committed to it. Alternatives to combining one's soft compatibilism with soft libertarianism include granting that incompatibilist species of freedom and responsibility are conceivable that may be rationally preferred by some people to any compatibilist species while being agnostic about the existence of such species in the real world, and taking an agnostic stance on the conceivability claim as well.

19. On life-hopes, see Honderich 1988.

20. Kane contends that "the desire to be independent sources of activity in the world, which is connected . . . to the sense we have of our uniqueness and

importance as individuals," is an "elemental" libertarian desire (1996, p. 98). Here I am following his lead.

21. Recall my observation in chapter 1 (sec. 2) about the notion of ultimacy at work here. As Wilma sees things, actions for which she is ultimately responsible have, in Kane's words, "their ultimate sources in" her (1996, p. 98), in the sense that the collection of agent-internal states and events that explains these actions is not deterministically caused by anything outside her. In Wilma's view, if these actions satisfy robust alleged sufficient conditions for responsibility that a sophisticated compatibilist finds convincing, the addition of "ultimacy," in this sense, yields ultimate responsibility for them.

22. Van Inwagen (1983, p. 223) is such a hard libertarian. Even though the conjunction of the agnostic autonomist thesis that there are free agents and the proposition that determinism is true *entails* compatibilism, my claim here is intended as a psychological one. Hence, my use of "probably."

FIVE

A Daring Soft Libertarian
Response to Present Luck

In the preceding chapter, I mentioned the possibility of combining soft libertarianism with modest libertarianism. The main business of the present chapter is the development of a considerably less modest soft libertarian view—*daring soft libertarianism,* or DSL, for short. DSL grants the main moral of Frankfurt-style cases and tackles the problem of present luck. I have asked (ch. 3) how it can be that an agent may act freely and morally responsibly at a time at which pertinent cross-world differences are just a matter of luck. DSL offers an answer.

1. Leeway

Derk Pereboom contends that although event-causal libertarianism, un-like compatibilism, may "provide leeway for decision and action," it "lacks any significant advantage over compatibilism in securing moral responsibility because it does no better in providing the enhanced control that would be required" (2001, p. 55). Event-causal libertarianism, he argues, "docs not provide agents with any more control than compati-bilism does, and hence a way must be found to enhance an agent's control to the appropriate degree" (p. 56). Similarly, Randolph Clarke argues that if "broad incompatibilism" (2003, p. xiv)—the thesis that determinism is incompatible both with free will and with moral responsibility—is true, then no event-causal libertarian view secures for agents the sorts of freedom and control most closely associated with moral responsibility. "The active control that is exercised on [this libertarian] view is just the same as that exercised on an event-causal compatibilist account. [The] view fails to secure the agent's exercise of any further positive powers to causally influence which of the alternative courses of events that are open will become actual" (Clarke 2003, p. 220). As I have mentioned (ch. 3, sec. 6), Pereboom holds that agent causation, if it were to exist, would do the enhancing for which he calls, and Clarke contends: "The requirement of agent causation . . . provides for the agent's exercising when she acts, in addition to the active control secured by an event-causal view, a further power to causally influence which of the open alternatives will be made actual" (pp. 220–21). However, both Pereboom and Clarke are skeptical about agent causation. Pereboom argues on empirical grounds that it is extremely unlikely that anyone has agent-causal power (2001, ch. 3). This is part of his argument for the thesis that we lack free will and moral responsibility. In Clarke's judgment, relevant arguments collectively "incline the balance against the [conceptual] possibility of substance causation in general and agent causation in particular" (2003, p. 209). However, he maintains that, in light of difficulties in understanding causation, "we cannot have a *great deal* of confidence" in this judgment (pp. 209–10).

In chapter 3, I argued that agent causationists have not solved the problem of present luck: what they say about the "enhanced control" secured by agent causation leaves the problem intact. This observation, together with serious grounds for skepticism about the actuality and even the conceptual possibility of agent causation, should give pause to all libertarians who are inclined to believe that every conceivable kind of event-causal libertarianism would be too much like compatibilism to be acceptable. Such libertarians who are inclined to believe that every conceivable kind of pause to wonder whether "leeway"—or something associated with it other than "enhanced control"—can do more work than they think. Leeway, as Pereboom intends it to be understood, is incompatible with determinism: it is a matter of agents' having open to them alternative futures that are consistent with the combination of the present state of the universe and the laws of nature.

2. Luck and Modest Libertarianism

In the present section, I prepare the way for my discussion of daring soft libertarianism by exploring a modest libertarian response to luck. I begin with a story about Beth, an indeterministic agent of the kind described in my summary of modest libertarianism in chapter 1.

Recently, Beth deliberated about whether it would be better on the whole to quit her job as a lawyer in a large urban law firm and accept a position at a firm in a small town in another state.[1] During a two-week span, Beth spent many hours mulling over the matter. She had been worrying that her job too often brings prudence and morality into conflict. Largely for that reason, she decided to take the offer of a new job seriously. Beth was confident that she would be much less likely to compromise her moral principles working in the small-town firm, but she was fond of city life and she would miss her friends. Beth considered a wide range of quality-of-life issues in addition to the salient moral matter. At one point, she came to believe that the pressure on her at work to compromise her moral principles was so severe and stressful that, even given other quality-of-life issues, the case for moving was strong enough that it might well be a waste of time to continue deliberating about the matter. However, she decided to take another pass at the issue.

When Beth visited the small town toward the beginning of her deliberation, she spent all of her time with the lawyers who worked there and their families and friends. It occurs to her now—at time *t*—that it might be worth the time and trouble, before coming to a decision, to return to the town and explore it on her own. This thought, *T*, is indeterministically caused. After reflecting on *T*'s merits, judging *T* to be warranted, and judging further that she ought to return, Beth makes the trip. She discovers a level of bigotry in the town that she is unwilling to live with, and she judges it best on the whole to stay put. (The local lawyers and their families and friends are so accustomed to the bigotry that those who once noticed it no longer do.) Given the kind of agent Beth is, an intention to reject the offer is deterministically produced, as is Beth's phoning the firm with the news. Incidentally, things subsequently go very well for Beth. A few days later, a senior partner in her firm surprises everyone by resigning, and with him goes much of the pressure Beth felt to compromise her moral principles.

In some possible worlds with the same past and laws of nature, of course, thought *T* does not occur to Beth at *t*, and she proceeds to judge it best to accept the job offer and then acts accordingly. This difference at *t* between those worlds and the actual world is just a matter of luck. Does that undermine modest libertarianism?

Compare propositions *A1* and *A2* from chapter 3 with comparable propositions about Beth:

A1. The difference at noon between world *W*, in which Ann
performs a noontime coin flip, as she promised, and any world,
Wn, with the same past and laws of nature in which Ann does
not so act and instead decides at noon not to toss the coin
then is just a matter of luck.

B1. The difference at *t* between world *W*, in which Beth has
thought *T* then, and any world, *Wn*, with the same past and laws
of nature in which Beth does not have thought *T* then is just a
matter of luck.

A2. Ann is not morally responsible in *Wn* for deciding at noon to
hold on to the coin and for not doing what she promised.

B2. Beth is not morally responsible in *Wn* for accepting the job
with the small firm at $t + n$.[2]

I have already accepted *B1*. A difference between Ann and Beth that
is relevant to the second pair of propositions merits attention. As I
explained in chapter 3 (sec. 2), Ann's decision in *Wn* not to toss the
coin is plausibly viewed as a manifestation of a breakdown of agency
that goes beyond the irrationality of paradigmatic akratic decisions. As
a less prosaic writer than I might put it, Ann, but not Beth, has a
problem with her will. Ann is so constituted as an agent that breakdowns of the pertinent kind are psychologically possible for her, and
she suffers such a breakdown in *Wn*. Beth, on the other hand, is so
constituted that some thoughts that have some bearing on a topic she is
deliberating about may or may not come to mind during deliberation.
(Recall that on the modest libertarian view at issue, many relevant
considerations may be deterministically caused to come to mind during
her deliberation.) Ann's problem as a decision maker seems to get her
off the moral hook in *Wn*. And Beth is free of that defect.

Should it be held, even so, that Beth is not morally responsible in
Wn for accepting the job offer? It is true that in some worlds in which
she has better luck at *t* than she does in *Wn*—for example, some worlds
in which she has thought *T* at *t*—she instead rejects the job offer some
time after *t*. Does that speak strongly in favor of her not being morally
responsible for accepting the job? I think not.

Not every bit of luck that an agent has in a causal stream leading to an
action precludes moral responsibility for that action. Ava luckily finds two
$10 bills on an empty street and puts one of them in a poor box. Her luck
does not preclude her being morally responsible and praiseworthy for her
charitable act. Betty unluckily loses $20: she sees it fly out of her shirt

pocket and car window as she is driving to work on a crowded highway. That bit of bad luck puts Betty in a bad mood, and she takes it out on her coworkers in small ways all morning. Her bad luck does not preclude her being morally responsible and blameworthy for her grumpy acts.

Of course, the lucky events featured in the preceding two examples happen in the external world, not in the agents. The luck there may be termed *agent-external* luck. The luck featured in the stories of Ann and Beth is agent-internal and, more specifically, psychological. Does all agent-internal psychological luck in a causal stream leading to action preclude moral responsibility for that action? No. Today, Bill luckily remembers where he hid a treasure map years ago: he was indeterministically caused to remember. Bill was arrested shortly after he hid it, and he has just completed a twenty-year prison sentence. After he retrieves and sells the treasure, Bill gives 25 percent of the proceeds to charity. His psychological luck does not preclude his being morally responsible and praiseworthy for his charitable act. Booker hears a line from a blues song on his radio as he is driving to work: "If it wasn't for bad luck, I wouldn't have no luck at all." Next he hears, "Hard luck and trouble is my only friend/I been on my own ever since I was ten." Booker had been having what he regarded as a string of bad luck. As an indeterministically caused consequence of all this, an image of his father's abandoning his mother and him when Booker was ten comes vividly to mind. That unlucky mental occurrence puts him in a foul mood, and he takes it out on his coworkers in small ways. As in the previous "bad mood" scenario, the featured unlucky occurrence—this time a psychological one—does not preclude the agent's being morally responsible and blameworthy for his moody acts.

What about Beth in the actual world? Like Bill, she makes good use of a lucky psychological event. Bill takes advantage of the lucky memory when he uses the information it carries to find the treasure. And Beth takes advantage of her lucky thought *T*—that it might be worth the time and trouble, before coming to a decision, to return to the small town on her own. Her having that thought provides her with the opportunity for reflection on it, and she takes advantage of that opportunity. If Bill had not remembered where he hid the treasure, he would not have found it and therefore would not have performed his impressive charitable deed. But that obviously is entirely consistent with his being morally responsible and praiseworthy for his actual charitable deed. Now, I have not said (*C*) that if Beth had not had thought *T* at *t*, she would have accepted the job in the small town.

There are possible worlds with the same past and laws of nature as the actual world in which she does not have that thought at t and she subsequently takes the job, but they might not include the closest worlds with the same past and laws in which Beth does not have thought T at t. Perhaps some worlds in which she has T a millisecond— or a minute, or an hour—later and subsequently rejects the job offer are closer. But suppose that counterfactual C is true. Then would Beth's lucky thought in the actual world preclude her being morally responsible for rejecting the job offer?

Consider a world with the same past and laws of nature in which Beth does not have thought T at t, and just after t she judges it best to accept the job. An intention to accept the job is deterministically caused, as is Beth's execution of that intention. Of course, given the deterministic causation, conventional libertarians will deny that Beth is (directly) morally responsible for accepting the job. But the question I want to raise now is whether Beth's bad *luck*—T's not coming to mind even though it could have—precludes her being morally responsible for accepting the job. Now, Beth thought carefully and rationally about her situation and based her judgment and action on a wealth of information. If she had been luckier—if T had occurred to her—she might subsequently have acquired an important further piece of information to factor into the mix, the fact about bigotry, for reflection on T might have led her to make an eye-opening return trip to the small town, as it did in the actual world. But the fact that a judgment is made on the basis of incomplete information is not the sort of thing that philosophers have regarded as uniformly blocking moral responsibility for actions performed in accordance with the judgment. That is an unsurprising fact: few, if any, of our evaluative judgments are made on the basis of *complete* relevant information. So it is difficult to see why it should be believed that T's unluckily not coming to mind precludes Beth's being morally responsible for accepting the job. One who believes that Beth is morally responsible for accepting the job may wish to take up the question of whether she deserves blame, praise, or neither for accepting it. That question is not pursued here.

Can it consistently be held both that, given the details of Ann's case, Ann's bad luck in Wn precludes her being morally responsible in Wn for deciding at noon to hold on to the coin and for not doing what she promised and that, given the details of Beth's case, Beth's bad luck in Wn does not preclude her being morally responsible in Wn for accepting the job? Yes, for the instances of bad luck are of different kinds.

It is false that every agent-internal, psychological kind of bad luck an agent has in a causal stream leading to action precludes moral responsibility for that action, as I have explained, and Ann's bad luck is made possible by an agential defect that Beth lacks. So one can consistently believe *A2* and disbelieve *B2*.

A2 suggests worries about whether Ann freely decides as she does in *Wn* and about whether she freely performs her noontime coin flip in *W*. These worries are recorded in propositions *A3* and *A4* in chapter 3 (sec. 6). People who worry that *B2* is true may similarly worry that Beth does not freely accept the job in *Wn* and does not freely reject it in the actual world. The following two items correspond to *A3* and *A4*:

> *B3.* In *Wn*, Beth does not freely accept the job at $t + n$. (That she does not freely do this explains why she is not morally responsible for doing it.)
>
> *B4.* In *W*, Beth does not freely reject the job offer. (Just as Beth's bad luck at t in *Wn* blocks moral responsibility, so does her good luck at t in *W*. After all, given exactly the same laws of nature and exactly the same past, in some worlds in which she has worse luck at t than she does in *W*, she subsequently accepts the job offer. And that Beth does not freely reject the job offer explains why she is not morally responsible for rejecting it.)

In *Wn*, because *T* unluckily fails to come to mind, Beth fails to gather additional relevant information about the small town. But it is generally granted that very few free decisions are made in the light of *complete* relevant information. So, just as it is difficult to see why *T*'s unluckily not coming to mind should be believed to preclude Beth's being morally responsible for accepting the job, it is difficult to see why it should be believed to preclude her freely accepting the job. Furthermore, just as Bill's luckily remembering where he hid the map is not at odds with his freely making the donation he makes, *T*'s luckily coming to mind in the actual world is not at odds with Beth's freely rejecting the job offer.

3. Daring Soft Libertarianism

As I observed in chapter 1 (sec. 2), in an agent with the psychological architecture that modest libertarians describe, certain decisions have, in Robert Kane's words, "their ultimate sources in" the agent (1996,

p. 98), in the sense that the collection of agent-internal states and events that explains these decisions is not deterministically caused by anything outside the agent. This point about these decisions is supposed to contribute to the agents' "ultimate responsibility" for them. The indeterministic nature of the deliberation that issues in these decisions secures the absence of a deterministic connection to the agent's past that is relevant to the "ultimacy" component of ultimate responsibility. But the absence of a deterministic connection of this kind can be secured, during deliberation, in ways that do not involve the agent's brain's operating indeterministically. Suppose that some questions that are peripherally relevant to the topic of an agent's deliberation may or may not be raised by an external source. Imagine that the source is an indeterministic device that operates the entire time the agent, Radu, is deliberating, and the internal workings of his brain are deterministic. Radu has the device playing like a radio as he deliberates. When the device asks a question, Radu considers it, if he believes it to merit consideration. In some cases, throughout much of the time he is deliberating, more than one deliberative outcome is causally open to him, and the same is true of various courses of overt action. In these cases, what Radu judges best is influenced by how he answers at least some of the questions the device raises or would have been influenced by some of his answers if some of the questions that the device could have raised had been raised.

Radu may, on some occasions, satisfy a robust compatibilist set of sufficient conditions for free action and moral responsibility, and on some of these occasions, it is causally open what he will judge best while he is deliberating. In these respects, he resembles the sort of agent modest libertarians highlight. One naturally worries that Radu is too much like an agent in a deterministic world to be regarded by any libertarian as acting freely and morally responsibly; and given the similarity between Radu and a modest libertarian agent, the same worry arises about the latter agent. One possible reaction to this worry is that modest libertarianism gives libertarians all the openness they can get without introducing into an agent a kind of openness that entails freedom-precluding and responsibility-precluding luck, and libertarians therefore should settle for modest libertarianism. I believe that this reaction is overly pessimistic. In the remainder of this chapter, I develop a more daring soft libertarian view, DSL.

The modest libertarianism that I have described is consistent with a compatibilist view of a portion of a process that may issue in free actions, a portion that begins with the appearance of a rationally acquired belief that it is best on the whole to A, includes the immediate acquisition of an intention to A, and ends shortly thereafter in an A-ing that executes that intention. It is consistent, for example, with the following claim: Beth freely rejected the job offer, her rejecting it was deterministically caused by its immediate antecedents, and its immediate antecedents were deterministically caused by something that included the indeterministically caused event of her acquiring the belief that it is best on the whole to reject the job offer. In the present section, I use section 2's discussion of modest libertarianism as a partial introduction to a more daring soft libertarian view that embraces present luck rather than following modest libertarianism in shunning it.

Daring soft libertarians (DSLs) try to stare down the problem of present luck. They claim that present luck is entailed by an agent's having a kind of initiatory power that they value and that its presence in a case of action does not preclude the action's being freely performed or the agent's being morally responsible for it. The softness of their libertarianism makes their situation less treacherous than that of conventional libertarians. Soft libertarians do not assert that free action and moral responsibility require the falsity of determinism.

Daring soft libertarianism of the kind I am about to invent is focused on deciding.[3] My daring soft libertarians especially value a power to make decisions that are not deterministically caused—a certain *initiatory* power. They are causalists about actions, including decisions, and for reasons of the sort set out in chapter 3, they believe that agent causation leaves the problem of present luck intact. Not wanting to be saddled with a questionable species of causation for which they have no use, they opt for event-causal soft libertarianism. However, they want to avoid the problems with Kane's event-causal libertarianism (see ch. 3, sec. 2). For example, they believe that although people sometimes try to bring it about that they decide to A, people never try to decide to do what they judge it best to do while also trying to decide instead to do what they are tempted to do.[4] According to their causal theory of action, actions are events with the right sort of causal history, decisions are made for reasons, and deciding for a reason R to A requires that R (or the agent's apprehension of R, or the neural realizer of R or of the agent's apprehension of R) play a part in causing the decision (see Mele 2003a). (What explains the disjunction is that DSLs may disagree with one another about the nature of reasons and about whether mental states and events, as opposed to their neural realizers, can be causes.

I will not try to sort out these disagreements.)[5] The initiatory power at issue is at work only when the proximate causes of a decision do not deterministically cause it.

DSLs have a no-nonsense attitude toward the problem that present luck poses for traditional libertarianism. Recall, from chapter 1 (sec. 1), the image of a tiny indeterministic neural roulette wheel in an agent's head. There the wheel is strictly a decision wheel. This time it includes more than decisions. Imagine that just prior to a certain agent's making a decision, there is a probability that what happens next is that he decides to A and there are probabilities of various alternative events, some of which are decisions and some of which are not. Larger probabilities get a correspondingly larger segment of the wheel than do smaller probabilities. A tiny neural ball bounces along the wheel. Its landing in a particular decision segment is the agent's making the corresponding decision, its landing in a segment for continued deliberation is the agent's continuing to deliberate, and so on. When the ball lands in the segment for a highly probable decision, its doing so is not *just* a matter of luck. After all, the mechanism's design is such that the probability of that happening is very high. But the ball's landing there is *partly* a matter of luck. And the difference at issue at *t* between a world in which the ball lands there at *t* and a world with the same past and laws of nature in which it lands in a segment for something else at *t* is just a matter of luck.

Recall the concepts of *basically* free action and action for which an agent is *basically* morally responsible (ch. 1, sec. 1). By definition, *basically* free actions are free A-ings occurring at times at which the past and the laws of nature are consistent with the agent's not A-ing then. Similarly, A-ings for which an agent is *basically* morally responsible are A-ings for which he is morally responsible that occur at times at which the past and the laws of nature are consistent with his not A-ing then. These notions are essentially incompatibilist. As DSLs see it, extant detailed event-causal libertarian views and agent-causal views of the production of basically free and morally responsible actions are meant to incorporate features that distinguish them from the roulette wheel model of free and morally responsible action and models of its kind. I call such models *time-of-action neural randomizer models.* One avenue to explore in developing DSL accounts of basically free and basically morally responsible action starts with the working assumption that some such model *does* apply to agents in basic instances of free and morally responsible action.

If Frankfurt-style cases of the kind featured in chapter 4 are successful, basically free action is blocked in them, and the same is true of action for which the agent is basically morally responsible. At least, that is so if what I called *normal action-descriptions* are assumed—for example, "Bob's deciding to steal the car," as opposed to "Bob's deciding on his own to steal the car" and "Bob's deciding otherwise than on his own to steal the car" (ch. 4, sec. 2). (I simplify discussion by assuming this.) But something very similar is left open, the agent's performing a free action, the proximal causes of which do not deterministically cause it, and the agent's being morally responsible for that action. When and only when an agent freely *A*-s at a time at which he has at least a nonrobust alternative possibility, the action is *basically* free*. Similarly, when and only when an agent *A*-s at a time at which he has at least a nonrobust alternative possibility and he is morally responsible for his *A*-ing, the agent is *basically* morally responsible* for his *A*-ing. Basically* free *A*-ing differs from basically free *A*-ing in that the latter, but not the former, requires that *not A*-ing be open to the agent at the time of action, given the past and the laws of nature. There is a parallel difference between basic* and basic moral responsibility for an action. Basicness* is somewhat more inclusive than basicness: its requirement for alternative possibilities at the time of action is weaker. In the case of an agent who *A*-s on his own at *t*, the possibility of his *A*-ing at *t* because a Frankfurt-style mechanism made him do that is enough to satisfy the weaker requirement. Because DSLs find some Frankfurt-style cases persuasive, they prefer working with basicness*.

As I have mentioned (ch. 1, sec. 1), it is open to libertarians to hold that an agent's basically free actions that are suitably related to later actions of his that are not basically free confer freedom on those later actions and that moral responsibility can be conferred in this way, too. DSLs take this position, and they take the same position on *basically** free and morally responsible action. They see an agent's being able to perform some actions whose proximal causes do not deterministically cause the actions as a necessary condition for his having a kind of initiatory power that they value. For them, the importance of this initiatory power is not limited to cases in which it is exercised; it is also important insofar as the basically* free and morally responsible actions that depend on its exercise confer an incompatibilist kind of freedom and moral responsibility on some subsequent actions. This point merits emphasis, because DSLs—who not only are theorists but also are agents—would like to make themselves such that their considered judgments about what it is best to do are consistently part of a mix that *deterministically* causes corresponding intentions that, in turn, are part of a mix that deterministically causes corresponding attempts.[6] They hold that they would make such deterministically caused attempts freely and morally responsibly, on an incompatibilist conception of free action and moral responsibility: the freedom and moral responsibility would be conferred. And they believe the same of actions that are successful attempts of this kind.

Given that DSLs would like to make themselves into agents of the kind just described, why do they value the ability to perform basically* free and morally responsible actions? Recall Wilma's report (ch. 4, sec. 3) that she values a measure of independence from the past, a kind of independent agency that includes the power to make a special kind of causal contribution to some of her actions and to her world— contributions that are not themselves parts of the unfolding of deterministic chains of events that were already in progress in the distant past. Basically* free actions are not parts of such chains. Nor are the deterministically caused actions that DSLs would like to enable themselves to perform: the fact that these actions are suitably influenced by past basically* free actions the agent performed precludes their being parts of such chains.[7] Now, Wilma herself does not have aspirations that go beyond modest soft libertarianism. She is happy to have the absence of a deterministic link to the distant past ensured by causally undetermined, rationally formed, effective better judgments. But traditional libertarians want more than this, and so do daring soft libertarians, even if they do not place the same requirements on freedom and moral responsibility as their traditional cousins do.

In short, DSLs view the power to perform basically* free and morally responsible actions as a requirement for having a kind of free and morally responsible agency that they value more highly than any compatibilist species of agency, but they also value working to make it the case that they are not subject to luck in an important practical sphere, even though success in this effort would cut them off from *further* basically* free and morally responsible actions in this sphere. This is not paradoxical, as is easily seen from a common perspective on moral credit. Aristotle's virtuous agent has made himself such that akratic action is not psychologically possible for him, and this agent is regarded as deserving moral credit for his virtuous actions.[8] Some ordinary libertarians find it very intuitive that such an agent deserves moral credit for the actions that flow from his virtuous constitution only if he deserves some moral credit for that constitution and that he deserves credit in the latter connection only if some basically* free and morally responsible actions of his played a significant role in his making himself as he is.

DSLs appeal to the game blackjack as a rough analogy of part of what they have in mind. Players compete only with the dealer, whose every move is dictated by the rules. Unlike the dealer, the players have options: for example, they can hit (request another card), stand (refuse additional cards), double their bets in certain situations, and split pairs (e.g., two aces) into two hands. Blackjack involves a mixture of luck and skill. What cards one gets is a matter of luck, and skilled players have memorized and are guided by reliable tables about when they should hit, stand, and so on. Very skilled players keep track of the cards they have seen—they "count cards"—and they adjust their playing strategy accordingly.

Just as luck—though not necessarily indeterministic luck—is an essential part of (legal) blackjack, being subject to present luck, according to DSLs, is an essential part of being an agent who is capable of performing basically* free actions and actions for which he is basically* morally responsible. But whereas luck is an ineliminable part of (legal) blackjack, DSLs seek, as agents, to eliminate luck in an important sphere. To return to the image of the roulette wheel, they seek to replace an indeterministic wheel connecting considered judgment and action with a deterministic one. Now, the blackjack player who wants to maximize his chances of winning (legally, of course) should learn how to minimize the potential consequences of bad luck and to maximize the potential consequences of good luck. So he should learn to count cards, and he should memorize a good set of blackjack tables and play accordingly. What should DSLs do about luck, given their aspirations as agents? One thing they should do, apparently, is to try to become so self-controlled that there is no longer a chance that they will act akratically.

4. Daring Soft Libertarianism and the Problem of Present Luck

DSLs embrace present luck. How do they respond to the worry that its presence in an instance of action is incompatible with the action's being freely performed and with the agent's being morally responsible for it?

In this section, I begin to work my way toward an answer. Because present luck is especially important to DSLs in the sphere of akratic action and its contrary—continent action—I start with a brief preparatory discussion of that sphere.

Strict akratic action may be defined as free, intentional action that is contrary to a conscious belief that the agent has at the time to the effect that it would be best to *A* (or best not to *A*)—best from the perspective of his own values, desires, beliefs, and the like, as opposed, for example, to a common evaluative perspective that he does not endorse. More briefly, strict akratic action is free, intentional action that is contrary to the agent's *CB*. An agent who refrains from *A*-ing and freely and intentionally *B*-s, even though his *CB* favors *A*-ing, acts akratically. So, in normal cases, does an agent who freely *decides* to *B* rather than *A*, despite having a *CB* that favors *A*-ing. That decision itself, in normal cases, is contrary to the agent's *CB* in a straightforward sense. For a decision to *B* to be akratic, the agent need not consciously believe that a better option than *deciding* to *B* is open to him; the conscious belief that an alternative to *B*-ing is a better course of action will do, other things being equal.[9]

I investigate DSL's resources for explaining strict akratic actions shortly. Brief attention to a conventional libertarian's resources provides useful background. Recall Kane's thesis (discussed in ch. 3, sec. 2) that in basic instances of free decision, agents simultaneously try to make each of two competing decisions, and throughout the process it is causally open which attempt will succeed. On this event-causal libertarian view, an agent who is tempted to act contrary to his *CB* may try to decide in accordance with his *CB* while also trying to decide to take the tempting course of action. Whether he decides akratically or not is a matter of which effort succeeds.

I illustrate this feature of Kane's view with a variant of Bob's story from chapter 3 (sec. 6). Recall that after Bob agreed to toss a coin at noon to start a football game, Carl offered him $50 to wait until 12:02 to toss it. Bob was tempted by the $50, but he also had moral qualms about helping Carl cheat bettors. He judged it best on the whole to do what he agreed to do, and in the current version of the story, he tried to decide to toss the coin at noon while also trying to decide to wait until 12:02 to toss it.[10] The latter effort was successful: at noon, Bob decided to toss the coin at 12:02 and to pretend to be searching for it in his pockets in the meantime. In a possible world that does not diverge from the actual world before noon, Bob decides at noon to toss the coin straightaway and acts accordingly.

The problem of present luck stares us in the face. The difference between Bob's deciding at noon to toss the coin in two minutes and his deciding at noon to toss it straightaway is just a matter of luck. But as DSLs see it, the psychology that Kane postulates is a greater problem. They doubt that agents ever try to decide to *A* while also trying to decide to do something else instead. DSLs want a more credible view of what happens in agents in the sphere of akratic and continent action.

In Mele 1992 (ch. 12), I argued that a common route from the acquisition of a *CB* in favor of *A*-ing to an intention to *A* is a default route. The basic idea is that "normal human agents are so constituted that, in the absence of preemption," acquiring a *CB* in favor of *A*-ing "issues directly in the acquisition of an intention to *A*" (p. 231). In simple cases involving little or no motivational opposition, the transition from *CB* to intention is smooth and easy. In such cases, having acquired a *CB* in favor of *A*-ing, agents have no need to think further about whether to *A*; nor, given the agents' motivational condition, is there a need to exercise self-control in order to bring it about that they intend to *A*. No special intervening effort of any sort is required. The existence of a default procedure of the sort at issue in normal human agents would help to explain the smoothness and ease of the transition. Indeed, we should expect an efficient action-directed system in beings who are capable both of acquiring deliberative *CB*-s and of performing akratic actions to encompass such a procedure. Special energy should be exerted in this connection only when one's *CB* encounters significant opposition. When one akratically fails to intend in accordance with one's *CB*, opposition is encountered: something blocks a default transition; something preempts the default value of the *CB*.

In Mele 1992 (pp. 233–34), I also distinguished among three kinds of cases in which an agent's *CB* is opposed by competing motivation: (1) a default process unproblematically generates a continent intention even in the face of the opposition; (2) a continent intention is formed even though the default route to intention is blocked by the opposition; (3) the motivational opposition blocks the default route to intention and figures in the production of an akratic intention. What I needed was a principled way of carving up the territory. I suggested that a continent intention is produced (in the normal way) by default, as opposed to being produced via a distinct causal route, when and only when (barring causal overdetermination, the assistance of other agents, science fiction, and the like) no intervening exercise of *self-control* contributes to the production of the intention (p. 233). (Sometimes opposing motivation is sufficiently weak that no attempt at self-control is called for.) If the move from *CB* to intention does not involve a special intervening effort on the agent's part, the intention's presence typically may safely be attributed to the operation of a default procedure.

Self-control also figures importantly in explaining why, when a default route from *CB* to intention *is* blocked, we sometimes do, and sometimes do not, intend on the basis of our *CB*-s. Barring the operation of higher-order default processes, overdetermination, interference by intention-producing demons, and so on, whether an agent intends in accordance with his *CB* in such cases depends on his own efforts at self-control. In simple cases of self-indulgence, he makes no effort at all to perform the action favored by his *CB* or to form the appropriate intention. In other cases, an agent whose *CB* favors *A*-ing might attempt in any number of ways to get himself to *A* or to get himself to intend to *A*. He might try focusing his attention on the desirable results of his *A*-ing or on the unattractive aspects of his not *A*-ing. He might generate vivid images of both or utter self-commands. If all else fails, he might seek help from a behavioral therapist. Whether his strategies work depends on the details of the case.[11]

Consider the following case (from Mele 2002, p. 156). Because she has had one shot of whiskey already—and very recently—at a party and needs to drive home soon, Drew believes that it is best to switch now to coffee. She believes both that she can switch from whiskey to coffee now and that she can have another whiskey instead; in Drew's opinion, it is up to her which of these she does. She knows that it is risky to drive under the influence of two shots, and she believes that, in light of the risk, her reason for having a second shot—that she would enjoy it— does not justify having one. Although Drew believes that she should switch to coffee, she thinks, "I've had a bit too much to drink before, and all has gone well. It really would be best to switch to coffee, but I'll indulge myself. Just one more shot, then a cup of coffee, then I'll drive home." Still believing that it would be best to switch to coffee now, Drew decides to drink another shot and drinks one. She does not feel compelled to drink. She feels that she is deciding freely and that she is freely drinking the whiskey. Drew makes no attempt to exercise self-control in support of her acting as she believes best, even though she has a modest desire to make such an attempt.

If strict akratic action is possible, this would seem to be a case of it. Imagine that the story just told is instantiated in a possible world with the same natural laws as the actual world and the same past up to the moment at which Drew decides to drink another shot. In the actual world, at that very moment, Drew decides to switch to coffee (and she switches). In another possible world with the same past and laws, she remains undecided about what to do a little longer. Suppose that Drew's brain works indeterministically in a way that helps to account for the possibility of these worlds. Is that consistent with Drew's having freely decided to switch to coffee and with her being morally responsible for that decision? DSLs of the kind under consideration now answer *yes*. How well can they support that answer?

As DSLs see it, the occurrence of basically* free akratic and continent actions entails cross-world luck at the time of action, and such luck does not preclude freedom or moral responsibility. In their view, various relevant probabilities are grounded primarily in various features of Drew's psychological condition at the time, t, at which she acquires her *CB* in favor of switching to coffee. Relevant probabilities include the probabilities that Drew will straightaway decide to drink another whiskey, straightaway decide to switch to coffee, straightaway decide to exercise self-control in support of switching to coffee, and remain undecided for a time about what to do. The features of Drew's psychology that partly ground or account for these probabilities include the strengths of various desires she has at t: for example, her desire to drink another whiskey, her desire to avoid increasing her chance of being in an accident as she drives home and her chance of being pulled over by the police and arrested for driving under the influence, her desire to avoid breaking the law, and her desire to exercise self-control in support of her acting as she believes she should. Other pertinent psychological features include, but are not limited to, Drew's degree of confidence at t that switching to coffee would be best and the strength of any generic desire she may have at t to do whatever she thinks is best. DSLs point out that these features do not come out of the blue and that they are products in part of Drew's past behavior. For example, it is very plausible that the strength of Drew's desire at t to avoid increasing the chance of an accident is influenced by her beliefs about previous occasions on which she drove under the influence, beliefs that she would lack if she had not engaged in this risky behavior in the past.

In remarking on Drew's past behavior, DSLs are not overlooking the point that if luck is in play in agents' present basically* free and basically* morally responsible actions, this also is true of their past actions of these kinds. DSLs maintain that agents play an indeterministic role in shaping the probabilities that they will act continently and that they will act akratically insofar as they play an indeterministic role in shaping things that ground these probabilities. Many agents have a capacity for present influence on relevant future probabilities of action, and it is often true that their past behavior has influenced present probabilities of action. Regarding influence of the former kind, notice that someone who has just acquired a *CB* in favor of *A*-ing may have, in addition to a probability that he will straightaway decide to *A* or nonactionally acquire an intention to *A* and a probability that he will straightaway decide to pursue a tempting course of action instead, a high probability of remaining undecided for a while. While he is undecided, there may be a chance that he will try to bring it about that he intends to do what he believes he should. If he tries in a promising way to do this, he thereby increases the probability that he will *A*. Other things being equal, an agent who makes such an effort at self-control has a better chance of continently *A*-ing than he would if he were to make no such effort. To be sure, if the attempt is a basically free action, then there was a chance that the agent would not make it at that time, and if it was a basically* free action, there might have been a chance that the agent would make it unfreely. These observations do not undermine the claim about present influence.

Past influence on present probabilities of action is considerable. For example, the strengths of Drew's desire for another whiskey and her desire not to increase the risk of an accident are likely to have been influenced by past decisions she made in similar situations, by her reflection on the consequences of those decisions, and by decisions about future behavior made partly on the basis of such reflection. Of course, if these decisions are basically free actions, there was a chance, when Drew made them, that she would not make them, and if they are basically* free actions, there might have been a chance, when she made them, that she would not freely make them. But these facts do not undermine the claim that they have an influence on the strengths of present relevant desires.

Part of what DSLs are driving at in their claims about influence is that probabilities of actions—practical probabilities—for agents are not always imposed on agents. Through their past behavior, agents shape present practical probabilities, and in their present behavior they shape future practical probabilities. The relationship between agents and the probabilities of their actions is very different from the relationship between dice and the probabilities of outcomes of tosses. In the case of dice, of course, the probabilities of future tosses are independent of the outcomes of past tosses. However, the probabilities of agents' future actions are influenced by their present and past actions.

A similarity between modest and daring soft libertarianism merits mention. One attractive feature of modest libertarianism is that it gives agents the opportunity to override bad luck before the time of action. For example, if a consideration relevant to an agent's decision problem unluckily fails to come to mind by *t*, an agent may increase the probability that it does come to mind before he reaches a decision by engaging in further deliberation, and if a silly desire unluckily becomes salient in consciousness (in a case in which the desire would have no effect on deliberation or action if it were not to become salient), the agent may reflectively discount it. DSLs emphasize another kind of opportunity that agents have regarding luck: the opportunity to learn from events associated with their bad luck—especially from basically* free decisions contrary to their rational *CB*-s. An agent who executes such a decision—say, a decision to drive under the influence—with bad consequences may learn from reflection on the consequences. (Of course, a drunk driver who kills himself in a car crash has no opportunity to learn from his mistake.) Another agent who drives under the influence against his *CB* but gets home safely and without being arrested may learn from reflection on what could have happened if he had been less fortunate. And both agents can think, effectively, about how to decrease the probability that they will drive under the influence again.[12]

DSLs maintain that in the vast majority of cases of basically* free actions and actions for which agents are basically* morally responsible, agents have some responsibility for the relevant practical probabilities. They have, for example, some responsibility for the chance that they will act akratically and for the chance that they will act continently. These chances are not dictated by external forces, and they are influenced by basically* free and morally responsible actions the agents performed in the past. DSLs take these claims to soften worries about present luck, but they realize that they have more work to do.

5. Objections and Replies

How should DSLs respond to the claim that the influence of agents' actions on their present probabilities of action is of no use to DSLs because an agent's being subject to cross-world luck at the time of action precludes his acting freely and morally responsibly at that time, no matter how the pertinent practical probabilities came to be as they are? Return to the case of Ann and the coin (ch. 3, sec. 4). Ann is rightly convinced both that she has a good reason to toss the coin at noon as she promised and that she has no significant reason not to do what she promised. The only thing that speaks in favor of deciding not to toss it then is a very weak desire to discover what it would feel like to break a promise for no good reason, and Ann regards that desire as silly. In the actual world, W, Ann tosses the coin at noon. In a possible world Wn, she decides at noon to hold on to the coin. In that world, as I have explained (ch. 3, sec. 4), Ann seems to suffer a breakdown of agency that is beyond the sphere of akratic action. The objection to DSL under consideration entails not only that Ann's decision in Wn is unfree but also that Ann does not freely toss the coin in W. DSLs accept the claim about Wn: they do not see actions that are manifestations of radical breakdowns of agency as free. But they are well within their rights to ask why they should agree that Ann does not freely toss the coin in W.

Their opponents might claim that an agent performs a basically* free action only if he could have performed an alternative basically* free action at the time. However, if some Frankfurt-style cases are successful, they undermine this requirement, and the requirement is rejected on independent grounds even by some traditional libertarians (Clarke 2003, pp. 125–26). An argument would certainly need to be advanced for it. The opponents might ask how the possibility of performing an unfree action can be relevant to basically* free action, but soft libertarians have already answered a closely related question (see ch. 4, sec. 2), and that answer applies straightforwardly here. Opponents who deem the answer unsatisfactory should defend their opinion about it.

A critic of DSL might claim that even if it is possible for agents to A as a basically* free action in cases in which the only alternative actions open to them at the time are unfree actions, it is impossible for agents to A as a basically* free action when their alternatives to A-ing include a free action favored by the agent's *CB*. Such a critic might hold, for example, that all basically* free actions are performed in accordance with the agent's *CB* and that akratic action is impossible because action contrary to one's *CB* necessarily is unfree. This, of course, is far from obviously true; again, an argument is needed.

It may be objected that DSLs are not entitled to make any claims about the influence of past basically* free actions on present probabilities of action until they have shown that there is good reason to believe that basically* free actions are possible. However, DSLs should reply that the point they have made thus far in that connection is simply that we should not believe that basically* free action is impossible on the grounds that, necessarily, indeterministic agents' probabilities of action are externally imposed or that indeterministic agents necessarily are related to their present probabilities of action roughly as dice are related to present probabilities about how they will land if tossed. Can DSL accommodate basically* free akratic actions? If indeterministically caused actions contrary to the agent's *CB* were like outcomes of tosses of dice, they might plausibly be deemed to be only apparently akratic and actually unfree. If agents were to house neural randomizers with unchanging probabilities of continent and akratic action or with probabilities that change independently of what agents learn from their mistakes and successes, they would be subject to luck in a way that seems to preclude their being basically* morally responsible for actions contrary to their *CB*-s and to preclude their performing basically* free akratic actions. But DSLs postulate neural equipment of a kind that agents are capable of molding through, for example, reflection and efforts of self-control. They contend that morally responsible agency is possible and that, over time, agents can take on increased moral responsibility for their probabilities of action in the sphere in which *CB*-s clash with temptation, probabilities that evolve in ways sensitive to what agents have learned and their efforts at self-control.

How does an agent come to be morally responsible for anything? This is a question for any theorist who believes that at least some human beings are morally responsible agents. More fully, how do we get from being neonates who are not morally responsible for anything to being the free, morally responsible agents we are now, if we are indeed free and morally responsible agents? I return to this question in section 6 and point out now that one thing that is required is an *S*-ability to adjust our behavior in light of what we learn from our past behavior. DSLs are claiming that this ability includes an *S*-ability to mold our probabilities of akratic and continent action. (This is not to say that agents themselves think in terms of molding probabilities.)

How, according to DSLs, do basically* free akratic actions differ from actions manifesting radical breakdowns of agency, as in the world in which Ann strangely decides at noon to hold on to the coin? Two kinds of radical breakdown scenario may be distinguished: those in which the agent's focal action is contrary to his *CB* and those in which it is not. Consider a case of the second kind. Cathy, who is in her mid-fifties, had always been a sweet, harmless person. She had never liked her loud, obnoxious neighbor, George, but she had never wanted to hurt him. Today, as Cathy is doing her normal Saturday morning gardening, it strikes her that the world would be at least a slightly better place without George and that killing him would be a good thing to do today, and she acquires a desire to kill him. As Cathy continues her pruning, digging, and watering, she spends an hour or so devising a plan for killing George. Later, she attends her customary Saturday tea and bridge session, takes her granddaughters to a movie, and goes home to finish preparing a meal for her grandkids and their parents. After saying goodnight to her visitors and watching the 10:00 news, Cathy executes her plan for George's murder. She slips her hands into some new latex gloves, breaks into George's house, sneaks into his bedroom, and slits his throat with a knife she found in his kitchen. She then walks home, destroys the gloves, crawls into bed, and falls asleep.

This is all very strange, and the fact that the murder was wildly out of line with Cathy's history and character contributes to the strangeness. Why, we want to know, did Cathy do what she did? We might be given a "reasons-explanation" of a standard kind: Cathy killed George because she wanted to make the world at least a slightly better place and believed that killing him would accomplish that. But that is not what we want to know. Evidently, Cathy was moved to kill George by, among other things, the desire and belief just mentioned. But why?

Readers may be expecting an answer featuring a fanciful kind of hypnosis, brainwashing, or psychosurgery. But, in fact, there was simply an extremely improbable, indeterministically caused pair of glitches in Cathy's head that day—so improbable that this sort of thing had never happened before on Earth. Normally, when Cathy has thoughts about doing something or other that for her would be very strange—for example, speeding in her car just for the fun of it or seducing a friend's husband—she simply sets it aside as a fleeting fantasy. As a consequence of her first glitch that day, the thought of killing George was not set aside. As a consequence of the second, Cathy became so bizarrely fixated on and emotionally detached from the thought of killing George that killing him seemed to her to be an absolutely normal, unpleasant activity— rather like filling out her income tax forms. If we had to attach an everyday label to Cathy's psychological condition at the time of the killing, it would be "insanity." One final detail: it was possible the whole day, even as Cathy was in the process of executing her deadly plan, that she would snap out of her bizarre psychological condition, but there was nothing she could do to snap herself out of it.

An adjustment to Cathy's scenario turns it into a case of acting contrary to one's *CB*. The only difference (aside from differences for which this one is logically sufficient in the context) is that in addition to believing that killing George would be a good thing to do today, Cathy believes that, on the whole, it would be better not to kill him today. What tips the scales in the direction of the latter belief for Cathy is the belief that killing George at the end of a long and busy day would be very tiring. (Last month, Cathy judged that it would be best not to fill out her income tax forms at the end of a long, busy day, but she did it anyway.)

What led to the stories about Cathy was the question how, according to DSLs, basically* free akratic actions differ from actions manifesting radical breakdowns of agency. One difference between actions of the former kind and Cathy's killing George, apparently, is that the former are not relatively direct products of extremely improbable but enormously powerful flukes. A related difference—the connection being the power of the fluke—is that Cathy's insanity gets her off the hook for the killing. Cathy seems not to be morally responsible for the killing and not to have performed it freely, in a sense of "freely" closely associated with moral responsibility. However, basically* free actions are, by definition, free in that sense, and the agents of such actions are morally responsible for them.

If, holding Cathy's psychological condition and behavior fixed, they had been products of a fanciful kind of unsolicited brainwashing, hypnosis, or psychosurgery, the scenario would have featured an *extreme takeover* rather than an extreme breakdown. In one version of an extreme takeover scenario, the killing is contrary to Cathy's *CB*. Even so, the etiology of the killing precludes its being an akratic action. It also is noteworthy that extreme scenarios of the breakdown and takeover varieties do not afford agents the opportunity to learn from their experience in the way that scenarios featuring garden-variety akratic actions do (provided that the akratic actions do not result in the agent's death or incapacitation). Agents can typically learn from their akratic mistakes and make progress in dealing with similar temptations in the future. Subjects of extreme breakdowns and takeovers can hope that they are never again subjected to such forces, but they cannot learn how to deal with these forces.

Ann's strangely deciding at noon to hold on to the coin despite her promise and her assessment of her situation may seem not to be momentous enough to sustain a diagnosis of (temporary) insanity. However, even if that impression is correct, it may be that as far as intrinsic features alone of the pertinent glitches are concerned, Ann is the locus of glitches of the same kind as Cathy's. If the two agents' glitches are related in this way, then Ann's strange decision to hold on to the coin can be made much more momentous by adjusting the stakes while holding the intrinsic features of her glitches fixed. In an adjusted scenario, Ann would love to have a million dollars and she knows that the reward for tossing the coin at noon, as she promised to do, is a million dollars. With that much at stake and only a very weak desire— which she regards as silly—to learn what it feels like to break a promise for no good reason speaking in favor of holding on to the coin, Ann's deciding not to toss the coin would seem to be a product of temporary insanity. The decision is not merely irrational and not merely surprisingly irrational; it is shockingly and astoundingly irrational. Akratic decisions are much more consonant with psychological normalcy.

In Mele 1987, I offered a compatibilist account of the possibility of strict akratic action and a compatibilist theory about how strict akratic actions are caused. The account and theory rest partly on two theses, both of which I defended there:

1. The motivational strength of our desires is not always in line with our evaluation of the "objects" of our desires (i.e., the desired items).
2. Typically, *CB*-s are formed, in significant part, on the basis of our evaluation of the objects of our desires.

(Notice that both theses are consistent with incompatibilism.) Given 1 and 2, an agent may have a stronger desire to *A* than to *B*, even though his *CB* favors *B*-ing rather than *A*-ing. If such an agent proceeds to act on the stronger desire, he acts contrary to his *CB*. If his action is intentional and free, he acts akratically. The same is true of the agent's *deciding* in accordance with the stronger desire in this case—his deciding to *A*. If he *freely* decides to *A*, his decision is an akratic action. If it is assumed that there is a tight—even if indeterministic—connection between an agent's strongest proximal motivation at a time and what he does at that time, a key to understanding how we can act akratically is understanding how preponderant motivation and better judgment can part company. I will not rehearse my compatibilist view of akratic action in any detail here. The point I want to make is that DSLs can apply a modified version of it to basically* free akratic decisions. (Recall that DSL is focused on deciding.) The main difference is that the actual or imagined phenomenon that DSLs have in their sights is a *basically** free species of action and therefore is performed at a time at which the past and the laws leave open at least a nonrobust alternative possibility.

(So, for example, a strong desire's being part of something that prox-imally deterministically causes the decision is excluded.)

6. Little Agents

In the preceding section, I asked how we get from being neonates, who do not even act intentionally, much less freely and morally responsibly, to being free, morally responsible agents. In Mele 1995, I sketched a pair of overlapping answers to this question (pp. 227–30)—one for compatibilists and the other for libertarians. The main question for DSL in this connection is whether it can accommodate the possibility of a neonate's developing into an agent capable of performing basi-cally* free actions for which he is basically* morally responsible.

Normal parents eventually come to view their children as having some degree of moral responsibility for what they do. The word "de-gree" is important here. Normal four-year-olds are not as well equip-ped for impulse control as normal eight-year-olds, and they have a less developed capacity for anticipating and understanding the effects of their actions. When normal four-year-olds snatch an appealing toy from a younger sibling's hands, most people take them to be morally responsible and blameworthy for that, but not as responsible and not as blameworthy as their normal eight-year-old siblings are for doing the same thing. (This is true at least of most people with a robust memory of significant dealings with children of these ages.) A simple way to account for this difference in how people regard these children is in terms of their grip on the fact that, given the differences in the chil-dren's emotional and intellectual development, resisting an impulse to snatch a toy tends to be significantly harder for the younger children.

In some cases, four-year-olds may have an urge to snatch a toy from a younger sibling and nonactionally acquire an intention to do so. (Recall my claim in ch. 1, sec. 3 that whereas some intentions to A are formed in actions of deciding to A, others are nonactionally acquired.) In others, they may have an urge to snatch it, think (very briefly) about whether to do so, and decide to take it. Consider the first time a normal child, Tony, makes a decision about whether to snatch a toy from his younger sister. He has occasionally acted on nonactionally acquired intentions to grab his sister's toys, but this time he gives the matter some thought and makes a decision. Tony knows that his father is nearby; and, on the basis of some unpleasant experiences, he associates taking the toy with his sister's screaming and his father's scolding him. He decides not to snatch it and feels a little frustrated. Imagine that Tony's father saw that he was tempted to take the toy and was inconspicuously watching his son to see what he would do. When he saw Tony move away from his sister and pick up something else to play with, he praised him for his good behavior. The father was not simply trying to reinforce the good behavior; he believed that Tony really deserved some credit for it.

Suppose now that owing to Tony's being an indeterministic decision maker and to his being tempted to take the toy, there was a significant chance at the time that he would decide to take it. In another world with the same past and laws of nature, that is what he decides to do, and he proceeds to grab the toy (with predictable results). Does that entail that Tony has no moral responsibility at all for deciding not to take the toy? Well, he is only a child, and if he can be morally responsible for anything, he can be so only in ways appropriate for young children, if moral responsibility is possible for young children. It does not seem at all outlandish to believe that Tony would deserve, from a moral point of view, some blame in the world in which he decides to snatch the toy and acts accordingly—but blame appropriate to his age and the nature of his offense, of course. If he does deserve some such blame, he has some moral responsibility for the decision. Similarly, the father's belief that Tony deserves some moral credit for his good decision is far from outlandish. If he does deserve such credit, it is of a kind appropriate to his age and the nature of his action, and he has some moral responsibility for the decision.

The difference at t (the time of Tony's decision) between the actual world and a world with the same past and laws in which Tony decides at t to snatch the toy is just a matter of luck. That should be taken into account when asking about Tony's moral responsibility for deciding not to take the toy. Only a relatively modest degree of moral responsibility is at issue, and the question is whether the cross-world luck—or the luck together with other facts about the case—entails that the degree is zero. I doubt that the knowledge that all actual decision-making children are indeterministic decision makers like Tony would lead us to believe that no children are morally responsible at all for any of their decisions.

Views according to which agents' past decisions can contribute to their moral responsibility for their present decisions naturally lead us to wonder about the earliest decisions for which agents are morally responsible. When we do wonder about that, we need to keep firmly in mind how young these agents may be and how trivial their good and bad deeds may be by comparison with the full range of good and bad adult deeds. Tony's making the right or the wrong decision about the toy is not that big a deal, and that is something for theorists to bear in mind when trying to come to a judgment about whether Tony is morally responsible for his decision. If, when pondering whether an indeterministic decision maker can make a first decision for which he is morally responsible, a theorist is focusing on scenarios in which adults make decisions about important moral matters, cross-world luck at the time of decision should strike the theorist as at least seriously problematic on grounds associated with the worries presented in chapter 3. But this focus is very wide of the mark.

Galen Strawson describes true or real moral responsibility as "*heaven-and-hell* responsibility," a kind of responsibility such that, if we have it, "it makes sense to propose that it could be just—without any qualification—to punish some of us with (possibly everlasting) torment in hell and reward others with (possibly everlasting) bliss in heaven" (2002, p. 451). Obviously, no sane person would think that little Tony deserves torment in hell—eternal or otherwise—for his bad deeds or heavenly bliss for his good ones. But Tony might occasionally deserve some unpleasant words or some pleasant praise; and, to use Strawson's expression, "it makes sense to propose" that Tony has, for some of his decisions, a degree of moral responsibility that would contribute to the justification of these mild punishments and rewards—even if those decisions are made at times at which the past and the laws leave open alternative courses of action, owing to Tony's being an indeterministic decision maker.

If no one can be morally responsible for anything, then, of course, Tony is not morally responsible to any degree for deciding not to take the toy. But if people are morally responsible for some things, they have to develop from neonates into morally responsible agents, and Tony's decision not to take the toy is a reasonable candidate for an action for which this young agent is morally responsible.[13] If Tony is basically morally responsible to some degree for deciding not to take the toy, and if an agent is basically morally responsible for an action only if he does it freely, then Tony freely decides not to take the toy.

Perhaps I have not been sufficiently explicit about certain themes in my discussion of little Tony. Moral responsibility is very commonly and very plausibly regarded as a matter of degree. *If* young children and adults are morally responsible for some of what they do, it is plausible, on grounds of the sort I mentioned, that young children are not nearly as morally responsible for any of their deeds as some adults are for some of their adult deeds. When we combine our recognition of that point with the observation that the good and bad deeds of young children are relatively trivial in themselves, we should be struck by the implausibility of stringent standards for deserved moral praise and blame of young children—including standards the satisfaction of which requires the absence of present luck. And once even a very modest degree of moral responsibility is in the picture, DSLs can begin putting their ideas about the shaping of practical probabilities to work.

What DSLs say about agents' shaping of their practical probabilities is meant to help us understand, among other things, how we get from being little free agents like Tony to being the mature free agents we are, if, in fact, we are free agents. The free agency at issue is an incompatibilist kind, not a compatibilist kind to which DSLs are open, given their softness. The process, if it is real, would seem to be very gradual, and I will not try to trace it. DSLs claim that, other things being equal, as the frequency of the indeterministically caused free actions of little agents increases and as the range of kinds of situations evoking such free actions expands, the agents take on greater moral responsibility for associated practical probabilities of theirs and for their morally significant free actions. This, DSLs say, helps to account for the fact that the moral credit and blame that little free agents deserve for their indeterministically caused free actions tend to increase over time.

In chapter 3 (sec. 6), I considered the claim that when we take Bob's past into account, we may see that the cross-world difference between his cheating at noon in the actual world, *W1*, and his flipping the coin at noon, as promised, in a world, *W2*, with the same past and laws of nature is *not* just a matter of luck, because the practical accessibility itself of these worlds to Bob at the time is partly explained by basically free actions he performed at earlier times. As I mentioned, it may be claimed, for example, that if, in certain past situations, Bob had performed—as he could have—better free actions than he in fact performed, the cheating worlds would not have been practically accessible to him at noon. My reply was that this claim moves the worry about present luck back in time. Relocating the problem in that way is not illegitimate, but to relocate it without then addressing it at its new location is to ignore the problem. My discussion of little Tony addresses the relocated problem from the perspective of DSLs.

I did not, in chapter 3, explicitly answer the question whether it true that if Bob has a history of the right sort, then the cross-world difference in noontime actions is not just a matter of luck. Now, given that Bob does have a history of the right sort, DSLs maintain that what probabilities of action obtain at the time is not just a matter of luck. But probabilities of action are one kind of thing, and the difference at noon between Bob's cheating then in *W1* and his flipping the coin then in *W2* is another. Suppose that if Bob had performed different free actions in the past, as he could have, his probabilities of action at noon would have been different and that, at one time, a history was open to Bob—one including his performing relevant character-influencing basically free actions—such that, if that history had been actual, it would have resulted in Bob's having, at the time, a probability of 0 of cheating and a very high probability of tossing the coin, as promised. (There might have been some small chance of Bob's accidentally failing to toss the coin at noon: for example, the coin might accidentally slip out of his hand.) The supposition would reveal something about Bob, but it is irrelevant to the question whether, holding fixed *the actual past* and the laws of nature, the difference at noon between Bob's cheating then, as he does in *W1*, and Bob's flipping the coin then, as he does in *W2*, is just a matter of luck. And again, the actual past and the laws are held fixed when testing for basically (and basically*) free and morally responsible action. Even if the practical accessibility of the worlds open to Bob at the pertinent time is partly explained by basically free actions he performed at earlier times, the cross-world difference in Bob's noontime actions in *W1* and *W2* is just a matter of luck.

7. Conclusion

DSLs grant that if, in the actual world, an agent decides at *t* to *A*, whereas in another possible world with the same laws of nature and the same past he decides at *t* not to *A*, then the cross-world difference at *t* is just a matter of luck. But they hold that the fact that the difference is just a matter of luck is compatible with its being true that the agent decided freely and morally responsibly at *t*. To be sure, hard event-causal libertarians and agent-causationists can make this compatibility claim, too. According to DSLs, the main problem with the most detailed event-causal libertarian view on offer, Kane's, is not that it is subject to the problem of present luck but rather that its account of what agents do in cases of basically free action for which they are basically morally responsible is unsatisfactory. Kane's doubled trying maneuver fails to solve the problem of present luck anyway, and there is good reason to believe that no real agent who lacks a serious brain disorder tries to decide to A while also trying to decide to do something else instead. (The same goes for trying to bring it about that one decides to A while also trying to bring it about that one decides to do something else instead.) DSLs have a similar attitude toward agent-causal libertarianism. As they see it, the only thing that this view might have seemed to have going for it is that it might secure a kind of "enhanced control" that solves the luck problem. But DSLs, on grounds of the sort adduced in chapter 3, are convinced that agent causationists leave the problem intact. So in light of independent worries about agent causation, they set it aside. DSLs are inclined to agree with Clarke that relevant arguments collectively "incline the balance against the [conceptual] possibility of... agent causation" (2003, p. 209). They also agree with Clarke (pp. 206–7) that there is no evidence for the existence of agent causation. DSLs, unlike Clarke (whose task in Clarke 2003 is to assess the conceptual adequacy of libertarian views), contend that, in fact, human beings sometimes act freely. And how is one to defend the claim that human beings sometimes engage in a kind of free action that requires the existence of a species of causation for which there is no evidence?

As I said in chapter 1 (sec. 2), modest libertarians hold that if (*ML1*) an agent's A-ing satisfies a set of alleged sufficient conditions for free action that a sophisticated compatibilist would endorse and that many sophisticated folks who have no commitment to incompatibilism would find very attractive, including the condition that the agent A-s on the basis of a rational deliberative judgment that it would be best to A, and (*ML2*) while the agent was deliberating, it was causally open that he would not come to the conclusion that it would be best to A, then (*ML3*) the agent freely A-s. (The specific compatibilist proposal that I offered [Mele 1995, p. 193] is summarized in ch. 7, sec. 1.) Modest libertarianism does not include a position on the possibility of free actions that are not performed on the basis of a judgment about what it would be best to do. Proponents of daring soft libertarianism substitute the following for *ML2*: (*DSL2*) the agent's A-ing is a decision the proximate causes of which do not deterministically cause it. They maintain that the combination of *ML1* and *DSL2* is conceptually sufficient for the agent's decision's being basically* free. They maintain, as well, that there are basically* free akratic decisions.

NOTES

1. Dennett discusses a similar case (1978, pp. 293–94).

2. Of course, the following proposition also is comparable to A2: (B2*) Beth is not morally responsible in *Wn* for having thought *T* at *t*. However, my concern here is intentional actions.

3. DSL is similar in some ways to an event-causal libertarianism that Clarke describes as "unadorned" and "centered" (2003, chs. 3 and 5–7). Three prominent ways in which DSL differs from the unadorned, centered event-causal libertarianism that Clarke discusses are that the former view, but not the latter, includes a detailed reply to the problem of present luck, accommodates Frankfurt-style cases, and is a species of soft libertarianism.

4. There are *special* cases in which agents try to bring it about that they decide to *A*. For example, Joe occasionally has thought hard about whether it would be best on the whole to quit smoking and judged that quitting soon would be best. As he knows, he always put the matter off after reaching this point; he has never decided to quit. Tonight, on New Year's Eve, Joe is again reflecting on the issue. Once again, he judges that it would be best to quit soon. He also believes that if he can get himself to decide to quit, he will have a decent chance of quitting. Joe decides to ask his doctor what he can do to bring it about that he decides to quit. After a session with his doctor, Joe embarks on a twelve-step program that he believes will give him a reasonable chance of bringing this about.

5. On competing theories of the nature of reasons for action and how they may be squared with causal theories of action and of action explanation, see Mele 2003a, chs. 3–5.

6. Some DSLs hold that it is the neural realizers of these judgments and intentions that do the causal work rather than the judgments or intentions themselves, but I will ignore this complication. Henceforth, unless I indicate otherwise, readers should understand assertions of mental causation disjunctively, as assertions that either the mental item at issue or its neural realizer does the causal work.

7. Perhaps an action can be causally overdetermined by a deterministic chain that stretches into the distant past and a chain with at least one indeterministically caused link. To simplify discussion, I stipulate that *suitable* influence by past basically free actions includes the absence of such overdetermination.

8. See *Nicomachean Ethics* 1152a1–8, in light of *Nicomachean Ethics*, bk. 2, ch. 1.

9. In special cases, alternative decisions, as opposed to alternative courses of nondecisional action that the agent can decide between or among, are rendered salient for the agent. If an agent believes that a mind reader will reward him with a good book for deciding at *t* to raise only his left hand at $t + n$ (whether or not he actually raises it) and will reward him with a good bottle of whiskey

for deciding at t to raise only his right hand at $t + n$, he may reflect on which decision it would be better to make. If he consciously believes that the former decision would be a better one to make than the latter, but freely makes the latter, he decides akratically. (Presumably, the focus of the practical reflection would be whether it would be better to bring it about that he has a good book or a good bottle of whiskey.)

10. Again, readers who have trouble with the idea that agents try to decide to A may suppose that the agent is trying to bring it about that he decides to A.

11. Parts of this paragraph and the preceding two are borrowed from Mele 1992, pp. 231–34. For a discussion of the practical potential of strategies such as these in effective self-control, and of pertinent empirical literature on the topic, see Mele 1987, pp. 23–24 and chs. 4–6. For more on intentions by default, see Mele 1992, ch. 12.

12. Agents in deterministic worlds also can learn from events associated with their bad luck, but, of course, they cannot perform basically* free actions.

13. Some readers may regard Tony as not sufficiently cognitively developed to have any degree of moral responsibility for his pertinent actual and counterfactual deeds. Some such readers may be satisfied if, for example, Tony were to believe the universal proposition that it is wrong for any child to take a toy away from another child just because he wants to play with it. I am willing to be accommodating.

Compatibilism
Objections and Replies

There are two popular arguments for incompatibilism. One is the consequence argument, introduced in chapter 4. The other is an argument to the effect that regarding free action and moral responsibility, there is no important difference between cases of manipulation in which agents A unfreely and are not morally responsible for A-ing and ordinary cases of A-ing in deterministic worlds. I call it the *manipulation argument* (following Kapitan 2000, p. 81). In section 1, I comment briefly on the consequence argument. In section 2, I argue that the most fully developed version of the manipulation argument—Derk Pereboom's recent version (2001)—is unpersuasive. In section 3, I introduce an idea—the *no-chance idea*—that is at least loosely associated with the consequence argument. That section sets the stage for my discussion of different kinds of compatibilism in sections 4 through 6.

1. The Consequence Argument

Here, again, is a short version of Peter van Inwagen's consequence argument: "If determinism is true, then our acts are the consequences of the laws of nature and events in the remote past. But it is not up to us what went on before we were born, and neither is it up to us what the laws of nature are. Therefore, the consequences of these things (including our present acts) are not up to us" (1983, p. 16). If this argument is to yield the conclusion that determinism is incompatible with free action and moral responsibility, it needs a premise along the following lines: If our acts are not up to us, we do not perform them freely and are not morally responsible for them.

There is a large body of literature on the consequence argument. Much of it concerns the validity of various inference rules used in various versions of the argument. I bypass that literature and repeat a point I made in Mele 1995 (p. 249). In what sense, according to the consequence argument, are the laws of nature and events in the distant past "not up to us"? Presumably, in the sense that—or in a sense that entails that—we have *no control over them*. But it does not follow from (1) the supposition that these things are not up to us in this sense and (2) the supposition that our actions "are the consequences of" these things, that (3) our actions are "not up to us" in the *same* sense. We proximately control ordinary actions of ours, as I have explained (ch. 1, sec. 1), and that fact is compatible with the truth of 1 and 2 (see Slote 1982). Incompatibilists can claim that any acceptable reading of "up to us" entails *indeterministic* control. However, that kind of control is viewed by compatibilists as at best an excessive requirement for free action and moral responsibility. An argument for the claim is needed.

Suppose it is claimed that free action and moral responsibility require indeterministic control because they require robust alternative possibilities at the time of some actions. My reply may be inferred from my position on Frankfurt-style cases in chapter 4. If I am right, it is possible for there to be free, morally responsible agents who never have robust alternative possibilities. That possibility entails that it is false that there is a need for robust alternative possibilities that justifies the requirement of indeterministic control: incompatibilists need to look for other grounds for that alleged requirement. The manipulation argument bears directly on the dispute between compatibilists and incompatibilists about the kinds of control required for free action and moral responsibility.

2. The Manipulation Argument

Derk Pereboom contends that "the best type of challenge to compatibilism" is that determinism "is in principle as much of a threat to moral responsibility as is covert manipulation" (2001, p. 89).[1] He argues that, regarding moral responsibility, there is no important difference between cases of covert manipulation in which agents are not morally responsible for A-ing and ordinary cases of A-ing in deterministic worlds (pp. 112–26). His strategy in what he calls his "four-case argument" (p. 117) is to describe three cases of progressively weaker manipulation in which, he contends, the agent, Plum, is not morally responsible for killing his victim, Ms. White, and to compare them to a related deterministic case that involves no manipulation. Pereboom argues that what blocks Plum's moral responsibility for killing White in the first three cases is the fact that "his action results from a deterministic causal process that traces back to factors beyond his control" and that, because this fact also obtains in the fourth case, Plum is not morally responsible for that killing either (p. 116).

In Mele 1995, I offered a collection of jointly sufficient conditions for autonomous action, on a compatibilist view of such action. One condition, in the case of deliberative action, is that the deliberation that gives rise to the action not be driven by compelled or coercively produced attitudes (p. 193). A related condition is that the agent's capacity for control over his inner life not be bypassed by processes that instill in him deliberative habits of certain kinds (pp. 182–85). I believe that *if* Pereboom's primary intuition about his first three cases is correct, a better explanation of it is framed in terms of features like these of Plum's deliberation and that such an explanation reveals a noteworthy difference between these cases and the fourth. I defend that belief after providing further background.

In Pereboom's first case, Plum is "created by neuroscientists [who] 'locally' manipulate him to undertake the process by which his desires are brought about and modified—directly producing his every state from moment to moment" (2001, pp. 112–13). They "manipulate him by, among other things, pushing a series of buttons" (p. 113). In the second, the scientists who create Plum "cannot control him directly," but they have "programmed him to weigh reasons for action so that he is often . . . rationally egoistic, with the result that in the circumstances in which he now finds himself, he is causally determined to undertake the moderately reasons-responsive process and to possess the set of first- and second-order desires that results in his killing Ms. White" (pp. 113–14). Pereboom writes: "Causal determination by factors beyond Plum's control most plausibly explains his lack of moral responsibility in the first case, and I think we are forced to say that he is not morally responsible in the second case for the same reason" (p. 114).

Is Pereboom's judgment about "causal determination"—that is, deterministic causation—warranted? Consider an analogue of case 1 in which the manipulators fall short of initiating *deterministic* causal chains. In case 1a, the neuroscientists locally manipulate Plum and produce "his every state from moment to moment," but they do this by means of an indeterministic mechanism. There is an extremely good chance that each push of a button will have the result the neuroscientists want, but each push also has a tiny chance of incapacitating Plum. These are the only possible outcomes of the button pushes. As it happens, Plum is not incapacitated. If Plum is not morally responsible for killing White in case 1, then he is not morally responsible for killing her in case 1a either. And the correct explanation of his lacking moral responsibility for the killing in case 1a plainly does not appeal to deterministic causation. That the causation in case 1 is deterministic is not essential to Plum's lacking moral responsibility in it.

Consider an indeterministic analogue of case 2. In case 2a, the program the scientists install in Plum is indeterministic. It works just like the program in case 2 except that there is a tiny chance every few seconds that the program will incapacitate Plum. As it happens, Plum is not incapacitated. If Plum is not morally responsible for killing White in case 2, he is not morally responsible for killing her in case 2a either. Surely, blending this possibility of incapacitation into case 2 does not transform it from a case of nonresponsibility into one of responsibility. Here again, that the causation in Pereboom's case is deterministic is not essential to Plum's lacking moral responsibility for the killing.

I reproduce Pereboom's third case of manipulation in full because I am not sure how to interpret it:

> Plum is an ordinary human being, except that he was determined by the rigorous training practices of his home and community so that he is often but not exclusively rationally egoistic (exactly as egoistic as in Cases 1 and 2). His training took place at too early an age for him to have had the ability to prevent or alter the practices that determined his character. In his current circumstances, Plum is thereby caused to undertake the moderately reasons-responsive process and to possess the first- and second-order desires that result in his killing White. He has the general ability to grasp, apply, and regulate his behavior by moral reasons, but in these circumstances, the egoistic reasons are very powerful, and hence the rigorous training practices of his upbringing deterministically result in his act of murder. Nevertheless, he does not act because of an irresistible desire. (p. 114)

I explain my interpretive uncertainty shortly. My point about cases 1 and 2 should be echoed now. Imagine that the causal chain linking "the rigorous training practices of his upbringing" to Plum's killing of

White falls short of being deterministic. At various points along the way, and at the time of the murder, there was a tiny chance that Plum's training would cause an incapacitating mental breakdown. That is the only noteworthy difference between this scenario (case 3a) and case 3. Again, Plum is not incapacitated. If Plum is not morally responsible for killing White in case 3, the same is true of case 3a. Surely, blending this possibility of a mental breakdown into case 3 would not transform it from a case of nonresponsibility into one of responsibility. As in cases 1 and 2, the deterministic causation in case 3 is dispensable.

Pereboom's fourth case, set in a deterministic world, is case 3 without "the rigorous training practices" (p. 115). Here is his punch line: "The best explanation for the intuition that Plum is not morally responsible in the first three cases is that his action results from a deterministic causal process that traces back to factors beyond his control. Because Plum is also causally determined in this way in Case 4, we should conclude that here too Plum is not morally responsible for the same reason" (p. 116). I have argued that we lack adequate grounds for accepting the claim that the deterministic causation in cases 1, 2, and 3 is what produces the intuition that Plum is not morally responsible for killing White. So far, at least, the claim that the manipulation in those cases is what does the intuition-producing work looks very plausible. If my arguments hit their mark, Pereboom's four-case argument does not warrant the conclusion that, in case 4, "Plum is not morally responsible" for killing White and that he lacks moral responsibility for this because the killing was deterministically caused.

Identifying what might block Plum's moral responsibility for killing White in Pereboom's first three cases is a bit more complicated than some readers may now think. In Mele 1995, I pointed out that the responsibility-undermining effects of intentional manipulators can be matched by blind forces—for example, by a brain disorder or a spontaneously generated electromagnetic field (pp. 168–69). Imagine a variant of case 1 (case 1b) in which a strange, spontaneously generated electromagnetic field he is passing through on a cruise ship directly produces Plum's "every state from moment to moment" or a variant of case 2 (case 2b) in which that field programs Plum's infant brain in such a way that it operates just as it operated in the original story. Presumably, if Plum is not morally responsible for killing White in cases 1 and 2, he is not morally responsible for killing her in 1b and 2b, and the same is true of the connection between cases 1a and 2a—indeterministic versions of cases 1 and 2—and variants of those cases (1c and 2c) in which the spontaneously generated electro-magnetic field stands in for the neuroscientists. What interesting properties do the four cases in the 1 series (cases 1 though 1c) have in common, aside from Plum's not being morally responsible for killing White, if he is not morally responsible for that? Half are deterministic and half are indeterministic. Half involve agents who intentionally manipulate Plum, and half do not. In the 1 series, Plum is not even partly in control of "the process of reasoning" that happens in his head. Rather, "his every state from moment to moment" is directly produced—either deterministically or indeterministically—by the neuroscientists or the electromagnetic field. What about the 2 series (cases 2 though 2c)? Here, too, half the cases are deterministic, half are indeterministic, half involve agents who intentionally manipulate Plum, and half do not. In each case in this series, Plum played no role at all in shaping his procedure for weighing reasons (say, through trial and error over the years he has been in the business of deliberating). Unlike normal agents, Plum had no control throughout his history as an agent over this important aspect of his deliberative style. Rather, the procedure is imposed on him—either deterministically or indeterministically—by the neuroscientists or the electromagnetic field. Facts such as these about what Plum does not control in the two series of cases do seem to account for his nonresponsibility in them, if it is true that he lacks moral responsibility for the killings in both series. (Again, my claim is that *if* Plum is not morally responsible for killing White in cases 1 and 2, the same is true of his killing White in all cases in the 1 and 2 series.)

I do not see how it can reasonably be claimed that an agent who is out of the control loop in the way Plum is in the 1 series is morally responsible for the fruits of "his reasoning."[2] Plum's control abnormality in the 2 series is subtler. Normal agents learn how to weigh reasons for action. For example, a young agent who weighs reasons very egoistically may suffer as a consequence and learn that things go better for him when he weighs the interests of others more heavily as reasons. His deliberative style might gradually become significantly less egoistic, and, along the way, his less egoistic actions might have reinforcing consequences that help to produce in him increased concern for the welfare of those around him. This increased concern would presumably have an effect on his evolving deliberative habits. The story of the normal evolution of a particular agent's deliberative style is a long one. The point here is that in the 2 series Plum is cut off from such evolution regarding his procedure for weighing reasons. If anything properly generates the judgment that Plum is not morally responsible for the killings in the 2 series, it is this point, for it is the only relevant apparent threat to moral responsibility that all four cases in the series have in common.[3]

I have concentrated primarily on cases 1 and 2 in Pereboom's four-case argument because of my uncertainty about how case 3 is to be interpreted. How powerful are the effects of "the rigorous training practices"—the manipulation—supposed to be? Pereboom reports that Plum's "training took place at too early an age for him to have had the ability to prevent or alter the practices that determined his character." Because the scenario is deterministic, this suggests that Pereboom, for the purposes of his four-case argument at least, is willing to understand the ability to prevent something that was not prevented and the ability to alter something that was not altered in such a way that agents can have these abilities in a deterministic world. When Plum grew older, was he able, on a compatibilist reading of "able," to alter his "character"? More specifically, was he able—perhaps partly through reflection on his values and experiences—to make himself less egoistic and more sensitive to moral reasons? Pereboom does not say. If the rigorous training practices did not render Plum unable to do these things, and if he was able—in a compatibilist sense—to do them, typical compatibilists have no good reason to agree that Plum is not morally responsible for the killing. If, however, the manipulation was such as to render Plum unable to attenuate its effects, some compatibilists can agree that Plum is not morally responsible for the killing. But they should hasten to add that the deterministic causation in the story is dispensable. A story in which the manipulation indeterministically causes Plum to lack the pertinent compatibilist abilities, through no fault of his own, would also be a story in which, according to compatibilists of the relevant kind, Plum is not morally responsible for the killing (see Mele 1995, chs. 9 and 10).

I can imagine someone objecting that the fact that there are indeterministic versions of Pereboom's manipulation cases in which Plum is no more responsible for killing White than he is in Pereboom's deterministic cases has nothing to do with the merits of his four-case argument. Not so. Recall Pereboom's claim that "The best explanation for the intuition that Plum is not morally responsible in the first three cases is that his action results from a deterministic causal process that traces back to factors beyond his control" (2001, p. 116). Some incompatibilists may find this very plausible. But what about compatibilists? They should find Pereboom's claim no more plausible than the claim that the best explanation for Scarlet's car's being damaged in the following three cases is that it was struck by an object that was, among other things, *wet*: (case 1) Scarlet's car was struck by a falling large wet lead pipe and was damaged as a result; (case 2) Scarlet's car was struck by a falling large wet wrench and was damaged as a result; (case 3) Scarlet's car was struck by a falling large wet metal candlestick and was damaged as a result. (In each case, the object fell ten feet.)

The claim that I have just invited readers to recall immediately precedes Pereboom's assertion that "Because Plum is also causally determined in this way in Case 4 [where there is no manipulation], we should conclude that here too Plum is not morally responsible for the same reason" (p. 116). As it happens, in case 4 of the Scarlet chronicles, her car was struck by a falling large wet sponge. Peacocke concludes that Scarlet's car is damaged in this case, too. But, of course, she is wrong. It was such things as the hardness and weight of the falling objects, not their wetness, that did the work. Similarly, for all Pereboom has shown, it is the manipulation, not the deterministic causation, that does the intuition-driving work in his cases.

Pereboom has failed to justify his diagnosis of the source of the alleged intuition that Plum is not morally responsible for killing White in his cases of manipulation: the deterministic causation in those cases is dispensable, as I have explained. Consequently, he has failed to provide adequate support for his theses that Plum is not morally responsible for killing White in case 4 and that this is so because "his action results from a deterministic causal process that traces back to factors beyond his control" (p. 116). Pereboom's four-case argument for incompatibilism fails.

Obviously, the failure of Pereboom's manipulation argument does not entail that all manipulation arguments for incompatibilism will fail. I selected it for examination here because it is the most carefully developed manipulation argument currently on offer. (For my reply to earlier manipulation arguments, see Mele 1995, pp. 187–91.)[4]

3. The No-Chance Idea Introduced

The topic of the present section is an idea that is at least loosely associated with the consequence argument. I call it the *no-chance idea*, or NCI, for short.

NCI. Suppose that determinism is true of our universe. Then (1) shortly after the big bang, there was no chance that anything that has happened (as of the time of your reading this) would not happen, right down to the smallest detail. Consider everyone's past actions, for example. Shortly after the big bang, there was no chance that they would not perform those actions. Moreover, (2) there was no chance of this because of the following fact about all past actions: shortly after the big bang, there was no chance that any of their causes—remote or proximate—would not occur or exist and no chance that any of their causes would not have the effects they had. Given 2, no agents are morally responsible for any of their past actions.

For the purposes of this argument, "chance" is defined in such a way that there was a chance a thousand years ago of x happening today if and only if the conjunction of a complete description of the state of the universe at that time and a complete statement of the laws of nature is consistent with x happening today.

Consider indeterministic Frankfurt-style cases (ch. 4) and, more specifically, the claim that in some such cases, even though there was no chance that the agent would not A at t, the agent was morally responsible for A-ing, which he did at t.[5] This claim does not directly threaten NCI, because in these cases there was a chance that what caused the agent's A-ing would not cause it. These cases include a chance that the potential intervener or potentially effective process would instead cause the agent's A-ing. Given that indeterministic Frankfurt-style cases have no obvious use in compatibilist challenges to the no-chance idea, how should compatibilists go about challenging NCI? There is the obvious and reasonable strategy of asking incompatibilists for an *argument* that has 2 as a premise and the assertion that agents in deterministic universes are not morally responsible for any of their past actions as a conclusion. More aggressive lines of reply also are open to compatibilists.

One common compatibilist charge against incompatibilists is that they confuse deterministic causation with compulsion or constraint.[6] Compatibilists can argue that this confusion is at work in NCI. They can argue, for example, that fans of NCI mistakenly regard 2 as entailing that agents in deterministic universes are compelled to do whatever they do. Stock examples of compulsion are a kleptomaniac's stealing something because he has an uncontrollable urge to steal it and an addict's using a drug because of an irresistible desire to use it. Compatibilists typically hold that actions such as these in deterministic universes are importantly different from, say, an ordinary philosopher's giving an ordinary lecture or making a routine trip to work in a deterministic universe. On a familiar conception of things, there was no chance that any of these agents would not do what they did, given that their universes are deterministic. And, even so, compatibilists see the compelled actions as importantly different from the ordinary ones. Until proponents of NCI produce an argument that has 2 as a premise and the proposition that no agent in a deterministic universe is morally responsible for any of his past actions as a conclusion, compatibilists can reasonably say that it is not incumbent on them to try to show that 2 is compatible with moral responsibility. But this is not the way of progress. John Fischer and Mark Ravizza (1998) have produced the most detailed extant compatibilist account of moral responsibility. (They embrace semicompatibilism, a species of compatibilism.) Implicit in their account is an answer to the question why 2 should be thought to be compatible with moral responsibility. In the following section, I evaluate their account. In section 5, I apply their account and a potential successor to the question about 2.

4. Fischer and Ravizza on Moral Responsibility

Semicompatibilism, again (see ch. 1, n. 27), is the view that determinism is compatible with free action and moral responsibility even if it is incompatible with agents' ever having been able to act otherwise than they did (Fischer 1994; Fischer and Ravizza 1998). In a book symposium on Fischer and Ravizza 1998, I raised some problems for their semicompatibilist position on moral responsibility. Two of the critical claims I advanced are that a necessary condition they offer for moral responsibility is too strong and the sufficient conditions they offer are too weak (Mele 2000). They reply in Fischer and Ravizza 2000. Although my claim about their sufficient conditions is more germane to NCI, I examine their replies to both claims here. Both claims are relevant to a certain tension in their view that merits attention.

Fischer and Ravizza contend that "taking responsibility" is a necessary condition of moral responsibility and requires that the agent "accept that he is a fair target of the reactive attitudes as a result of how he exercises [a certain kind of] agency in certain contexts" (1998, p. 211). One version of this requirement—the one that is my concern—is for people who "engage in significant metaphysical reflection about the relationship between causal determinism and the fairness of our social practices of applying the reactive attitudes" (1998, p. 211). Here it is:

(R) Such an "individual must view himself as, prima facie at least, an apt candidate for the application of the reactive attitudes, and be willing to put aside his residual doubts, for all practical purposes" (p. 227). Fischer and Ravizza assert that whereas their "reactive attitudes" condition for nonreflective agents involves a judgment about what our social practices are, the counterpart condition for reflective agents involves these agents' making a "metaphysical judgment" (p. 226). For reflective agents "the question is *not* simply about the given social practices; the question is whether these practices can be *justified*, all things considered" (p. 226, emphasis altered).

In Mele 2000, I offered an apparent counterexample to *R* (pp. 447–49). It features a philosopher, Phil, who is converted from a compatibilist believer that he and most people are morally responsible agents to a hard determinist during a visit to London in which, over the course of several months, Ted Honderich persuades him that determinism is true and Galen Strawson convinces him that determinism is incompatible with moral responsibility.[7] Phil is intellectually committed to hard determinism—he is no less committed to it than, for example, most philosophical atheists are to atheism—and he is convinced that indignation, gratitude, and the like are unjustified and that there are no fair targets of the reactive attitudes. By hypothesis, Phil is mistaken and the world abounds with morally responsible agents who are fair targets of the reactive attitudes.

Phil's conversion does not drastically change his life. Among other things, he continues to care about pleasure, pain, well being, and the like—both his own and others': he does not believe that the changes in his philosophical convictions have rendered these things unimportant. Phil continues to be a good husband and father, to donate money to various charities, to spend time building Habitat for Humanity houses, and, in general, to treat people well. Also, occasionally, but no more frequently than in his compatibilist days, Phil indulges in repeating unfavorable rumors about people, tells small lies to make things easier for himself, and so on.

I suggested in Mele 2000 that, other things being equal, and assuming widespread moral responsibility in his world, Phil is plausibly deemed morally responsible for the good and bad actions just mentioned. Seemingly, not only does Phil falsely believe that no one around him is "an apt candidate for the application of the reactive attitudes" and that no one around him is morally responsible for anything but also he falsely believes that he is not "an apt candidate for the application of the reactive attitudes" and that he is not a morally responsible agent. If matters are as they seem, a theoretically reflective skeptic about moral responsibility does *not* need to satisfy R in order to be morally responsible.

Fischer and Ravizza reply that, in a certain respect, Phil is like an addict who "sees that he has an irresistible urge to take a drug" and takes it "because he knows that it is futile to resist" and like "a sailor who knows that his rudder is broken" (2000, pp. 468–69). (The sailor also appears in their treatment of "taking responsibility" in their book [1998, p. 221], as does a serial killer who sees himself as "controlled by 'a monster inside'" [p. 220].) Phil, they claim, is "similar to the addict and sailor in lacking a certain kind of self-engagement in his behavior, understood subjectively. . . . Insofar as the reactive attitudes are a response to behavior with this particular sort of quality, Phil is not an apt target for them" (2000, p. 469).[8]

Suppose for the sake of argument that there is a kind of self-engagement—kind K—that the addict, the sailor, and Phil all lack. Is it in virtue of the addict's and the sailor's lacking that kind of self-engagement that they are not apt targets of the reactive attitudes for their relevant behavior and are not morally responsible for it—~AT&~MR for it, for short? In the course of replying to an objection of mine that I discuss shortly, Fischer and Ravizza write: "if the individual really is not responsible for the phobia or addiction, and it issues in genuinely irresistible urges, then intuitively the individual is not morally responsible for the relevant behavior" (2000, p. 471). I agree, and I assume accordingly that the factors identified in the antecedent of the sentence just quoted also suffice for the agent's not being an apt target of the reactive attitudes for the relevant behavior. What about the sailor? The combination of his not being morally responsible for the broken rudder and his knowing that the rudder is broken suffices for his being ~AT&~MR for not trying to use the rudder and for suitably related motions of his boat.

If the facts that the addict's urges are irresistible and he is not responsible for the addiction that issues in them and that the sailor knows that his rudder is broken and is not responsible for its condition entail that these two agents lack self-engagement of kind K in the relevant contexts, so be it. That does not entail that it is in virtue of lacking self-engagement of kind K—a kind that Phil also lacks—that they are ~AT&~MR for the conduct at issue. And reflection on salient differences between Phil and these other two people may help those who view Phil as AT&MR for the good and bad actions I mentioned to get a handle on why it is that although they are willing to accept that all three lack self-engagement of kind *K*, they believe that only the latter two are ~AT&~MR for their pertinent conduct. A salient difference between Phil and the addict is that Phil is reasons-responsive regarding the good and bad actions at issue, whereas the addict is not reasons-responsive regarding his using the drug. And whereas the sailor lacks a way to guide his ship, Phil does have ways to guide his conduct.

In short, even if there is a kind of self-engagement that all three agents lack, it is consistent with this that Phil, unlike the addict and the sailor, is AT&MR for the relevant conduct. That in virtue of which Phil lacks self-engagement of kind *K* may be significantly different from that in virtue of which the other two agents lack it, and different in such a way that although they are ~AT&~MR for their relevant conduct, he is AT&MR for some of his conduct. Moreover, given the specific differences I mentioned, it is by no means a stretch of the imagination to suppose that although there is a kind of self-engagement that all three agents lack, one of them is AT&MR for relevant conduct and two are not. I return to self-engagement shortly in comparing Phil with another agent about whom I disagree with Fischer and Ravizza.

As I mentioned, I also argued in Mele 2000 that Fischer and Ravizza's sufficient conditions for moral responsibility are too weak. They argue that "an agent is morally responsible for an action insofar as it issues from his own, moderately reasons-responsive mechanism" (1998, p. 86). An agent makes a mechanism "his own" by "taking responsibility" for it (p. 241). "Moderate reasons-responsiveness consists in regular reasons-receptivity, and at least weak reasons-reactivity, of the actual-sequence mechanism that leads to the action" (p. 89). My specific concern now is weak reasons-reactivity, where *reactivity* to reasons is "the capacity to translate reasons into choices (and then subsequent behavior)" (p. 69). A mechanism of an agent is at least *weakly* reasons-reactive provided that although it issues in the agent's *A*-ing in the actual world, there is some possible world with the same laws of nature in which a mechanism of this kind is operative in this agent, "there is a sufficient reason to do otherwise, the agent recognizes this reason, and the agent does otherwise" (p. 63) for this reason.

I observed in Mele 2000 (p. 450) that even in extreme cases of phobia or addiction we can usually imagine *some* reason such that if a troubled agent who *A*-ed had had that reason for *B*-ing, he would have *B*-ed for that reason rather than *A*-ing. His relevant mechanism's reacting positively, in a possible world, to a good reason for *B*-ing, on

Fischer and Ravizza's view, is sufficient for weak reasons-reactivity. I offered the following story for consideration:

> Fred's agoraphobia is so powerful that he has not ventured out of his house in ten years, despite his family's many attempts to persuade him to do so and the many incentives they have offered him. Owing to his fear, he often has decided not to do things that he believed he had good reason to do (and then behaved accordingly), including some things that he believed he morally ought to do. For example, he recently decided to stay at home (and stayed there) rather than attend his beloved daughter's wedding in the church next door. Now, in some possible world with the same laws, there was a raging fire in Fred's house on his daughter's wedding day. Fred, it turns out, is even more afraid of raging fires than of leaving his house. Judging that he had a good reason to leave his house, he decided to do so, for that reason; and then, making a heroic effort, he walked next door to the church. (p. 450; see Mele 1992, p. 87)

Fred's relevant mechanism is weakly reasons-reactive. Nothing in Fred's story precludes its also being regularly reasons-receptive and its being Fred's own mechanism.[9] Suppose it has these two features, too. Then, on Fischer and Ravizza's view, Fred is morally responsible for staying home during his daughter's wedding (in the actual world). My suggestion in Mele 2000 is that, other things being equal (e.g., Fred is not morally responsible for his agoraphobia), because Fred's fear is so debilitating that it would take something as frightening as a raging fire to move him to decide to leave his house or to leave it intentionally, he is *not* morally responsible for staying home during the wedding.

An important plank in Fischer and Ravizza's reply is their assertion that "being morally responsible does not entail being praiseworthy or blameworthy" (2000, p. 471). They say that they "would not be inclined" to judge that Fred is "blameworthy for staying inside and not going to his daughter's wedding" (p. 472). However, they "are inclined to say that [Fred] is interestingly different from someone whose urges are genuinely irresistible. . . . The way we mark this distinction is to say that Fred is morally responsible, whereas someone subject to significant manipulation, or someone with irresistible urges, is not morally responsible. Whatever language one uses for the distinction, there is some important distinction here to mark" (p. 471).[10]

I agree that Fred is different from someone whose pertinent mechanism, which issues in his *A*-ing in the actual world, is such that there is *no* possible world with the same laws of nature in which a mechanism of this kind operates in this agent, "there is a sufficient reason to do otherwise, the agent recognizes this reason, and the agent does otherwise" for this reason (Fischer and Ravizza 1998, p. 63). Of course, agreeing with Fischer and Ravizza about this difference or distinction—I name it *D*—is consistent with holding that both Fred and this other agent fall short of moral responsibility for their pertinent conduct. Now, if Fred is said to be morally responsible for staying home during his daughter's wedding but not blameworthy for that, I obviously have less to disagree with than I would if blameworthiness were claimed. And if "morally responsible" is just a term of art to mark *D*, there may be nothing substantive to disagree with: philosophers are entitled to use their terms of art as they wish, as long as they make it clear what they are doing.[11] However, this is not the end of the matter.

Fischer and Ravizza's account of moral responsibility has the consequence that Fred is morally responsible for staying home during his daughter's wedding, whereas Phil is not morally responsible for such things as his lying and his charitable deeds. And that is an extremely peculiar consequence. Fred has a terrible psychological problem. His agoraphobia is so severe that, I believe, the desire he has on his daughter's wedding day to stay indoors would count as irresistible by everyday standards (see Mele 1992, ch. 5), even if he would resist it in some scenarios featuring extreme danger. Phil, by contrast, is a psychologically healthy agent with (by hypothesis) some false theoretical beliefs. I have friends who share Phil's view that moral responsibility is an illusion—for example, Derk Pereboom and Galen Strawson. From time to time, I have reactive attitudes toward them: positive ones, I hasten to add—they are nice guys. And I believe those attitudes to be justified. This belief of mine might be false, of course. Alternatively, Derk and Galen may secretly—or without realizing it—see themselves as morally responsible for some of their behavior. However this may be, Fred certainly seems to be a much clearer case of an agent who lacks moral responsibility for a certain deed than Phil does. Of course, because Fred sees himself as an apt target of some reactive attitudes for staying home during his daughter's wedding whereas Phil sees himself as not being an apt target of the reactive attitudes for anything, Fred has a kind of self-engagement that Phil lacks. I regard this as good evidence that self-engagement cannot do all the theoretical work Fischer and Ravizza want it to do.

An attractive strategy for avoiding the problem I have been developing is to beef up the reasons-reactivity condition in such a way that Fred and agents with equally severe psychological maladies of the pertinent kind do not count as reasons-reactive enough to be morally responsible for the relevant behavior. This would remove the extremely peculiar consequence that I identified—that Fred is morally responsible for staying home during the wedding whereas Phil is no longer morally responsible for anything. Fischer and Ravizza's appeal to moderate reasons-responsiveness is motivated partly by a problem with Fischer's earlier "weak reasons-responsiveness view" (1994), and further tightening up would seem to be in order. As I observed in Mele 2000 (p. 451, n. 2), in the course of constructing an analysis of irresistible desire in Mele 1992, ch. 5, I argued that an agent's desire to A (e.g., to stay in his house) may properly count as irresistible even if he would successfully resist it in some extreme scenarios. If Fischer and Ravizza were to be persuaded of this, they might find a principled way of motivating acceptance of a reasons-reactivity constraint on moral responsibility that is moderately stronger than weak reasons-reactivity and strong enough to exclude Fred's missing the wedding from the sphere of things for which he is morally responsible.[12] Of course, I have also suggested that Phil *is* morally responsible for his lying and his charitable deeds, but that is a distinct issue.

Imagine that, for Fischer and Ravizza, "moral responsibility" really is a term of art to mark difference or distinction D—the difference between someone like Fred and someone whose pertinent mechanism, which issues in his A-ing in the actual world, is such that there is *no* possible world with the same laws of nature in which a mechanism of this kind operates in this agent, "there is a sufficient reason to do otherwise, the agent recognizes this reason, and the agent does otherwise" for this reason (1998, p. 63). Even then, an objection is in the offing. As the reader has surmised, I take Phil to be praiseworthy for some of his good actions and blameworthy for some of his bad actions. (I am assuming that praiseworthy and blameworthy behavior are common in Phil's world.) I also agree with Fischer and Ravizza that Fred is not blameworthy for missing the wedding. Compare Phil's wrongly repeating an unfavorable rumor about someone (his A-ing) with Fred's staying at home on his daughter's wedding day (his B-ing). For reasons of the sort I adduced earlier when discussing moral responsibility, Phil's deed seems to be a much clearer case of one for which its agent is blameworthy than Fred's deed does. If Phil is blameworthy for A-ing whereas Fred is not blameworthy for B-ing, it can reasonably be objected that Fischer and Ravizza should abandon their (imagined) practice of using "moral responsibility" as a term of art to mark distinction D and adopt a practice that brings their use of "moral responsibility" more into line with true judgments about the blameworthiness (and praiseworthiness) of agents for their actions. The idea is that an acceptable account of moral responsibility would support the contrastive judgment I made about blameworthiness in the cases of Phil and Fred.

This objection moves the debate forward to the question whether someone like Phil, who, for theoretical reasons, does not view himself as an apt target of the reactive attitudes for any of his behavior, can nevertheless be blameworthy or praiseworthy for some of it. Now, if Phil's belief that he is an inappropriate target of the reactive attitudes were to derive from a conviction that his action-producing mechanisms are not even weakly reasons-reactive, he might be off the hook for repeating the rumor. An agent with this conviction views himself as someone whose action-producing mechanisms are such that there is no possible world with the same laws of nature in which mechanisms of these kinds operate in him, "there is a sufficient reason to do otherwise, [he] recognizes this reason, and [he] does otherwise" for this reason. Such an agent is a kind of fatalist, and internalizing a fatalist view of this kind presumably would be psychologically very damaging. An agent with this view of himself would realize (as we philosophers do about ourselves) that there are relevant possible worlds in which there are excellent reasons to act otherwise than he acts in the actual world, and he would be convinced that his action-producing mechanisms either are such that he is incapable of recognizing these reasons or are such that if he is capable of recognizing some of them, he is incapable of acting on them. He would see himself as an agent whose action-producing mechanisms are frighteningly inflexible and limiting. But recall that the version of Fischer and Ravizza's "taking responsibility" condition that I have been discussing is for people who "engage in significant metaphysical reflection about the relationship between causal determinism and the fairness of our social practices of applying the reactive attitudes" (1998, p. 211), and it is false that being an agent in a deterministic world entails being devoid of action-producing mechanisms that are at least weakly reasons-reactive, as Fischer and Ravizza themselves would observe. Phil may have been converted to the common incompatibilist idea that moral responsibility requires a kind of openness of the future that determinism precludes. In any case, Phil views his action-producing mechanisms as, by and large, at least weakly reasons-reactive, and he is right about that. His mechanisms are also regularly reasons-receptive, as he recognizes.

Recall that, for Fischer and Ravizza, "an agent is morally responsible for an action insofar as it issues from his own, moderately reasons-responsive mechanism" (1998, p. 86). Given the properties I attribute to Phil, it can safely be assumed that the mechanism at work when he repeats the harmful rumor is moderately reasons-responsive. What precludes Phil's being morally responsible for the action, in Fischer and Ravizza's view, is that the mechanism does not count as "his own" in their sense. It is not "his own" because that requires his seeing himself as an apt target of the reactive attitudes and he does not have that view of himself. However, it is hard to see why that fact about Phil precludes his being blameworthy for repeating the harmful rumor. It may be suggested that because someone like Phil cannot benefit in his practical reasoning or decision making from such beliefs as that the subject, Sara, of the rumor might rightly be indignant at him if she were to learn that he repeated it, he is impoverished in his practical resources in a way that gets him off the hook. Possibly, but I would like to see an argument for that suggestion. Bear in mind that Phil does care about pleasure, pain, and well being, and he can benefit in his practical reasoning and decision making from, among other things, the belief that his repeating the rumor is likely to cause Sara some pain.

Fischer and Ravizza say that "it is hard to know how to argue for the contention that the reactive attitudes are responses only to behavior" of agents who see themselves as apt targets of the reactive attitudes (2000, p. 469). This is not quite what they mean: they would accept that Sara can feel *unjustified* gratitude toward someone who, unbeknownst to her, does not see himself this way, and gratitude is a reactive attitude. Their intended contention is about *justified* reactive attitudes. The point I want to make is that if it is hard for them to know how to argue for this contention, then, in light of the problems I have raised for it, they should consider abandoning it.

In Mele 2000 (pp. 449–50), I speculated about the possibility that basic human psychology is such that no configuration of properties sufficient for moral responsibility is present in human beings who have never accepted that they are fair targets of the reactive attitudes. Suppose it were discovered that, owing to our basic psychological makeup, we simply cannot learn to regard the interests of others as at all important and achieve any moral sensitivity unless we are sensitive to emotions of other people and learn to see ourselves as apt targets of some reactive emotions. Even if this discovery would warrant the claim that, in human beings, being a morally responsible agent requires at least having seen oneself as a fair target of the reactive attitudes, I observed that philosophers should wonder whether moral responsibility *conceptually* requires a "reactive attitudes" condition. I asked whether a hypothetical, isolated community of emotionless beings—hence, beings with no reactive attitudes—might include morally responsible agents. Because the beings I imagined have no idea what reactive attitudes are, they do not take themselves to be fair targets of the reactive attitudes. But might they, even so, have desires for the welfare of others, beliefs that they morally ought to do certain things, a robust reasons-responsive capacity to act on those beliefs, a view of themselves as agents, and further properties contributing to a mix sufficient for moral responsibility?

Fischer and Ravizza reply that although they find an analysis of moral responsibility in terms of the reactive attitudes "natural and plausible" and "adopt it as a working hypothesis in the book," they "are not certain that it is the correct analysis of our culture's shared concept of moral responsibility" (2000, p. 470). So they would not insist that our culture's shared concept of moral responsibility is such that no possible emotionless being counts as morally responsible. That is a healthy attitude. I will express caution, too. I have not argued against the thesis that one "must see [oneself] as morally responsible in order to be morally responsible" (Fischer and Ravizza 2000, p. 467). Assessment of this "subjective thesis" is complicated, given that what one sees when one sees oneself as morally responsible depends on what moral responsibility is, and for all I know, the correct analysis of moral responsibility does entail this subjective thesis.[13] What I have argued for in this connection is skepticism about the view that, on the assumption that moral responsibility is to be analyzed in terms of the reactive attitudes, being a morally responsible agent entails seeing oneself as an apt target of the reactive attitudes.

5. Application to the No-Chance Idea, Proposition 2

I said that I would apply Fischer and Ravizza's account of moral responsibility and a potential successor to the question why proposition 2 in NCI—NCIp2, for short—should be thought to be compatible with moral responsibility.

NCIp2. If determinism is true of our universe, then shortly after the big bang, there was no chance that anyone would not perform the actions he has performed (as of the time of your reading this), and there was no chance of this because of the following fact about all past actions: shortly after the big bang, there was no chance that any of their causes—remote or proximate—would not occur or exist and no chance that any of their causes would not have the effects they had.

I mentioned that compatibilists can appeal to a familiar compatibilist criticism of incompatibilism—that it confuses deterministic causation with compulsion or constraint—and argue that proponents of NCI mistakenly take NCIp2 to entail that agents in deterministic universes are compelled to do whatever they do. The basis of such an argument is present in Fischer and Ravizza's work. Their requirement of weak reasons-reactivity of the relevant actual-sequence mechanism is supposed to draw—or contribute importantly to drawing—the line between compelled and uncompelled actions. If that mechanism also is regularly reasons-receptive and the agent's "own," then, according to Fischer and Ravizza, the agent is morally responsible for the action at issue. From their point of view, a plausible diagnosis of where theorists go wrong in thinking that the absence of chance featured in NCIp2 entails the absence of moral responsibility is in their failing to see that noncompulsion does not require that there have been a chance that what caused one's action would not cause it and instead requires a certain kind of flexibility of the mechanism that issues in the action.

I have argued that Fischer and Ravizza need a stronger reasons-receptivity requirement. For a relevant mechanism that issues in an agent's A-ing in the actual world to satisfy their requirement, it is enough that there be a possible world—no matter how remote—with the same laws of nature in which a mechanism of this kind operates in this agent, "there is a sufficient reason to do otherwise, the agent recognizes this reason, and the agent does otherwise" (1998, p. 63) for this reason. Fred satisfies this requirement and the others. So he is counted—wrongly, by my lights—as morally responsible for staying home on his daughter's wedding day. A beefed-up reasons-receptivity requirement may be framed in terms of the relative closeness of relevant possible worlds. Possible worlds as remote as the one identified in which Fred attends the wedding are reasonably viewed as too remote to secure moral-responsibility-level reasons-reactivity for the agent. Working out the details of a stronger, plausible reasons-reactivity requirement does not promise to be an easy project, but moral responsibility is not an easy issue. In any event, a compatibilist requirement of this kind provides a putative basis for distinguishing between compelled and uncompelled actions in deterministic worlds and a perspective from which fans of NCI can be charged with conflating deterministic causation with compulsion.

Do I think that experienced incompatibilists who favor NCI would be likely to abandon it and their incompatibilism, if they were to be presented with a plausible compatibilist distinction between compulsion and deterministic causation? No; I have been immersed in this issue long enough to have learned that experienced incompatibilists— like experienced compatibilists—rarely are persuaded to climb over, or even onto, the fence. It is much more likely that incompatibilists presented with a distinction with the imagined properties would grant the distinction and claim that the compulsion of an action and the deterministic causation of an action are each incompatible with moral responsibility for the action—that noncompulsion does not go deep enough and that being a morally responsible agent requires that it be up to the agent what he does in a sense of "up to" that is incompatible not only with compulsion but also with determinism (see Mele 1995, p. 137; van Inwagen 1983, p. 17).

Of course, what theorists are likely to claim is one thing, and how well they are likely to defend their claims is another. The consequence argument for incompatibilism is problematic, as I have explained. Pereboom's manipulation argument for incompatibilism fails, as I have shown. And I have not yet seen an argument with NCIp2 as a premise and incompatibilism about moral responsibility as the conclusion.

6. Semicompatibilism and Traditional Compatibilism

I have focused on Fischer and Ravizza's semicompatibilist view of moral responsibility because it is the most fully developed extant compatibilist account of moral responsibility. For my purposes thus far in this chapter, what separates semicompatibilism from traditional compatibilism has not been an issue. It is easy to imagine a traditional compatibilist analogue of a semicompatibilist analysis of an agent's being morally responsible for an action. A bit of background will help explain why.

What separates semicompatibilists from traditional compatibilists is a disagreement about "was able to do otherwise"—or "could have done otherwise," where "could" is the "could" of ability. According to a standard incompatibilist view, an agent who A-ed at *t* in a world *W* was able at *t* to do otherwise then only if in another possible world with the same past and laws of nature as *W*, he does otherwise at *t*. Obviously, an agent whose world is deterministic could never have done otherwise than he did, on this reading of "could have done otherwise." Traditional compatibilists and semicompatibilists agree that being morally responsible for A-ing does not require that the agent could have done otherwise than A in this sense. They disagree about a related issue. The former hold that there is "a could have done otherwise" requirement on moral responsibility and free action, and they endeavor to develop one that is compatible with determinism; the latter hold that moral responsibility and free action are compatible with determinism, even if determinism is incompatible with its ever being the case that an agent could have done otherwise. In response to a traditional compatibilist's proposed account of the "could have done otherwise" requirement—an account intended to specify something such that if all the other conditions for moral responsibility and freedom with respect to his A-ing are satisfied by an agent, adding satisfaction of this condition to the mix renders the action free and one for which the agent is morally responsible—semicompatibilists can side with incompatibilists in arguing that the account is not of something that deserves the label "could have done otherwise." If a semicompatibilist were to accept the proposed account (as intended by its proponents) and to agree that determinism is compatible with its being true that agents could have done otherwise in that sense, "semi" should be dropped from the name of his or her view.

Incidentally, traditional compatibilists who regard some Frankfurt-style cases as coherent can consistently claim that there is a sense in which the featured agents could have done otherwise that is crucial for freedom and moral responsibility. Like semicompatibilists, they can tie free agency and moral responsibility to reasons-responsiveness and understand the latter in terms of reasons-receptiveness and reasons-reactivity. Part of their disagreement with semicompatibilists is about the possible worlds relevant for tests of these capacities. Some traditional compatibilists may claim that "counterfactual controllers" are absent from relevant possible worlds in Frankfurt-style cases, on the grounds that the potential controller's plans and powers are irrelevant to the agent's pertinent capacities or abilities, properly understood: the counterfactual controllers may simply mask the agent's actual abilities (Smith

1997, pp. 310–12; 2003).[14] Traditional compatibilists are, in principle, in a position to advance views of reasons-responsiveness and its connection to moral responsibility and free action that differ from semicompatibilist views mainly in asserting that this reasons-responsiveness is sufficient for "could have done otherwise." Traditional compatibilist views along these lines may yield accounts of morally responsible action and free action that are every bit as subtle as accounts that semicompatibilists are in a position to offer (see Smith 2003).

Again, traditional compatibilists, unlike semicompatibilists, agree with traditional incompatibilists that moral responsibility and freedom require that agents at least sometimes have been able to do otherwise than they did. Can compatibilists who accept this requirement agree that if our universe is deterministic, then, shortly after the big bang, there was no chance that anything that has happened would not happen? Yes. They might believe that it is correct to hold the past and the laws fixed for the purposes of ascertaining whether there was a *chance* of something happening but not for the purposes of ascertaining whether an agent was *able* to do otherwise than he did. They might regard what an agent is able to do at a time as partly a matter, for example, of what he would do at that time if he had slightly different reasons for action but not take the same view about what there is a chance of the agent doing.

One way to interpret a salient difference between semicompatibilism and traditional compatibilism features NCIp2. Traditional compatibilists view the absence of chance identified there as compatible with the ability to do otherwise and with moral responsibility and free action, and semicompatibilists view it as compatible with moral responsibility and free action, even if it is incompatible with the ability to do otherwise.

The leading arguments for incompatibilism leave compatibilism in the running. In the following chapter, I turn to a proposed set of sufficient compatibilist conditions for free action.

NOTES

1. See Pereboom 2001, p. 133, for his assessment of the relative merits of his manipulation argument and the consequence argument.

2. Fischer claims that Plum is morally responsible, but not blameworthy, for killing White in case 1 (2004, p. 158). I suspect that he does not fully appreciate the significance of the detail that the neuroscientists directly produce Plum's "every state from moment to moment." Fischer and Ravizza (2000) diagnose another case of undesirable action (to put it mildly) as a case in which

the agent is morally responsible but not blameworthy. See section 4 of this chapter for discussion.

3. Some readers might take Plum's being created by neuroscientists to preclude his being morally responsible for killing White. But that feature of the case is dispensable. Plum might have come to exist in the normal way, and the neuroscientists might have got to work on him at birth. Readers may be toying with a version of case 2 in which Plum's deliberative style in a deterministic world *evolves* as a result of "programming." If some such case is constructed in which Plum kills White and is not morally responsible for that, should we infer from this fact about the case that the killing's being *deterministically* caused precludes moral responsibility? No. If Plum lacks moral responsibility for the killing in this case, a pertinent indeterministic version of the case can be constructed in which he also lacks moral responsibility for it. (Readers have been given a recipe for constructing such cases.) Of course, if in some case of manipulation in a deterministic world an agent satisfies the best extant compatibilist set of alleged sufficient conditions for being morally responsible for *A*-ing and yet is not morally responsible for *A*-ing, that set of conditions is inadequate. In chapter 7 (sec. 4), I construct and examine a case-based manipulation-style argument for incompatibilism that avoids the central problem with Pereboom's four-case argument.

4. The present section derives from Mele 2005a, an article that attracted a good bit of attention in "The Garden of Forking Paths" free will blog (http://gfp.typepad.com). I discovered that some people misunderstood the structure of my basic argument. Pointing out that because intuitions are caused, I applied standard methods for assessing causal claims to the following assertion seemed to help: "The best explanation for the intuition that Plum is not morally responsible in the first three cases is that his action results from a deterministic causal process that traces back to factors beyond his control" (Pereboom 2001, p. 116). I have said how I think people would respond to certain versions of these three cases in which deterministic causation is subtracted and manipulation retained. Suppose manipulation were subtracted and deterministic causation retained. Incompatibilists would make incompatibilist judgments about the three modified cases, and compatibilists would make judgments consistent with compatibilism. Whereas eliminating manipulation from the three cases while retaining deterministic causation gets one nowhere, eliminating deterministic causation while retaining manipulation is revealing.

5. On deterministic Frankfurt-style cases, see ch. 4, sec. 2.

6. See Audi 1993, chs. 7 and 10; Ayer 1954; Grünbaum 1971; Mill 1979, ch. 26, esp. pp. 464–67; and Schlick 1962, ch. 7. Also see Hume's remarks on the liberty of spontaneity versus the liberty of indifference (1739, bk. II, pt. III, sec. 2).

7. Strawson also holds that moral responsibility is impossible independently of the truth or falsity of determinism, as I have mentioned.

8. Fischer and Ravizza also discuss my "apparent suggestion that Phil continues to apply the reactive attitudes" (2000, p. 467). I do not see this suggestion in Mele 2000, and I set this issue aside here.

9. By "receptivity to reason," Fischer and Ravizza "mean the capacity to recognize the reasons that exist" (1998, p. 69). "Regular reasons-receptivity... involves a pattern of actual and hypothetical recognition of reasons... that is understandable by some appropriate external observer. And the pattern must be at least minimally grounded in reality" (p. 90).

10. Notice that Phil, too, is "interestingly different from someone whose urges are genuinely irresistible." Yet, Fischer and Ravizza do not "mark this distinction" by saying that Phil is morally responsible.

11. The point made in the preceding note indicates that Fischer and Ravizza do not (always) use "morally responsible" simply to mark *D*.

12. There are independent reasons for Fischer to revise his understanding of irresistible desires. He writes: "An irresistible urge is one whose intensity or intrinsic motivational force... explains why the action takes place; there is no possible scenario (including those whose pasts differ in their details from the actual past) in which the agent fails to act on the desire, given its motivational force" (2004, p. 159). This will not do. An agent who acts on an irresistible desire in the actual world will not act on it in a possible scenario in which, because of a neuroscientist's interference, he is unable to act on it, even though it has the same intrinsic motivational force. Also, consider the following from Mele 1992:

S, who is in the habit of brushing his teeth after his morning shower, has just finished showering and now has a desire of unremarkable strength to brush his teeth. A demon allows *S* to conceive of intentionally not brushing his teeth but renders him unable to conceive of any further alternative to brushing his teeth (e.g., shaving or dressing). Moreover, he renders *S* unable to want not to brush his teeth. Finally, the demon does all this without increasing the absolute strength of *S*'s desire to brush his teeth.... *S*'s desire to brush his teeth is literally irresistible by him. The demon, by constraining, as he does, what *S* can conceive and want, renders *S* incapable of conquering his desire and renders the desire uncircumventable as well. Even if it is true that under normal circumstances an irresistible desire is so largely in virtue of some internal feature of the desire itself, it does not follow that a desire's irresistibility *must* be internally grounded in this way. Notice, moreover, that standard intuitions about irresistible desires are based on paradigm cases, cases that do not involve demons and the like. In paradigm cases, the irresistibility of a desire *is*, in significant part, a function of the strength of that desire. But an analysis of irresistible desire designed to accommodate even highly contrived examples must be sensitive to much more than intuitions fostered by paradigms. (pp. 99–100)

If I am right, S's desire to brush his teeth is irresistible, even though there are possible scenarios in which that desire has the same intrinsic motivational force and S fails to act on it. Consider a scenario in which there is no demon, the intrinsic motivational force of S's desire to brush his teeth very soon is the same, and S has a stronger desire to answer his ringing telephone now. S walks to his phone, leaving his toothbrush in its rack. The caller reports an emergency. Reacting to it at once is far more important to S than brushing his teeth. (If the reader likes, a neuroscientist can ensure that the intrinsic motivational force of S's tooth-brushing desire remains constant.)

13. As I understand Fischer and Ravizza's subjective thesis, its readers are meant to understand that someone who reports something he believes in saying "I am morally responsible for A-ing" may nevertheless not believe that he is— or not see himself as—morally responsible for A-ing. He may misunderstand moral responsibility, and the content of his belief may not in fact be that he is morally responsible for A-ing.

14. The actual intervention in the Mele-Robb story discussed in chapter 4 poses a problem for the claim that the agent's relevant abilities are simply masked there.

SEVEN

My Compatibilist Proposal
Objections and Replies

Peter van Inwagen writes: "It is conceivable that science will one day present us with compelling reasons for believing in determinism. Then and only then, I think, should we become compatibilists" (1983, p. 223). I believe that few libertarians would be moved to accept compatibilism by anything short of one or the other of two conversions: a conversion to the view that determinism is true or a conversion to the view that indeterministic agency is incompatible with—or, alternatively, cannot contribute anything important to—moral responsibility and free will. Showing that determinism is true is not a philosophical task.[1] Showing that indeterministic agency is incompatible with—or cannot contribute anything important to—free will and moral responsibility is a philosophical task, but given my openness not only to compatibilism but also to libertarianism, it is a task for others. As I see it, the project of developing particular compatibilist accounts of moral responsibility and free action has as its primary audience compatibilists and those who have not yet taken a side in the dispute about whether compatibilism is true. Attempting to win this audience over to a specific compatibilist account is a very different project from trying to persuade incompatibilists to switch sides.

In Mele 1995, as I have mentioned, I offered a set of compatibilist sufficient conditions for free or autonomous agency and a set of incompatibilist sufficient conditions for this. In this chapter, I summarize the compatibilist set and reply to some compatibilists' objections to it. Notice that I say *sufficient* conditions, not necessary and sufficient conditions. My project in Mele 1995 did not include offering a compatibilist *analysis* of free or autonomous agency. Motivating the thesis that determinism is compatible with free action does not require locating *minimally* sufficient conditions for free action. Motivating the assertion that conditions sufficient for free action are satisfiable by an agent in a deterministic world would turn the trick.

1. A History-Sensitive Compatibilism

My strategy in Mele 1995, again, involved constructing an account of an ideally self-controlled agent (self-control being understood as the contrary of *akrasia*), arguing that even such an agent can fall short of autonomy (or free agency), asking what may be added to ideal self-control to yield autonomy (or free agency), and developing two answers—one for compatibilists and another for libertarians. My compatibilist proposal adds the following to being an ideally self-controlled and mentally healthy agent who regularly exercises his powers of self-control: the agent has no compelled or coercively produced attitudes, his beliefs are conducive to informed deliberation about all matters that concern him, and he is a reliable deliberator (1995, p. 187).[2] When all this is true of an agent who nondeviantly *A*-s on the basis of a rationally formed deliberative judgment that it would be best to *A*, he *A*-s freely. So, at least, I proposed (p. 193).

I developed this proposal partly in response to a manipulation argument against compatibilism, and I examined several detailed stories about manipulated agents. One prominent concept at work in those stories is the concept of an agent's values. I complained that many philosophers who use the term "values" leave it to their readers to guess what they mean by it, and I offered glosses on the verb and the noun. As I understand valuing in Mele 1995 and in the present book, "*S* at least *thinly values X* at a time if and only if at that time *S* both has a positive motivational attitude toward *X* and believes *X* to be good" (p. 116). When values are understood as psychological states, I take them to have both of these dimensions by definition. This account of thinly valuing and the corresponding thin account of values are not meant to be major contributions to the theories of valuing and values; their purpose is to make my meaning clear.

I repeat (from Mele 1995, p. 145) the following tale of Ann and her manipulated colleague, Beth, because some of my critics have quite a bit to say about it. Ann is a free agent and an exceptionally industrious philosopher. She puts in twelve solid hours a day, seven days a week, and she enjoys almost every minute of it. Beth, an equally talented colleague, values many things above philosophy for reasons that she has refined and endorsed on the basis of careful critical reflection over many years. Beth identifies with and enjoys her own way of life, and she is confident that it has a breadth, depth, and richness that long days in the office would destroy. Their dean wants Beth to be like Ann. Normal modes of persuasion having failed, he decides to circumvent Beth's agency. Without the knowledge of either philosopher, he hires a team of psychologists to determine what makes Ann tick and a team of new-wave brainwashers to make Beth like Ann. The psychologists decide that Ann's peculiar hierarchy of values accounts for her productivity, and the brainwashers instill the same hierarchy in Beth while eradicating all competing values—via new-wave brainwashing, of course. Beth is now, in the relevant respect, a "psychological twin" of Ann. She is an industrious philosopher who thoroughly enjoys and highly values her philosophical work. Largely as a result of Beth's new hierarchy of values, whatever upshot Ann's critical reflection about her own values and priorities would have, the same is true of critical reflection by Beth. Her critical reflection, like Ann's, fully supports her new style of life.

Naturally, Beth is surprised by the change in her. What, she wonders, accounts for her remarkable zest for philosophy? Why is her philosophical work now so much more enjoyable? Why are her social activities now so much less satisfying and rewarding than her work? Beth's hypothesis is that she simply has grown tired of her previous mode of life, that her life had become stale without her recognizing it, and that she finally has come fully to appreciate the value of philosophical work. When she carefully reflects on her values, Beth finds that they fully support a life dedicated to philosophical work, and she wholeheartedly embraces such a life and the collection of values that supports it.

Ann, by hypothesis, freely does her philosophical work, but what about Beth? In important respects, she is a clone of Ann—and by design, not accident. Her own considered values were erased and replaced in the brainwashing process. Beth did not consent to the process. Nor was she even aware of it; she had no opportunity to resist. By instilling new values in Beth and eliminating old ones, the brainwashers gave her life a new direction, one that clashes with the considered principles and values she had before she was manipulated. Beth's autonomy was violated.[3] And it is difficult not to see her now, in light of all this, as heteronomous—and unfree—to a significant extent in an important sphere of her life. If that perception is correct, then given the psychological similarities between the two agents, the difference in their current status regarding freedom would seem to lie in how they *came* to have certain of their psychological features, hence in something *external* to their present psychological constitutions. That is, the crucial difference is *historical*; free agency is in some way history-bound.

In Mele 1995, I argued that this last sentence is true in some stories of this kind that involve relevant "unsheddable" values. (I discuss such values shortly.) So I faced an apparent problem. Richard Double (1991, pp. 56–57) contends that once agents' histories are allowed to have a relevance of the sort mentioned here to their freedom, their having *deterministic* histories also is relevant in a way that undermines compatibilism. It may be thought that if instances of manipulation of the sort present in the Ann-Beth story block free agency in certain connections, they do so only if they *deterministically cause* crucial psychological events or states and that determinism consequently is in danger of being identified as the real culprit.

This worry is misplaced, as my critique of Pereboom's manipulation argument in chapter 6 shows. Manipulation by means of indeterministic mechanisms can block moral responsibility and freedom. Furthermore, even compatibilists who embrace determinism can distinguish among different causal routes to the collections of values (and "characters") agents have at a time. They are also in a position to provide principled grounds for holding that distinct routes to two type-identical collections of values may be such that one and only one of those routes blocks acting freely in accordance with those values. An analogue of the familiar compatibilist distinction between *caused* and *compelled* (or constrained) *behavior* may be used here (see ch. 6, n. 6, for references). Perhaps in engineering Beth's values, her brainwashers *compelled* her to have Ann-like attitudes. Even so, a true and complete causal story about Ann's having the values she has might involve no compulsion. If Beth was compelled to have her Ann-like values whereas Ann was not, there are some apparent grounds, at least, for taking the latter alone to be responsible for having certain values and, perhaps, for actions that stand in certain relations to those values.

In this connection, I argued in Mele 1995 (pp. 166–72, 183–84) for the relevance of a notion of agents' capacities for control over their mental lives being *bypassed*. In ideally self-controlled agents—agents of the kind featured in my compatibilist set of sufficient conditions for free agency—these capacities are impressive. Such agents are capable of modifying the strengths of their desires in the service of their normative judgments, of bringing their emotions into line with relevant judgments, and of mastering motivation that threatens (sometimes via the biasing of practical or theoretical reasoning) to produce or sustain beliefs in ways that would violate their principles for belief-acquisition and belief-retention. They also are capable of rationally assessing their values and principles, of identifying with their values and principles on the basis of informed, critical reflection, and of modifying their values and principles, should they judge that to be in order. Most readers of this book have each of these capacities in some measure. All such capacities are bypassed in cases of value engineering of the sort at issue. In such cases, new values are not generated via an exercise or an activation of agents' capacities for control over their mental lives; rather, they are generated despite the agents' capacities for this.

It is time to discuss a complication to which I alluded. Even effective manipulation as severe and comprehensive as Beth's might not block freedom in the relevant sphere. To the extent to which one can successfully counteract the influence of brainwashing, having been a victim of it might not render any of one's actions unfree. Agents may be able to "shed" many attitudes produced by brainwashing—that is, to *eradicate* the attitudes or to *attenuate them significantly*. In Mele 1995, I argued that agents can autonomously possess attitudes that they are "practically unable" to shed and that, owing to their having different histories, agents who are psychologically very similar at a time may be such that although one of them autonomously possesses a practically unsheddable attitude, the other does not (pp. 149–73). The issue is complicated. I will not try to do it justice here, but I will say a bit more about it.

Imagine that Pat freely developed deep and admirable parental values. In some robust sense of "can," it may be true that, given how deeply entrenched Pat's parental values are, he can neither eradicate nor significantly attenuate them during t (a certain two-week span, say); that is, Pat's shedding those values during t, given his psychological constitution, is not a psychologically genuine option. Of course, it may be that if certain conditions beyond Pat's control were to arise, he would shed these values. He might become hopelessly insane, for example. Or government agents might use his parental values as a lever to motivate him to uproot those very values: they might convince him that the government will ensure his children's flourishing if he eradicates his parental values and that, otherwise, they will destroy his children's lives. Under these conditions (I am supposing), Pat would take himself to have a decisive reason for shedding his parental values, and if he thought hard enough, he might find a way to shed them. (Once he sheds the values, he might not care at all how his children fare, but that is another matter.) However, if, in fact, conditions such as these do not arise for Pat in the next two weeks, he will not shed his parental values during that period. Insofar as (1) the conditions that would empower Pat to shed these values are beyond his control—that is, insofar as his psychological constitution precludes his non-accidentally producing those conditions—and (2) the obtaining of those conditions independently of Pat's nonaccidentally producing them is not in the cards, he is apparently "stuck" with the values. Any agent who is stuck in this sense with a value (during *t*) may be said to be *practically unable* to shed it (during *t*), and values that one is practically unable to shed may be termed *practically unsheddable*—or *unsheddable*, for short. In Mele 1995 (ch. 9), I argued that although an agent like Pat may autonomously possess (during *t*) his parental values, this is not true (at least for a time) of another agent, who had been among the most uncaring parents imaginable until, last night, brain-washers installed unsheddable parental values like Pat's in him.

Imagine that Pat started his career as a father as a mediocre one. His own father had been very good to him, and Pat occasionally felt guilty about how little he did with and for his two children. After a couple of years as a mediocre parent, Pat freely embarked on a program of self-improvement. Part of his strategy was to spend more time with his kids, to make that more pleasant for himself by identifying and arranging activities that would be mutually enjoyable, and to focus his thinking about his kids, as much as possible, on their good properties and their welfare. For many parents, this sort of thing comes naturally, but for Pat it did not. To make a long story short, over the years, owing significantly to his self-improvement strategy, Pat became a wonderful father whose parental values were such that he could not do otherwise than make certain sacrifices for his children. Just today, he made such a sacrifice. He took out a huge loan to finance his daughter's first year at an exclusive liberal arts college.

Compare Pat with Paul, a selfish man who has for many years reflectively identified with his selfish values. Paul is a mediocre father of an eighteen-year-old daughter. At least, all that was true of him when he fell asleep last night. As he slept, Paul underwent some new-wave brainwashing. Paul's wealthy mother, without his knowledge, had hired a team of psychologists to determine what makes Pat tick and a team of brainwashers to make Paul like Pat. The psychologists decided that Pat's hierarchy of values accounts for his wonderful parental behavior, and the brainwashers installed the same hierarchy in Paul while eradicating all competing values. Paul is now, like Pat, an extremely caring parent with some unsheddable parental values. Largely as a result of Paul's new hierarchy of values, whatever upshot Pat's critical reflection about his own values and priorities would have, the same is true of critical reflection by Paul. His critical reflection would fully support his new values.

When Paul awakes, he recalls his daughter's wish to attend an exclusive liberal arts college, and he experiences a powerful desire to make that possible for her by taking out a huge loan. Naturally, Paul is amazed by this change. He wonders what accounts for his remarkable concern for his daughter's welfare and why he now cares so little about buying a new car for himself. Paul's hypothesis is that he simply has grown tired of his previous selfish mode of life, that he finally has come to see the light about the importance of father-daughter relationships, and that his powerful concern for his daughter's welfare had strangely been hidden from him. When he carefully reflects on his values, Paul finds that they fully support a life dedicated in significant part to his daughter's welfare, and he wholeheartedly embraces the idea of living such a life and the values that support it. When he thinks about his daughter's desire to attend the liberal arts college, it is obvious to him that he should take out the loan and that he very much wants to do so. Paul borrows the money later that day. Given his new parental values, he could not have done otherwise.

What I said about Beth may be echoed about Paul, and intuitions about his case may be even stronger, given the subject matter. Paul's own considered values were erased and replaced in the brainwashing process, and some of his new values are unsheddable. He did not consent to the process. Nor was he even aware of it; he had no opportunity to resist. By installing new values in Paul and eliminating old ones, the brainwashers gave his life a new direction that clashes with the considered principles and values he had before he was manipulated. He seems heteronomous— and unfree—to a significant extent, and he seems to be undeserving of moral credit for taking out the loan and to lack moral responsibility for that deed. Like Pat, Paul could not have done otherwise than borrow the money for his daughter's education, but whereas the history that accounts for this fact about Pat seemingly is compatible with his freely doing this and deserving moral credit for doing it, the process that accounts for the same fact about Paul seems not to be.

The focus of the discussion in Mele 1995 of the importance of history for a plausible compatibilism was what I called "psychological autonomy," especially the autonomous possession of particular values and autonomous deliberation. Psychological autonomy does not extend beyond the head. My view was that compatibilists would accomplish their main task "by showing how determinism is compatible with *psychological* autonomy. If [that compatibility] can be demonstrated, compatibilists can rest their case; the possibility of autonomous overt action raises no special worries about determinism beyond those raised by the possibility of psychological autonomy itself" (p. 193). I did not develop a position on conditions under which histories of certain kinds would render specific overt actions nonautonomous or unfree. However, if asked, I certainly would have been prepared to assert that Paul did not autonomously take out the college loan and did not freely do that. And I would have been prepared to assent to the following assertion, for example:

> *NF.* An agent who performs an overt action *A* does not freely *A*, if (1) he expresses unsheddable values in *A*-ing; (2) owing directly to those values, he could not have done otherwise than *A* in the circumstances (on a compatibilist reading of "could have done otherwise"); (3) those values were very recently produced in a way that bypassed his capacities for control over his mental life by value engineering to which he did not consent and are seriously at odds with autonomously acquired values of his that were erased in the process; (4) he retains no preexisting value that is promoted by his having the unsheddable values he expresses in *A*-ing; and (5) *A* is the first overt action he performs on the basis of his new values.

The notion at work here of an agent's *expressing* a value in an action has an essential causal dimension. By definition, an action *A* expresses a value *V* only if *V* (or its neural realizer) plays a nondeviant causal role in the production of *A*. Further support for *NF* emerges in the discussion of my compatibilist critics in sections 2 through 4.

I conclude this section with a brief discussion of another story about a woman named Beth. I told it elsewhere (Mele 2003c; see Mele 1995, pp. 156–62) in response to some claims Harry Frankfurt makes. Frankfurt contends that "to the extent that a person identifies himself with the springs of his actions, he takes responsibility for those actions and acquires moral responsibility for them; moreover, the questions of how the actions and his identifications with their springs are caused are irrelevant to the questions of whether he performs the actions freely or is morally responsible for performing them" (1988, p. 54). He reaffirms this in a recent article:

> If someone does something because he wants to do it, and if he has no reservations about that desire but is wholeheartedly behind it, then—so far as his moral responsibility for doing it is concerned—it really does not matter how he got that way. One further requirement must be added...: the person's desires and attitudes have to be relatively well integrated into his general psychic condition. Otherwise they are not genuinely his.... As long as their interrelations imply that they are unequivocally attributable to him...it makes no difference—so far as evaluating his moral responsibility is concerned—how he came to have them. (2002, p. 27)

Beth is waiting offstage. Consider Chuck first. Chuck is evil. He enjoys killing people, and he is wholeheartedly behind his murderous desires, which are "well integrated into his general psychic condition." When he was much younger, Chuck enjoyed torturing animals, but he was not wholeheartedly behind this. These activities sometimes caused him to feel guilty, he experienced bouts of squeamishness, and he occasionally considered abandoning animal torture. However, Chuck valued being the sort of person who does as he pleases and who unambivalently rejects conventional morality as a system designed for and by weaklings. He intentionally set out to ensure that he would be wholeheartedly behind his torturing of animals and related activities, including his merciless bullying of vulnerable people. One strand of his strategy was to perform cruel actions with increased frequency in order to harden himself against feelings of guilt and squeamishness and eventually to extinguish the source of those feelings. His strategy worked.

Compare Chuck with Beth. When she crawled into bed last night, she was a sweet person, as she always had been. But she awoke with a desire to stalk and kill a neighbor, George. Although Beth had always found George unpleasant, she is very surprised by this desire. What happened is that, while she slept, a team of psychologists that had discovered the system of values that make Chuck tick implanted those values in Beth after erasing hers. They did this while leaving her memory intact, which helps account for her surprise. Beth reflects on her new desire. Among other things, she judges, rightly, that it is utterly in line with her system of values. She also judges that she finally sees the light about morality—that it is a system designed for weaklings by weaklings. Upon reflection, Beth has no reservations about her desire to kill George and is wholeheartedly behind it. Furthermore, the desire is "well integrated into [her] general psychic condition" at the time. Seeing absolutely no reason not to stalk and kill George, provided that she can get away with it, Beth devises a plan for killing him, and she executes it—and him—that afternoon. That she sees no reason not to do this is utterly predictable, given the content of the values that ultimately ground her reflection.

Both Chuck and Beth satisfy Frankfurt's conditions for being morally responsible for the deeds at issue. That they differ markedly in "how [they] came to have" their relevant "desires and attitudes ... makes no difference," according to Frankfurt. However, I find that difficult to accept. Although (in the absence of further details that would get him off the hook) I see Chuck as morally responsible for his killings, I cannot help but see Beth as too much a victim of her manipulators to be morally responsible for killing George. Frankfurt may reply: "We are inevitably fashioned and sustained, after all, by circumstances over which we have no control" (2002, p. 28). But this assertion does not entail that we "have no control" at all regarding any of our "circumstances." (Frankfurt says "by," not "by and only by.") And whereas Beth exercised no control in the process that gave rise to her Chuckian system of values and identifications, Chuck apparently exercised significant control in fashioning his system of values and identifications. Frankfurt is committed to holding that that difference between Chuck and Beth is "irrelevant to the questions of whether [they perform the killings] freely or [are] morally responsible for performing them" (1988, p. 54), and it is open to him to contend that even if many people do have some control over some of their "circumstances," Chuck is simply morally responsible for an extra item that Beth is not morally responsible for—having become an evil person. The contention is that both are morally responsible for the killings and kill freely, and that Chuck, but not Beth, is morally responsible for having become a ruthless killer. In my opinion, this contention is unsustainable, and if compatibilists were to have nothing more attractive to offer than Frankfurt's—or any other—ahistorical view of moral responsibility and freedom, compatibilism would be in dire straits. For direct support for this opinion, see Mele 1995, chapters 9 and 10. The remainder of this chapter provides indirect support for it.

2. Dennett's Critique

Daniel Dennett evaluates my history-sensitive compatibilist proposal in his recent book (2003, pp. 281–84). Toward the end of the book, he writes: "Austin's putt, Kane's faculty of practical reasoning, and Mele's autonomy . . . have come in for the sort of detailed attention philosophers expect" (p. 307). However, inattention to important details has led Dennett astray, as I explain in this section.

Dennett asserts that "the practice of making oneself so that one could not have done otherwise is a key innovation in the evolutionary ascent through design space . . . to human free will" (2003, p. 216). We may believe Martin Luther's claim that he could not have done otherwise than register his protest while also believing him to have acted morally responsibly and freely at the time (p. 117). The operative interpretation here of "could not have done otherwise" is a traditional compatibilist one. The traditional compatibilist holds that an agent's world's being deterministic is compatible with its being true, in some cases, that he could have done otherwise than he did. This compatibilist also holds that there are some situations in which agents could not have done otherwise. Now, in some cases of the latter kind, one is not morally responsible for what one did and did not do it freely, and in other such cases, if Dennett is right, one is morally responsible for what one did and did it freely. For example, Luther's deed was not a free and morally responsible one, if he could not have done otherwise than nail the edict to the church door because, owing partly to a high fever, he was in the grip of a delusion that if he failed to do that, God would turn him into a turnip on the spot and feed him to the dogs. But in his actual circumstances, if Dennett is right, Luther acted freely and morally responsibly, even if he could not have done otherwise at the time than register his protest.

Given what I have said about Dennett's position, one might expect him to be receptive to my history-sensitive view of free and morally responsible agency. After all, "making oneself so that one could not have done otherwise" than take out a loan for one's daughter's education—in ordinary, real-world cases of this sort of thing—is very different from brainwashers making an agent that way last night. However, Dennett rejects the history-sensitive dimension of my position, and my question now is "Why?" My answer will be speculative, but I cannot do otherwise than speculate.

First, in commenting on my tale of two philosophers, Dennett overlooks an important detail about Beth's reaction to her new values. He writes: "Presumably part of [Beth's] psychological similarity with Ann . . . is an astonishingly rich set of false pseudo-memories of a fine, autonomy-guaranteeing moral education that never happened" (2003, p. 283). In fact, however, in my story (see Mele 1995, p. 145), Beth's reaction to her new values is the one I reported in the preceding section. I told her story that way to prevent readers from being distracted by worries about pseudo-memories that might lead to worries about personal identity. It is not surprising that someone who overlooks that part of my story hits on the hypothesis that massive pseudo-memories lie at the heart of an important difference between Ann and Beth.

Second, as far as I can tell, Dennett also overlooks the detail that the values at issue are unsheddable. He might be thinking that if Beth were told about the brainwashing, she would quickly undo its effects in light of that information. But the detail that the values are unsheddable entails that she is psychologically unable to do that.

Dennett's overlooking these details probably provides at most part of the answer to my question. He suggests tweaking the case of Ann and Beth by adding the detail that Ann was deceived into believing that she was brainwashed (2003, p. 283). This is an interesting suggestion. Consider a version of Pat's story that is tweaked in this way. Everything is the same up to *t*, including Pat's history and his having unsheddable parental values that lead him to take out the huge loan for his daughter, except that at *t*, not long before he borrows the money, someone successfully lies to him about his history. The liar convinces Pat that he is wrong to believe that he made himself a good father by successfully executing his long-term plan for self-improvement and that, instead, it was a series of brainwashing activities years ago that made him as he is. Is this a coherent story?

How would Pat react to this new belief? Well, suppose that you (dear reader) are a parent like the one Pat became. How would you react to your new false belief that your unsheddable parental values, which have been in place for years, are products of brainwashing that you unknowingly underwent years ago? Probably, you would resent the alleged invasion of your psyche—and perhaps much more so if you think that you would have acquired those values on your own had you been left to your own devices. Also, if you are inclined toward a history-sensitive position on free action and moral responsibility, you would be inclined to believe that some of the things you did for your kids years ago you did not do freely and were not morally responsible for doing. But I do not see how any of this—nor the false belief you have now about your history—is supposed to render unfree the things you proceed to do for your offspring.

Dennett writes: "If Ann's autonomy depends on the truth of her own beliefs about her own past, then Beth's problem is just that she has been lied to, not that she has been put into her enviable dispositional state by 'value engineering'" (2003, p. 284). However, Dennett has not offered convincing grounds for thinking that Ann's autonomy would be undercut by her falsely believing that her hierarchy of values is a product of brainwashing. The same goes for Pat and his imagined false belief about his parental values. And I have offered seemingly powerful grounds for holding that, in light of Paul's actual brainwashing, he unfreely takes out a college loan for his daughter, deserves no moral credit for so doing, and is not morally responsible for so doing.

As Dennett mentions (2003, p. 281), in Mele 1995 (pp. 166–72, 182–84) I distinguished between processes that bypass agents' capacities for control over their mental lives and processes that do not. I did so as part of my compatibilist answer to incompatibilist objections that some cases in which brainwashed agents obviously act unfreely satisfy compatibilist sufficient conditions for free action and that some such cases of brainwashed agents are no different, as far as freedom and moral responsibility go, from any case of an agent in a deterministic world. Of course, I argued that one important difference is that there is nothing about deterministic processes in general in virtue of which they bypass agents' capacities for control over their mental lives. In this, determinism is very dissimilar from the brainwashing that I discuss.

How might Dennett, a compatibilist, deal with incompatibilist objections of the sort I mentioned? He writes: "The genuinely autonomous agent is rational, self-controlled, and not wildly misinformed. The intuitive repugnance we feel in 'morality pills' and 'brainwashing,' in contrast to good old-fashioned moral education is perhaps due, then, to a dim appreciation of the utter impossibility of there being any such shortcut treatments that could actually preserve the informedness, flexibility, and open-mindedness that, in our experience, depends on a sound education" (2003, p. 284). His claim here seems to be, in part, that all such objections will feature a scenario that precludes satisfaction of a nonhistorical necessary condition of free, morally responsible action—a required amount of informedness, flexibility, or open-mindedness, or perhaps rationality or self-control.

Consider flexibility and open-mindedness. Any amount of these things that is required for acting freely is, for Dennett, consistent with the thesis that one who has made "oneself so that one could not have done otherwise" than *A* may freely *A*. For example, if Pat freely takes out the college loan, then, obviously, his inability to do otherwise does not entail that he is not flexible or open-minded enough to do this freely. And Paul, one may reasonably suppose, is no less flexible and open-minded than Pat. One is also entitled to suppose that Paul is no less rational than Pat.

What about self-control? If what Dennett means by that is simply autonomy, then his claim that "the genuinely autonomous agent is...self-controlled" is trivially true. It is appropriate to understand self-control here, with tradition, as (at least roughly) the power to see to it that one does not succumb to temptation against one's better judgment.[4] Paul might have just as much of that as Pat.

That leaves informedness. Pat truly believes that he has not been brainwashed, whereas Paul falsely believes this about himself. Imagine that after Paul has lived with and thought about his new values for a few hours, and before he takes out the loan, someone shows him a video of his being brainwashed and persuades him of the truth about how he acquired his new values. He is now no less informed than Pat, and I do not see why his now having this true belief *must* render him less flexible, less open-minded, less rational, or less capable of resisting temptation than he was just before he acquired it. (I return to this issue shortly.) So to the extent that I can identify Dennett's sufficient conditions for acting freely, he seems committed to the claim that Paul freely takes out the college loan for his daughter in this version of the case, even though, owing directly to the brainwashing, he could not have done otherwise. And to make that claim is to bite an extremely hard bullet. Or so it seems to me.

There is a way out for Dennett. He can go historical. If he were to defend a history-sensitive compatibilism, he could get some mileage out of his contention that "the practice of making oneself so that one could not have done otherwise is a key innovation in the evolutionary ascent through design space...to human free will" (2003, p. 216). Again, "making oneself so that one could not have done otherwise" is, in ordinary cases of that, very different from brainwashers making an agent that way last night. Perhaps the crucial difference between Pat and Paul—the one that explains why Pat but not Paul freely takes out the loan, is morally responsible for doing so, and deserves some moral credit for doing so—is that whereas, partly by means of free actions, Pat made himself such that he could not have done otherwise, Paul was made to be that way by unsolicited brainwashing.

Suppose that Paul had freely hired brainwashers to make him a wonderful father. Then all bets are off. The issue requires careful attention. I examined it in Mele 1995 (pp. 165–67), and I will not repeat the discussion here.

Is it possible for Paul eventually to freely make sacrifices for his daughter while being unable to do otherwise than make them? I believe so. I explored this issue in Mele 1995 (pp. 169–72), and I will not repeat myself here. But here is a hint about why the question might properly get an affirmative answer. Suppose that what Paul had always cared most about was his own happiness and he discovered over time that, as a consequence of acting in accordance with his new values, he is much happier than he used to be.

Is it important that people rather than blind forces replace Paul's selfish values with new unsheddable ones? I have already explained (ch. 6, sec. 2) that the answer is *no*. This, by the way, makes it clear that I do not accept the "Default Responsibility Principle" that Dennett attributes to me: "If no one else is responsible for your being in state *A*, you are" (2003, p. 281). If I am right, sometimes an agent is in state *A* and no one is responsible for that: the agent is not responsible for that, and no one else is either. In a review of Dennett 2003, Ronald Bailey (2003) reports that one of Dennett's theses "is nicely summed up by philosopher Alfred Mele's notion of a Default Responsibility Principle." Let me just say that I am not responsible for that principle and someone else is.

Dennett puts an imaginary interlocutor to work (2003). I would like one of my own. I call him Joe. Here is a question for him. Why don't pairs of stories like that of Pat and Paul move Dennett toward a history-sensitive compatibilism of the sort I've been discussing? Joe replies: "As Dennett showed years ago (1978, p. 44), it's conceptually impossible to brainwash someone into believing that he has a brother without producing a lot of pseudo-memories. What's his brother's name? What does he look like? And so on. Similarly, it's conceptually impossible to brainwash values into a person without producing a lot of pseudo-memories. Dennett regards your brainwashing stories as conceptually impossible, and rightly so. That's why he's not moved by them."

Recall that, for the purposes of my thought experiments, a person's valuing X is to be understood as his having a positive motivational attitude toward X and a belief that X is good. Dennett asserts that his thought experiment about "wiring into" someone the false belief that he has a brother "does not show that wiring in beliefs is impossible...but just that one could only wire in one belief by wiring in many" (1978, p. 44). This is certainly a stretch. I last saw my sister three months ago. I do not recall in any detail how she was dressed at the time. In principle, someone could insert in me the belief that she was wearing a red blouse without inserting many other beliefs. In any case, value insertion of the sort featured in my stories *does* involve the insertion of many evaluative beliefs.

"Let me make a separate point," Joe says. "Following Dennett's lead, you consider a version of Pat's case in which we deceive him into believing that his parental values are products of brainwashing. You have a nonchalant attitude toward such a drastic change in beliefs. That change would definitely be psychologically devastating to Pat and to any conceptually possible being who had been acting freely, and the devastation would definitely render any such being unfree—at least for quite some time. You say that the deceived Pat might freely take out the loan for his daughter, but you are dead wrong about that."

Joe seemingly is confusing a judgment about psychological reality with a judgment about conceptual impossibility. Joe needs to argue that it is *conceptually impossible* that Pat absorbs the shock well enough to take out that loan for his daughter and to do so freely. On the face of it, it is conceptually possible for Pat's attitude to be "my daughter's welfare first; reflection on my shocking discovery about myself later." But suppose Joe were able to show that, necessarily, Pat would be rendered unfree for some time by our deception of him. (Frankly, I see no way for Joe or anyone to construct a persuasive argument for this.) Then an *augmented* version of the history-sensitive compatibilism that I have been discussing might be a good bet for compatibilists. In addition to claiming that the absence of a certain kind of history is required for free and morally responsible actions performed on the basis of unsheddable values in cases in which one could not have done otherwise, one may claim that the absence of a certain kind of radical deception about the history of one's values also is required. This would be an advance, not a retreat.

3. Arpaly's Critique

Nomy Arpaly writes: "Anyone who wishes to argue that Beth is not morally responsible for her actions would need to explain why having been irrationally influenced by an evil human being exempts from responsibility in a way that having been influenced in a similar way by some unlucky chance of a force of nature does not" (2003, p. 129). In light of what I said in Mele 1995 (pp. 168–69) about cases in which "blind forces" erase some of an agent's values and replace them with new unsheddable values, as in a version of the electromagnetic field scenario discussed in the preceding chapter (sec. 2), this particular challenge to my history-sensitive compatibilist view is misguided.[5] However, the challenge may be reformulated in a way I articulate shortly. Of course, I do not accept the unqualified claim that "Beth is not morally responsible for her actions," and I doubt that Arpaly intends the claim to be read as unqualified. I see no reason to think that Beth is no longer morally responsible for her acts of kindness, for not returning extra change when she sees that a cashier has made an error, and so on. My view is that, at least for a time, Beth is not morally responsible for those actions of hers that express her new unsheddable values in cases in which, owing largely to those values, she could not have done otherwise than act as she did (on a compatibilist reading of "could have done otherwise"). Henceforth, as shorthand for this, I use the expression "*C*-express unsheddable values."

Arpaly asserts: "There are cases of profound conversions in a person's values that are just as inexplicable to their possessors, just as uninvited, and just as irrational as Beth's conversion" (2003, p. 127). Examples are "party animals" who become "industrious workers because of mysterious factors they regard as 'age' or 'the drying up of hormones,'" atheists who convert "to religion (or vice versa) as the result of an experience of extreme loneliness and pain," and "people who begin to value parenthood...the moment their (formerly unwanted) children are born." If these people are to be enough like Beth for Arpaly to get her challenge off the ground, the new values they acquire in their conversions need to be unsheddable. For example, a party animal who had cared little about work acquires overnight an unsheddable commitment to hard work. If Arpaly were to claim that, in her examples, agents with new unsheddable values are morally responsible for actions of theirs that

C-express those values, she could then challenge me to explain why, even so, Beth is not morally responsible for comparable actions of hers.

I am embarrassed to report that I know very little about party animals. But I suppose that if I were to learn of a party animal in my neighborhood who had cared very little about work until today and now is as committed to his work as Ann and Beth are to theirs, I would suspect that a personality-changing brain tumor is at work. If my suspicion is right, the converted party animal seems not to be morally responsible, at least for a time, for actions that *C*-express his new unsheddable values. Of course, Arpaly means to be appealing to cases in which the etiology of the conversion is considerably less far-fetched, and realistic cases are imaginable of people who had, for years, cared a lot about fun and little about work and now have an unsheddable commitment to hard work. In representative cases of this kind, a party animal eventually comes to view his life as unsatisfying, shallow, or silly; it occurs to him that things might be better if he were to put a lot of energy into his work; he gives that a try, and, over time, he acquires the unsheddable values of an "industrious worker." In a natural way of filling in the details of the story, the person's capacities for control over his mental life do a lot of work; they are not bypassed in the conversion. The agent acquires reasonable beliefs about the value of his party-animal life partly on the basis of his experiences, he considers throwing himself into an alternative routine as a way of improving his life, he elects to give that a try, he learns that hard work can be fulfilling, and so on. In the "tumor" version of the story, these capacities are bypassed, as they are in my story of Beth's brainwashing.

Apparently, the challenge issued here to a proponent of my view is to explain why Beth is not morally responsible for the industrious conduct that *C*-expresses her new unsheddable values, whereas the converted party animals are morally responsible for conduct of this kind. My reply has two parts. First, it is extremely plausible that in the tumor version of the party animal story, in which the agents' capacities for control over their mental lives are bypassed in the conversion process, the converted party animals are, at least for a time, not morally responsible for this conduct. They are just like Beth in this regard. Second, in realistic cases of party animals who become, over time, agents with the unsheddable values of an industrious worker, the agents' capacities for control over their mental lives are not bypassed in the conversion process. In this, they differ markedly from Beth. And this historical difference is a good candidate for accounting for the difference in moral responsibility, if some converted party animal with an unsheddable commitment to hard work is morally responsible for his pertinent conduct. Given my unfamiliarity with the life of a party animal, I make no evaluative judgments about it, but as I observed in Mele 1995 (p. 165), "An agent who, in the absence of brainwashing and the like, sees the error of his ways and radically transforms himself might properly be credited for his own good behavior. At least nothing that I have said closes this option."

What about conversions in the religious sphere? A philosopher friend once told me of her conversion from theism to atheism in her early twenties. She was knocked unconscious in a bad car accident; when she regained consciousness, she was an atheist. The first words out of my mouth were, "That reminds me of certain thought-experiments that feature belief-producing blows to the head. Why did your new, atheistic belief persist, given what you took to be its cause?" She reported feeling certain at the time that, whether she were to die or recover, the supernatural would have nothing to do with it. Theism suddenly seemed to her like a form of magic, and she disbelieved in magic. On reflection, she said, she judged this thought about theism to be warranted.

Another friend told me of a similar conversion that happened when he was fourteen. His girlfriend told him she thought she was pregnant. For a few weeks he prayed feverishly to God to end the pregnancy. Then it seemed incredible to him that God would end a pregnancy: after all, God is pro-life. His next serious thought, he said, was that God's existence is incredible. He thought it through and judged it to be extremely unlikely that there are any supernatural beings.

In both cases, a traumatic event led to a thought or belief that struck the person as an insight. And in both cases, the person evaluated that thought or belief and came to a conclusion about its merits. In real-life cases of people converting "to religion ... as the result of an experience of extreme loneliness and pain" (Arpaly 2003, p. 127), something similar may happen. The experience may generate an apparent insight that the person evaluates, and reflection on it may lead the person to accept what is, for him, a radically new view on the topic. If so, the process does not bypass the person's capacities for control over his mental life. Indeed, those capacities are centrally involved in it.

Suppose there are cases of religious conversion that involve no significant reflection. Perhaps an atheist is struck a violent blow to the head and, as a direct consequence, acquires a belief that God exists. Obviously, he does not autonomously acquire this belief, but does that

182 • *Free Will and Luck*

fact have any interesting implications for any of his actions?[6] In some versions of the story, he abandons his new belief on the basis of reflection. But suppose that whatever was done to his brain by the blow renders him incapable of doing this. Suppose also that this new theist, Ted, considers going to church and decides to give it a try. He attends a service, finds it interesting, and attends another a few weeks later.

Is Ted morally responsible for going to church? Well, there are people who blame churchgoers—not exactly for going to church, but for what they see as wishful thinking, self-deception, or something of the sort. People like this who know why Ted believes in God would not blame him for being a believer: his belief was produced by a blow to the head and sustained by the physical effects of that blow; wishful thinking and self-deception had nothing to do with it. There also are people who praise churchgoers for going to church. (Often, the praise is relatively modest.) They notice that lots of believers do not attend religious services, and they praise those who do. Would such people who know why Ted believes in God praise him for going to church? Maybe some of them would. It is true that Ted would not be attending religious services were it not for the blow to his head. But that is not the whole story about why he goes to church: after all, many believers do not go. Suppose something were added to Ted's story to match a salient feature of Beth's story. It is Beth's unsheddable *values* that drive her hard work, and on some occasions, she performs actions that C-express those values. Suppose now that the blow to his head also produces in Ted the most directly relevant values of a dedicated churchgoer, that the values produced in him are unsheddable, and that they are C-expressed in his churchgoing. Then, at least for a time, he seemingly merits no praise for going to church. Now, in the absence of an unsheddable value in a religious conversion story, the story is not sufficiently like Beth's story to serve as a basis for the challenge Arpaly wants to issue. And once unsheddable values are included—specifically, unsheddable values that the agent acquires in ways that bypass his capacities for control over his mental life and are C-expressed in some of his actions—the protagonist seems no more responsible for his pertinent actions than Beth does for hers.

That there are "people who begin to value parenthood...the moment their (formerly unwanted) children are born" (Arpaly 2003, p. 127) is not surprising at all, of course, as any evolutionary biologist will tell you. Now, in my examples of localized responsibility-blocking radical value change in Mele 1995, the new values not only are unsheddable but also are so extreme that they produce (or would produce, given the opportunity) uncommon or extraordinary behavior that is radically at odds with the agent's former behavior and values: Beth works on philosophy more than eighty hours a week, a woman who was very nice until she awoke this morning now has the values of a ruthless killer (pp. 156–62), and a man who had been a ruthless killer until he awoke devotes his days to working selflessly for many charitable organizations (pp. 164–65).[7] Probably, the great majority of new parents have at least very modest unsheddable values that, for example, place killing their infant child psychologically out of bounds. Unsheddable values can be modest (though in Mele 1995 I discussed only relatively extreme ones), and some modest unsheddable values may be ensured by the combination of a normal biochemical condition and a normal upbringing. If the new parents Arpaly has in mind initially have parental values like this, perhaps they deserve no praise for that and no praise for behavior that is no better than what is ensured by modest, unsheddable parental values of this kind. But having such values is consistent with parental activities ranging from the modest to the admirable, with patterns of behavior that nonaccidentally result in lofty parental values, and with patterns of behavior that are not suitable for having such a result. Other things being equal, then, they are consistent with praiseworthy and blameworthy parenting behavior.

The new parents Arpaly mentions might not be much like Beth at all. But suppose that the change in their values and their behavior was sudden and dramatic, as in Beth's story. A young mother was unreservedly committed to giving her child up for adoption and to having no further contact with him—until she saw his face. At that moment, she acquired unsheddable parental values as lofty as those of the most wonderful parents on Earth, and she cannot do otherwise than insist on keeping the child. In one version of the story, the mother was a very good and very loving young person, and various hardships explain her commitment to adoption: her raising the child, given her circumstances, would be heroic. The sight of the newborn infant's face activates this admirable young woman's enormous capacity for love and tenderness. Readers may wish to praise her for her values, for actions of hers that express them, or both. But this case is not much like Beth's at all. Some of Beth's deepest values were erased and replaced with new ones. This new mother's new values flow from an admirable aspect of her psyche. In another version of the story, a brain tumor causes the amazing values without activating any admirable capacity or disposition the young woman had. This version is much more like Beth's case, and at least for a time, the new mother apparently is not morally responsible for having the amazing values she has or for actions of hers that *C*-express them.

Arpaly asserts that my story of Ann and Beth "illustrates how reasoning in terms of autonomy can confuse, rather than clarify, important ethical issues" (2003, p. 126). As the foregoing indicates, I believe that it is Arpaly's reasoning that is confused. Attention to various important ways in which cases of (apparently) radical personal change differ from one another in their nonhistorical features would have helped eliminate some of the confusion. The same is true of attention to important similarities between some causal histories that feature manipulation by "an evil human being" (Arpaly 2003, p. 129) and some causal histories in which blind forces stand in for the bad guys.

4. Kapitan's Critique and the Zygote Argument

Given how much is built into the compatibilist sufficient conditions for free action offered in Mele 1995, including the agent's being ideally self-controlled and a reliable deliberator with a collection of beliefs conducive to informed deliberation about all matters that concern him, I did not worry about manipulated agents of this kind who have no unsheddable values. Because all of their values are sheddable, these agents would be able to undo the effects of value engineering, given a standard compatibilist position on ability.[8] Tomis Kapitan, a compatibilist, seems to take the view that I should have worried about such agents (2000, p. 90). I examine his critique after providing some background.[9]

Again, with "chance" defined as in chapter 6, section 3, the following is true: If a universe is deterministic, then shortly after the big bang (if there was a big bang), there was no chance that anything that subsequently happens in it would not happen. Compatibilists need to accommodate this point. In this connection, I tested my compatibilist proposal against an extreme scenario set in a deterministic universe in which a supremely intelligent being, Diana, creates a certain adult agent, Fred (Mele 1995, pp. 190–91). Diana creates Fred "precisely because [she] wants a certain event, *E*, to occur." She gives Fred, "at the time of creation, a particular collection of sheddable desires and values" because, partly in light of her knowledge of the state of the universe at that time, she knows that, owing partly to Fred's having those initial desires and values, there is no chance that a year later he will fail to judge, on the basis of deliberation, that it is best to *A*, no chance that he will not *A* on the basis of that judgment, and no chance that he will not bring about *E* by *A*-ing. Diana knows that Fred will *A* only if he lives his life in a particular way during that year, and she "knows just what collection of sheddable initial motivational states, together with the laws of nature and the state of Fred's universe at the time of his creation, will result in his living his life in that way." Finally, Fred satisfies my proposed set of collectively sufficient conditions for "compatibilist psychological autonomy: he is ideally self-controlled, he has no compelled* motivational states, his beliefs are conducive to informed deliberation about all matters that concern him, he is a reliable deliberator, and so on" (p. 190). (Again, compulsion* is compulsion that is not arranged by the agent.)

Given Fred's properties, he is capable of reflecting intelligently on his values and desires, and he is able—in a compatibilist sense of "able"—to shed those values and desires, develop new ones, and act on the new ones (Mele 1995, p. 190). He is able to do this; but there is no chance that he will, given that his universe is deterministic. Now, typical incompatibilists would reject the assertion that Fred is able to do these things; they hold that determinism is incompatible with the ability to do otherwise. Semicompatibilists who go beyond the claim that moral responsibility and free action are compatible with determinism *even if* determinism precludes the ability to do otherwise to the claim that compatibilism is true *even though* determinism precludes this ability also would reject the assertion about Fred's abilities.[10] But traditional compatibilists would accept that Fred is able to shed the pertinent values and desires (that is, that they are sheddable by him), able to develop new values and desires, and able to act accordingly.

Why might a traditional compatibilist take Fred's case to falsify the claim that my compatibilist conditions are collectively sufficient for free action? Kapitan (2000, p. 90) quotes the following remark of mine: "In one respect, Fred is like any autonomous agent at a deterministic world: his path is causally determined. He is *special* in having been endowed at the time of his creation with a collection of motivational attitudes for his creator's own purposes. But since these are sheddable attitudes, this detail of his creation does not render him nonautonomous, on the assumption that compatibilism is true" (Mele 1995, pp. 190–91). He then writes: "To the contrary, granting that Fred has the capacity to examine and revise his values, it remains that the creator has instilled

Fred with the values constitutive of this capacity." On any natural reading of this sentence, Kapitan infers from the assertion (K) that "the creator has instilled Fred with the values constitutive of this capacity" that the pertinent "detail of [Fred's] creation" *does* "render him non-autonomous."[11] But K is false. Although Fred's examinations of his values, like any agent's examinations of his own values, will be influenced by values that are already in place, his "capacity to examine and revise his values," like anyone's capacity to do this, is not *constituted* by his values. Assuming that the capacity at issue has constituents, various powers or abilities would certainly seem to be among them: for example, Fred's ability to recognize what he values, his ability to rank some of his values, and his ability to compare his values with other possible values. And, of course, Fred's values themselves are not powers or abilities. In Mele 1995, I discussed some cases of manipulation in which the implanted values are such that although the agent is able to reflect on them, he is not able to do otherwise than identify with them on the basis of such reflection and, accordingly, is not able to shed them (pp. 159, 169–72). Perhaps Kapitan is assimilating Fred to agents like this. Is that assimilation justifiable from a traditional compatibilist perspective?

We occasionally modify values and desires of ours. Sometimes we are told that, or wonder whether, we care too much—or too little—about our work, what others think of us, our children's success, how we dress, money, our health, or whatever. Sometimes, on reflection, we judge that we should care less—or more—about some of these things. Occasionally we make efforts to get ourselves to care less—or more. Someone who becomes convinced that he cares way too little about his health may try to get himself to care much more by spending time each day picturing opportunities that would be closed to him by poor health and thinking about the ways in which better health would improve his life, someone who judges that he cares way too much about work may attempt to fix that by reflecting periodically on the good things that his work leaves him little time for, and so on. Sometimes such efforts are successful, and no such effort would succeed if the values at issue were unsheddable (at the time). Fred's values, by hypothesis, are revisable in this way. And they differ from unsheddable values that some workaholics, misers, and health fanatics may have. How, exactly, the distinction is spelled out by a particular compatibilist depends on that theorist's preferred way of understanding what it is to have been able, in deterministic worlds, to do things that one did not do. I leave that open.

Kapitan writes: "The creator understands that Fred's pro-attitudes will produce the desired actions as outputs given certain environmental inputs, inputs which the creator knows Fred will be subject to. So, Fred is caused, indeed, deliberately caused, to behave in a certain way in much the same way that designers of robots program the responses of their machines to various stimuli" (2000, p. 90). This has the look of something straight out of an incompatibilist essay. Moreover, as far as I can tell, nothing about Fred precludes his intentional actions' satisfying Kapitan's own conditions for an action's being under its agent's control (2000, p. 83). Even so, it is an interesting question whether a typical compatibilist can motivate the view that Fred never acts freely, even though some agent in a deterministic universe—call him Norm—who is just like Fred in all relevant nonhistorical respects often acts freely.

There is a salient difference between Fred and Norm. Fred came into being in the strange way I described, and Norm came into being in the normal way (and was not subsequently manipulated). The question is what a typical compatibilist should make of this historical difference. On the view I proposed in Mele 1995, certain pairs of ideally self-controlled beings who are very similar in some important nonhistorical respects may nevertheless be such that one *A*-s freely while the other *A*-s unfreely. I motivated this idea by examining pairs of agents with some *unsheddable* values. If a traditional compatibilist were to show that the difference between Fred and Norm—ideally self-controlled agents with no unsheddable values—is such that Norm freely *A*-s whereas Fred *A*-s unfreely, I would have no objection to adding to my proposed set of collectively sufficient conditions a historical one that Fred does not satisfy. But can a traditional compatibilist show this while holding on to his or her compatibilism?

As I pointed out in Mele 1995 (p. 172), for some externalists about mental content, the creation of an adult agent like Fred is conceptually impossible. On their view, because Fred lacks a history, he has no thoughts at all—and therefore no values, for example—at the time of his creation (see Davidson 1987). Compatibilists with no commitment to internalism about mental content who regard Fred as a potential counterexample to their favorite set of sufficient conditions for free action have the option of excluding him from consideration on the grounds that he is impossible. In Mele 1995, I suggested that externalist worries about the possibility of beings like Fred could be set aside for

188 • *Free Will and Luck*

my purposes. Here, I wish to bypass the issue about mental content by switching to a case of engineering in utero.[12]

Diana creates a zygote Z in Mary. She combines Z's atoms as she does because she wants a certain event E to occur thirty years later. From her knowledge of the state of the universe just prior to her creating Z and the laws of nature of her deterministic universe, she deduces that a zygote with precisely Z's constitution located in Mary will develop into an ideally self-controlled agent who, in thirty years, will judge, on the basis of rational deliberation, that it is best to A and will A on the basis of that judgment, thereby bringing about E. If this agent, Ernie, has any unsheddable values at the time, they play no role in motivating his A-ing. Thirty years later, Ernie is a mentally healthy, ideally self-controlled person who regularly exercises his powers of self-control and has no relevant compelled or coercively produced attitudes. Furthermore, his beliefs are conducive to informed deliberation about all matters that concern him, and he is a reliable deliberator. So he satisfies a version of my proposed compatibilist sufficient conditions for having freely A-ed.[13]

Recall Kapitan's assertion that "Fred is...deliberately caused to behave in a certain way in much the same way that designers of robots program the responses of their machines to various stimuli" (2000, p. 90). Seemingly, if this is true of Fred, it is true of Ernie.[14] And one who infers from Kapitan's assertion about Fred that he unfreely A-s presumably would infer that Ernie A-s unfreely from a parallel assertion about him. Compare Ernie with Bernie, who also satisfies my compatibilist sufficient conditions for free action. The zygote that developed into Bernie came to be in the normal way. A major challenge for any compatibilist who claims that Ernie A-s unfreely whereas Bernie A-s freely is to explain how the difference in the causes of the two zygotes has this consequence. Why should that historical difference matter, given the properties the two agents share?

There is a related issue for compatibilists who lean the way Kapitan may be leaning. Diana assembles Z as she does in Mary so that E will happen. Of course, in doing this, thereby ensuring that Ernie will bring about E by A-ing thirty years later, Diana ensures a lot more than that. A complete description of the state of the universe just after Diana creates Z—including Z's constitution, of course—together with a complete statement of the laws of nature entails a true statement of everything Ernie will ever do. So is it just A that Ernie is supposed to do unfreely, given that Diana "deliberately caused" him to A? Or given that the means she selected for causing him to *A*—namely, assembling *Z* as she did in Mary—was no less a cause of all of his actions, is the claim that Ernie does *nothing* freely?

Recall my observation in chapter 6 (sec. 2) that the responsibility-undermining and freedom-blocking effects of intentional manipulators can be matched by blind forces. In some scenarios, values that are already in place are erased and replaced—either by manipulative agents or by blind forces—with a very different set of values that includes some unsheddable ones that are expressed in actions. These scenarios differ from Ernie's story in at least two salient ways. In Ernie's story no values are erased, and Ernie's *A*-ing does not express any unsheddable values. Even so, it is certainly very tempting for an incompatibilist to suggest that, as far as freedom and moral responsibility go, there is no important difference between Ernie's story and stories in which zygotes are created by blind forces; and, of course, it is the norm for zygotes to be created by blind forces.

Here, there is the basis for a manipulation argument for incompatibilism that avoids the problems with Pereboom's unsuccessful four-case argument. I call it *the zygote argument*. It runs, in skeleton form, as follows:

1. Because of the way his zygote was produced in his deterministic universe, Ernie is not a free agent and is not morally responsible for anything.
2. Concerning free action and moral responsibility of the beings into whom the zygotes develop, there is no significant difference between the way Ernie's zygote comes to exist and the way any normal human zygote comes to exist in a deterministic universe.
3. So determinism precludes free action and moral responsibility.

How might an incompatibilist defend premise 1? One predictable argument for it features the claim that Ernie is "deliberately caused to behave in a certain way in much the same way that designers of robots program the responses of their machines to various stimuli" (Kapitan 2000, p. 90). (Hence, my remark earlier that Kapitan, a compatibilist, sounds like an incompatibilist here.) An incompatibilist who fears that there may be readers who agree that Ernie does not freely *A* and is not morally responsible for *A*-ing but reject the claim that he *never* acts freely and morally responsibly is free to modify the story. In my story, Diana's aim is to create an agent who will bring about *E* at *t*. As I observed, Diana's assembling Z as she does in Mary—her means of achieving her aim—is a cause of all of Ernie's actions and not merely of his A-ing (by which he brings about E). In a modified version of the story, Diana has a much more extensive aim—to create an agent who performs *all* of those actions.

A defense of premise 2 might begin with the question how it can matter for the purposes of freedom and moral responsibility whether, in a deterministic universe, a zygote with Z's exact constitution was produced by a supremely intelligent agent with Diana's effective intentions or instead by blind forces. Imagine a deterministic universe U^* that is a lot like the one at issue, U, but in which Z comes into being in Mary in the normal way and at the same time. It is conceivable that, in U^*, throughout his life, Ernie does exactly what he does in U, down to the smallest detail. Suppose that this is so in U^*. Then, a proponent of the zygote argument might contend that, given the additional facts that, in both universes, Ernie has no say about what causes Z, no say about the rest of the universe at that time, and no say about what the laws of nature are, the cross-universe difference in what caused Z does not support any cross-universe difference in freedom or moral responsibility.

Although the argument I have sketched for premise 2 sounds a bit like the consequence argument, it is significantly different. The consequence argument is an argument for incompatibilism. The argument for premise 2 is, by itself, consistent with compatibilism. The thesis that the cross-universe difference in what caused Z does not support any cross-universe difference in freedom or moral responsibility is consistent with Ernie's acting freely and morally responsibly in both universes, as is premise 2.

Suppose an intuition check were to be run on premise 1. It is perhaps tempting to think that incompatibilists would uniformly deem 1 true and that compatibilists would uniformly deem 1 false. But Kapitan, a compatibilist, seemingly takes a comparable assertion about Fred to be true, and he might think the same about Ernie. Some philosophers and psychologists are running controlled intuition checks on untutored subjects.[15] I myself am doubtful about the significance of the judgments such subjects make about complicated theoretical matters. A more suitable audience for the question about premise 1 of the zygote argument might be people who have thought long and hard about freedom and moral responsibility and are agnostic about compatibilism. I call them *reflective agnostics*.

Here is a hunch. Reflective agnostics who have significant doubts about the compatibility of *indeterministic agency* with free and morally responsible action will, on average, be significantly more inclined to judge that premise 1 is false than will reflective agnostics who have a much brighter view of indeterministic agents' prospects for free and morally responsible action. My hunch is based partly on the following three conjectures. First, a significant majority of people who have thought long and hard about free action and moral responsibility— including a significant majority of such people who are agnostic about compatibilism—either believe that there are free and morally responsible agents or are more inclined to believe that than they are to believe that there are no such agents. Second, the more doubtful a person in this conjectured significant majority of agnostics is about indeterministic agents' prospects for free action and moral responsibility, the more likely he is to see the truth of premise 1 as a serious threat to freedom and moral responsibility. Third, the addition of Ernie's story to the collection of relevant things reflective agnostics have reflected on would not move many of these people out of the conjectured majority and would not—at least very quickly—give many of them a significantly brighter view of indeterministic agents' prospects for free action and moral responsibility.

That is a lot of guessing for a single paragraph. My point, in part, is that intuitions about free action and moral responsibility in particular stories are influenced by many things, and it would not be surprising if thoughtful people with different attitudes toward the seemingly tangential issue of *indeterministic* agents' prospects for free action and moral responsibility have different intuitions about whether Ernie is a free and morally responsible agent in his deterministic universe.

At this point, even patient readers may want me to put my cards on the table and say whether *I* believe that a full-blown version of the zygote argument would show that compatibilism is false. "Enough about how people with various views, opinions, or inclinations might react to the argument," a reader may say. "What about you?" Well, given what I have said thus far in this book, I certainly seem to fall into the reflective agnostic group, and I believe, as I have reported, that it is more credible that there are free, morally responsible agents than that there are no such agents. So if the conjectures I reported are on target, there is some likelihood that my attitude toward the argument is influenced by my optimism or pessimism about indeterministic agents' prospects for free action and moral responsibility. I reveal my attitude after a little more stage setting.

Premise 1 of the zygote argument is an assertion about a case. (Both the original case and the modified version of it are eligible for consideration here.) Suppose the assertion reports an intuition. Incompatibilists who have intuitions about Ernie intuit that he is not a free agent and is not morally responsible for anything. Now if they have that intuition partly because they already believe on independent grounds that determinism precludes free action and moral responsibility, then its value as an *intuition* in this context is called into question. After all, the zygote argument is supposed to use an intuition about Ernie as a step toward the conclusion that incompatibilism is true. Suppose that incompatibilists have the intuition reported in premise 1—that because of the way his zygote was produced in his deterministic universe, Ernie is not a free agent and is not morally responsible for anything—partly because they already believe on independent grounds that incompatibilism is true. What intuition (if any) would they have about Ernie if they were *not* incompatibilists? Well, if they were not incompatibilists, they would be compatibilists or agnostics. If they were compatibilists, they would probably have compatibilist intuitions about Ernie. I return to such intuitions shortly. And if they were agnostics, my preliminary judgment about what intuitions they would have would be shaped by the conjectures I reported. To the extent that assent to premise 1 rests on independent prior assent to incompatibilism, the zygote argument is question begging. In effect, I have suggested that it might be tested for question beggingness by running it by (perhaps purely hypothetical) reflective agnostics.

One does not need to be an incompatibilist or agnostic to find premise 2 very plausible. Rather than produce an argument for this claim, I challenge the reader to produce an argument against it.[16] I should point out, however, that a nonhistoricist compatibilist like Frankfurt has no theoretical commitment that speaks against 2, and the same is true of a historicist compatibilist who endorses the compatibilist sufficient conditions for free and morally responsible action that I have offered. It may be claimed that 2 is false on the grounds that normal agents *truly* believe that they came into being in some normal way, whereas Ernie *falsely* believes this. (See section 2 for discussion of a related claim by Dennett.) Testing this claim is left as an exercise for the reader, but I suggest that readers consider some additional cases when conducting their tests, all set in deterministic universes. In one, someone persuades Ernie of the truth about his zygote when he is an adult, a week or so before he *A*-s. In another, someone persuades him of this truth when he is a child. In others, Bernie—recall that he is a lot like Ernie with the notable exception that he came into being in a normal way—is deceived into believing that his zygote was produced in the way Ernie's was. Both early and late deception may be considered.[17]

If it is assumed that premise 2 is true, what should compatibilists say about premise 1? They should say that it is false. Compatibilists believe that there are free, morally responsible agents in some deterministic worlds and that the zygotes of many of them, at least, came to be in the normal way. Given their compatibilism and the assumption that premise 2 is true, Ernie should strike them as free and morally responsible (in light of his properties as an agent).[18]

Now, what about reflective agnostics, including me? A significant part of what prevents some of us from coming down off the fence and endorsing compatibilism might be cases like Ernie's. Reflective agnostics who are not moved at all by the consequence argument or by manipulation arguments like Pereboom's may feel a pull toward premise 1 while seeing no way around premise 2.

Thus far, I have not said what the event is that Ernie was built to produce (in the original story), event *E*. Different specifications of it may affect the strength of intuitions about the story.[19] Suppose that *E* is the death of Ernie's aunt and that Ernie poisoned her in order to inherit her money so that he could get himself out of serious financial trouble. Some reflective agnostics will feel pulled toward the judgment that Ernie is not blameworthy for the killing because Diana assembled his zygote as she did to ensure that he would do precisely that and because her creative activity did ensure that he would do that. Furthermore, because they judge that if Ernie had been morally responsible for the killing or had killed his aunt freely, he would have been blameworthy for the killing, they feel pulled toward the judgment that the action was not free and not one for which Ernie is morally responsible. These same agnostics might have a different attitude if *E* were a homeless shelter's receiving a $200 donation and *A* were Ernie's donating that money.[20] Other reflective agnostics may be more powerfully moved by Ernie's bad will in the killing scenario than by the details of his creation and be pulled toward the judgment that he is blameworthy and morally responsible for the killing and freely kills his aunt.

Scenarios like Ernie's—unlike the consequence argument, Pereboom's four-case argument, and manipulation arguments that I have examined elsewhere (Mele 1995, chs. 9 and 10)—prevent me from flatly endorsing compatibilism. But, for all I know, this would not be so if I were significantly less optimistic about indeterministic agents' prospects for free action and moral responsibility. Readers who have been patiently waiting for me to reveal my attitude toward the zygote argument will notice that I have just done so. I can be more explicit. Premise 1 has some intuitive pull on me, but not enough to move me to accept it. I am agnostic about premise 1, as I am about compatibilism.

Because I am laying my cards on the table, I need to return to a view about laws of nature that I said I would set aside in this book. In chapter 3 (n. 23), I announced that because necessitarianism about natural laws is far more popular than Humeanism, and because Helen Beebee and I (Beebee and Mele 2002) have done our best to situate Humean compatibilism in the debate about free will and moral responsibility, my discussion of compatibilism in this book presupposes necessitarianism. However, I am by no means convinced that a Humean view of laws should be rejected, and its truth would undermine the thought experiment about Ernie's zygote. According to a Humean view, some of the ontological ingredients of the laws of nature of Ernie's universe—namely, future regularities—are not in place at the time of his creation. The natural laws might turn out to characterize a deterministic or an indeterministic universe, and even on the hypothesis that the universe turns out to be deterministic, it is open at the time of Ernie's creation precisely what its laws will be. So Diana, who is supposed to benefit from her knowledge of the laws of nature in designing Ernie, is in no position to know the laws of nature: her complete knowledge of the past does not include knowledge of the laws, nor does it constitute a basis for deducing them. Even if Diana makes a true, educated guess about what the collection of natural laws will turn out to be on the basis of her complete knowledge of the past, it is open when she creates Ernie and right up to t both that she will be wrong about what the laws will be and that Ernie will not A at t. If Ernie were to B at t, something that is consistent with the entire past of his universe (given a Humean view of laws), that fact would be one of the facts to be accounted for by a web of contingent generalizations that appear as theorems (or axioms) "in each of the true deductive systems that achieves a best combination of simplicity and strength" (Lewis 1973, p. 73): that is, it would be among the facts to be accounted for by the laws of nature. On a Humean view of laws, in Gideon Rosen's words, "it may turn out in the end [that] the laws are as they are in part *because*" Ernie acted as he did (2002, p. 705). Some agnostics about compatibilism may find themselves in that position partly because they are agnostic about Humeanism about laws of nature.[21]

I close this section with a comment on a semicompatibilist view of sheddability. The compatibilist notion of sheddability at work in Mele 1995 conforms to the traditional compatibilist idea that determinism is compatible with agents' having been able to do otherwise than they in fact did. Thus, someone who did not shed a certain value in a deterministic world might have been able to shed it. I mentioned that a semicompatibilist of a certain kind denies that determinism is compatible with the ability to do otherwise. If the sheddability of an attitude that an agent did not shed is understood to entail that the agent was able to shed it, then such a semicompatibilist is committed to denying that this attitude was sheddable by the agent. However, semicompatibilists attempt to develop what amounts to an analogue of the ability of an agent to do otherwise, and a semicompatibilist analogue of sheddability is an option. Taking a hint from Fischer and Ravizza's (1998) semicompatibilist reasons-responsiveness view of moral responsibility, a theorist can distinguish between importantly different mechanisms for the assessment and revision of attitudes. Consider, for example, an agent in a deterministic world W whose mechanism for evaluation and revision of his desire for X is receptive to "the reasons that exist" (Fischer and Ravizza 1998, p. 69) for and against desiring X and is at least moderately reasons-reactive in this connection, where that is understood as a matter of there being some not too distant possible worlds with the same laws of nature as W in which a mechanism of this kind operates in this agent, "there is a sufficient reason" to attenuate or eradicate his desire for X, he "recognizes this reason," and he attenuates or eradicates it for this reason (p. 63). This agent is recognizably different from an agent in W whose mechanism for evaluation and revision of his desire for X is not receptive to any reasons against desiring X, and from an agent with a mechanism that can recognize some such reasons but does not react appropriately to them in any possible world with the same laws of nature as W or reacts appropriately only in very distant worlds with the same laws.

5. Conclusion

In this chapter, I have, among other things, defended the history-sensitive compatibilist proposal I offered in Mele 1995 against various

objections that compatibilists have raised to it. Do I believe that attention to my proposed compatibilist set of sufficient conditions for
free action will win libertarians over to compatibilism? For reasons of
the kind sketched in the introduction to this chapter, my answer is *no*.
In chapter 5, I offered libertarians something else—a libertarian view
that stares down the problem of present luck.

NOTES

1. Of course, a philosopher might argue as follows: (1) we sometimes act
freely and (2) free action is possible only in deterministic universes, so (3) our
universe is deterministic. However, the question whether 3 is true calls for
scientific investigation. People who hold that 2 is true should not regard
themselves as entitled to believe that 1 is true until they have good scientific
grounds for believing that our universe is deterministic.

2. I simplify a bit when I write "no compelled ... attitudes." What I actually
said was "no compelled* ... attitudes." Compulsion* is compulsion that is not
arranged by the compelled agent (1995, p. 166). By a "reliable deliberator," I
mean, roughly, a person who consistently deliberates in ways that "reliably
maximize his chances of locating efficient, effective means to his ends, whatever
those ends might be" (p. 183).

3. This use of "autonomy" is adequately captured by Feinberg's gloss on it:
"the sovereign authority to govern oneself" (1986, p. 28).

4. Dennett asks his readers to "imagine trying to devise an aptitude test that
would measure the flexibility of mind, general knowledge, social comprehension
and impulse-control that are arguably the minimal requirements of moral
agency" (pp. 290–91). The properties mentioned here overlap with the ones I
have just been discussing, and "impulse-control" appears instead of "self-control." This suggests that Dennett uses "self-control" to mean something similar
to "impulse-control" and that the traditional understanding I suggested of self-
control is at least a reasonable approximation of what Dennett has in mind.

5. As I mentioned in ch. 6, sec. 2, in Mele 1995, I argued that the responsibility-
undermining effects of intentional manipulators can be matched by blind forces.

6. I take no stand here on whether any beliefs are autonomously acquired.

7. The story of the formerly nice woman stops before there is any killing.

8. This point is relevant to my distinction in Mele 1995 between "being
compelled to *acquire* a value at a time and being compelled to *possess* a value
over a stretch of time" (pp. 158–59). A value that an agent is compelled to
acquire may or may not be sheddable, but, as I put it, "an agent's being
practically unable to abandon during *t* a pro-attitude [or value] of which he is
possessed throughout *t* is a necessary—but not a sufficient—condition of
his being compelled to possess that pro-attitude [or value] (over that interval)"
(p. 166). Some critics ignore the distinction. For example, Stefaan Cuypers

(in press) infers from the fact that the practical unsheddability of a pro-attitude or value is not an essentially historical matter that my sufficient condition for an agent's being compelled to possess a pro-attitude during an interval commits me to the following: "*S* autonomously possesses a pro-attitude *P*, only if . . . *P*'s generation lacks control bypassing." The inference is invalid, and he would not have made it if he had kept in mind that, on my view, an agent who was compelled to acquire a pro-attitude by means of manipulation that bypasses his capacities for control over his mental life may subsequently autonomously possess that pro-attitude.

9. Given my topic in this chapter, I focus on Kapitan's critique of my proposed compatibilist sufficient conditions for free or autonomous action. He also raises objections to other aspects of my position in Mele 1995, as he interprets it. I forgo replying to those objections in this book.

10. In an informal discussion, John Fischer writes: "I don't think that we could have done otherwise if determinism were true" (2000, p. 328).

11. Two observations are in order. First, Kapitan might not take the absence of autonomy to entail the absence of freedom. Second, in granting that Fred is able "to revise his values," Kapitan is apparently granting that his values are sheddable. Hence, my assertion earlier that he seems to take the view that I should have worried about manipulated agents with no unsheddable values who satisfy my proposed compatibilist sufficient conditions for free action.

12. A draft of the remainder of this section appeared in "The Garden of Forking Paths" free will blog (http://gfp.typepad.com) on June 28, 2004.

13. See Mele 1995, p. 193. As I pointed out in section 3, my focus on un-sheddable values in Mele 1995 was on relatively extreme ones. I ignored what, in section 3, I called *modest* unsheddable values. Some values that are unsheddable by an agent over a span of time may be so modest that only a mentally ill person would be able to shed them then. For example, after a friend raises the question whether Tony could slit his own throat just to see what it feels like, Tony acquires an explicit belief that refraining from slitting his own throat just to see what it feels like is a good thing and an explicit desire of reasonable strength never to slit his own throat just to see what it feels like. That belief-desire pair is a value, in my sense, and it is a modest one. If Tony were practically able to shed that value in the next few weeks, under the utterly normal circumstances in which he finds himself during that time, we would at least wonder whether he is sane. So I was wrong not to worry about agents with no unsheddable values (on grounds very different from Kapitan's). Consequently, rather than make it part of Ernie's story that he has no unsheddable values, I make it part of the story that if he does have any unsheddable values, they play no role in motivating his *A*-ing.

14. Of course, when applied to Ernie, the robot analogy is highly conten-tious. But the same is true when it is applied to Fred.

15. See Knobe in press, Malle and Nelson 2003, Nahmias et al. 2005, and Woolfolk et al. in press.

16. Some of my students suggested rejecting premise 2 on grounds related to the "Default Responsibility Principle" that Dennett mistakenly attributes to me (see sec. 2). They suggested that Diana is morally responsible for Ernie's *A*-ing, that Ernie is not also morally responsible for it, and that Bernie is morally responsible for his *A*-ing (partly because no one else is). A significant relevant difference between the ways in which the two zygotes come into existence, they say, is that Ernie's comes to be in a way that makes Diana morally responsible for what he does and Bernie's does not come to be in a way that makes anyone other than himself morally responsible for what he does.

The suggestion is easy to block. Just suppose that Diana is not morally responsible for anything because she has always been stark raving mad and has never had a grip on the difference between right and wrong.

17. Such cases are relevant if the rejection of 2 is based on the idea that what matters is the difference between having and lacking radically false beliefs of a certain kind about one's origins. See my discussion in section 2 of Dennett's position on the Ann-Beth scenario.

18. Gideon Rosen (2002) constructs a collection of stories that in some ways resemble a collection I discussed in Mele 1995 (pp. 189–91) and in other ways resemble Ernie's story. R. Jay Wallace (2002, pp. 721–25) presents a thoughtful compatibilist reply. Wallace makes it clear that he does not share Rosen's intuitions about his cases, and he concludes his reply as follows: "I can only invite readers to reflect for themselves on whether they share Rosen's intuition, and whether it seems to them a sufficient basis for his incompatibilist position, even while they bear firmly in mind the distinctions and interpretative complexities to which I have called attention" (p. 725). For a similar, informal exchange of ideas between Carl Ginet and John Fischer, see McKenna 2000, pp. 414–15. (I am grateful to Michael McKenna for calling my attention to the latter exchange.)

19. The strength of intuitions may also be affected by whether *E* benefits Diana, as Neil Levy suggested in conversation.

20. Are these attitudes inconsistent? That depends on whether correct standards for attribution of free and morally responsible action vary depending on the badness or goodness of the action.

21. Beebee and I explained that Humean compatibilists face a problem about present luck that is very similar to the problem typical libertarians face (Beebee and Mele 2002, pp. 218–21). My response to the latter problem in chapter 5 is easily adjusted for use by Humean compatibilists.

EIGHT

Conclusion

One of my aims in this book has been to identify and make vivid the most important conceptual obstacles for compatibilism and for libertarianism. That required not only highlighting these obstacles but also arguing that some objections to compatibilism and libertarianism are not all they are cracked up to be. I believe that the zygote argument, though it is sketchy, points to the most serious conceptual obstacle for compatibilism (presupposing necessitarianism about laws of nature). I also believe that the main conceptual obstacle for libertarianism is the problem of present luck. Of course, there is also the partly empirical worry—an important one—that even if some of the internal workings of human brains are indeterministic, the ways in which human brains in fact work indeterministically are not conducive to free action and moral responsibility. (I say *partly* empirical because the worry also has a conceptual component. Whether human brains work indeterministically in ways that are conducive to free action and moral responsibility depends not only on how brains work but also on what free action and moral responsibility are.)

My other main aim has been to present compatibilist and libertarian views—including proposed sets of sufficient conditions for free action—that meet the conceptual obstacles head on. In section 1, I provide brief summaries of the proposed sufficient conditions. In section 2, I discuss two thought experiments featuring imagined empirical discoveries.

1. Compatibilist and Libertarian Sufficient Conditions for Free Action

The compatibilist sufficient conditions for free action discussed in chapter 7 provide a partial basis for my proposed libertarian conditions in chapter 5. I start with the former.

> 1a. *Compatibilist sufficient conditions: Ideal-agent version.* An agent A-s freely if he nondeviantly A-s on the basis of a rationally formed deliberative judgment that it would be best to A, he is an ideally self-controlled and mentally healthy person who regularly exercises his powers of self-control, he has no compelled or coercively produced attitudes, his beliefs are conducive to informed deliberation about all matters that concern him, and he is a reliable deliberator.

On ideal self-control, see chapter 7, p. 164. Again, by a "reliable deliberator," I mean, roughly, a person who consistently deliberates in ways that "reliably maximize his chances of locating efficient, effective means to his ends, whatever those ends might be" (Mele 1995, p. 183). Even if no actual human being satisfies these conditions, the question is whether determinism is *compatible* with free action. My proposal is that a person who satisfies the conditions identified in 1a acts freely even in a deterministic world. As always, the freedom at issue is the sort most closely associated with moral responsibility: the topic is "moral-responsibility-level free action" (ch. 1, sec. 3).

If my proposal is true, compatibilism about moral-responsibility-level free action is true.[1] If such compatibilism is true, the door is wide open to realistic versions of 1a. Here is one:

> 1b. *Compatibilist sufficient conditions: Moderate version.* An agent A-s freely if he nondeviantly A-s on the basis of a rationally formed deliberative judgment that it would be best to A, has no compelled or coercively produced attitudes that influence his deliberative judgment, is well informed on the topic of his deliberation, and is mentally healthy.

If it is assumed that compatibilism is true, 1b is highly plausible, and it is very plausible that the conditions 1b articulates are often satisfied by real human beings.

As I have mentioned, I used my discussion of modest libertarianism as a way of setting the stage for daring soft libertarianism (DSL). Again, soft libertarians—unlike their hard counterparts—leave it open that free action and moral responsibility are compatible with determinism, and they maintain that the falsity of determinism is required for a more desirable kind of free action and a more desirable brand of moral responsibility (ch. 4, sec. 3). I introduced modest libertarianism (ch. 1, sec. 2) as an incompatibilist—hence hard libertarian—view before mixing it with soft libertarianism in chapter 4. When I use the expression "modest libertarianism" without qualification in this chapter, it designates the hard version.

Although DSL is primarily a response to the problem of present indeterministic luck that defends the compatibility of such luck with free decisions and moral responsibility, I also proposed sufficient conditions for free decision making in articulating DSL (ch. 5, sec. 7):

> 2a. *Daring soft libertarian sufficient conditions: Ideal-agent version.* An agent freely decides to A if he nondeviantly decides to A on the basis of a rationally formed deliberative judgment that it would be best to A, the proximate causes of his decision do not deterministically cause it, and he satisfies the conditions stated in 1a as fully as that is possible, given that the proximal causes of his decision do not deterministically cause it.

It may be thought that any decisions *ideally* self-controlled agents make on the basis of their best judgments would be deterministically proximately caused by something that includes that judgment. Hence the qualification in the final clause of 2a.

If 2a is acceptable, the following moderate version should be, too:

> 2b. *Daring soft libertarian sufficient conditions: Moderate version.* An agent freely decides to A if he nondeviantly decides to A on the basis of a rationally formed deliberative judgment that it would be best to A, the proximate causes of his decision do not deterministically cause it, he has no compelled or coercively produced attitudes that influence his deliberative judgment, he is well informed on the topic of his deliberation, and he is mentally healthy.

Unlike my presentation of modest libertarianism, my presentation of DSL includes a position on actions—specifically, decisions—that are contrary to the agent's best judgment. I offered a daring soft libertarian defense of the possibility of akratic—and therefore free—decisions that are not deterministically caused by their proximate causes (ch. 5, secs. 4 and 5).

Two decades ago, Peter van Inwagen wrote: "The human organism and human behaviour are such terribly complex things, and so little is known about the details of that terrible complexity (in comparison with what there is to be known), that it is hard to see why anyone should think that what we do know renders a belief that human behaviour is determined reasonable" (1983, p. 198). This was true then, and it is true today, even if much more is now known about human brains and behavior. It is also true that, for all we know, human brains do not work indeterministically in ways that are conducive to free action and moral responsibility. But by the same token, for all we know, they *do* work indeterministically in such ways. Given the assumption that compatibilism is true, it is very plausible, as I have observed, that human beings sometimes act freely and are morally responsible for some of what they do. Given the assumption that incompatibilism is true, our empirical knowledge is not up to the task of settling the issue whether it is more credible that there are free and morally responsible human agents or that there are no such agents.

2. Two Thought Experiments

John Fischer invites his readers to imagine that scientists discover that determinism is true (1994, pp. 6–7). I now invite you (dear reader) to imagine this. If some of your theoretical beliefs about free will and moral responsibility are influenced by intuitions you have about thought experiments, and if you take those intuitions seriously, Fischer's thought experiment merits your consideration.

What might hard libertarians think after due reflection on this imagined discovery? Van Inwagen says that he would become a compatibilist (1983, p. 223). He has been taken to task for this (Fischer and Ravizza 1998, pp. 253–54), but I admire his honesty. Part of the change in an erstwhile hard libertarian who joins van Inwagen in climbing over the fence to compatibilism might be a lowering of standards for free will and moral responsibility. How far they are lowered depends on how high they were, of course. Readers who have been persuaded that free action requires neither agent causation nor the distinctive features of Robert Kane's event-causal libertarianism should avoid embracing standards that include these things. Some hard libertarians may be attracted to daring soft libertarianism, provided that the softness is jettisoned. If proponents of DSL minus the softness—I dub this view DL—were to lower their standards for free action in response to the discovery that determinism is true, what would that amount to?

Proponents of DL (DLs, for short) require for free action and moral responsibility the occasional successful exercise of an initiatory power that, by definition, is at work only when the proximate causes of a decision do not deterministically cause it. This power gives agents causally open alternative futures, and unlike modest libertarianism, it gives them this openness at the moment at which some decisions are made. In successful Frankfurt-style scenarios featuring a decision to A, these causally open alternatives are limited to nonrobust alternative possibilities that include a decision to A (for example, an alternative possibility constituted by a decision to A that is caused by an alien brain implant); but in normal circumstances, decision makers sometimes have robust alternative possibilities, according to DSLs and DLs.

In chapter 5 (sec. 1), I mentioned Derk Pereboom's claim that event-causal libertarianism "does not provide agents with any more control than compatibilism does" (2001, p. 56) and Randolph Clarke's assertion that "the active control that is exercised on" an event-causal libertarian view "is just the same as that exercised on an event-causal compatibilist account" (2003, p. 220). Pereboom and Clarke would not regard DLs who lower their standards for free action after learning that determinism is true as lowering them much at all. If kinds of control are to be individuated partly on the basis of essential properties, then Clarke overstates his claim: the control exercised in making basically* free decisions is different in kind from the control "exercised on an event-causal compatibilist account," because the former kind of control is essentially indeterministic and the latter is not.[2] (Again, a *basically* free A-ing* is, by definition, a free A-ing performed at a time at which the agent has at least a nonrobust alternative possibility. See ch. 5, sec. 3.) Even so, the requirement of the initiatory power that I identified is entailed by the requirement of the agent causation of a decision and by Kane's view, but it does not entail either. So the gap between DL and compatibilist views of free and morally responsible agency is more modest than the gaps between these other libertarian views and compatibilist views. Consequently, other things being equal, it may be easier for DLs to make the move to compatibilism in light of the imagined scientific discovery of determinism's truth.

To suppose that some DLs would, on reflection, become compatibilists in the imagined conditions is not to suppose that they were really compatibilists in disguise. After all, van Inwagen certainly is not a compatibilist in disguise, even though he would become a compatibilist if it were known that determinism is true. Much conceptual reasoning is done under conditions of empirical uncertainty. If we were to know certain empirical truths, we might reason differently about conceptual theses we confidently deem true; on reflection, we might come around to the view that they are false. (This suggests that we should not rest content with our confidence about some conceptual issues until we have run for ourselves relevant thought experiments featuring imaginable empirical discoveries.)

I make the point that DL is not a disguised form of compatibilism because some friends and acquaintances have told me that DL cannot be accepted by *real* libertarians. If to be a real libertarian is to require for free and morally responsible agency either agent causation or dual indeterministic efforts to decide (à la Kane), then what these friends and acquaintances tell me is true. However, if my assessment in this book of these libertarian ideas is on target, committed incompatibilists who believe that there are free and morally responsible agents had better hope that there are other options for real libertarians.

What about DLs who would continue to reject compatibilism even after learning that determinism is true? What would keep them on the incompatibilist side of the fence? Perhaps the zygote argument (ch. 7, sec. 4). In a passage that I mentioned in chapter 5 (sec. 6), Galen Strawson asserts that if we have "*heaven-and-hell* responsibility . . . then it makes sense to propose that it could be just—without any qualification—to punish some of us with (possibly everlasting) torment in hell and reward others with (possibly everlasting) bliss in heaven [and] what we do is wholly and entirely up to us in some absolute buck-stopping way" (2002, p. 451). DLs need not believe in heaven-and-hell responsibility to be impressed by the zygote argument. They may believe that no human being is bad enough to deserve everlasting torment or good enough to deserve everlasting bliss, and they may believe that nothing is "wholly and entirely up to" free human beings, on a literal interpretation of the quoted words. They may see the zygote argument as a serious obstacle to what may be termed *down-to-earth* or *mundane* moral responsibility and to the sort of free action most closely associated with it.[3] Of course, the zygote argument is not a problem for modest libertarianism. So if some DLs are persuaded by that argument, that cannot explain why they endorse DL rather than settling for modest libertarianism. In some moods, I suspect that the idea that being a free agent requires sometimes deciding freely at moments at which one has at least nonrobust alternative possibilities derives more from the alleged feeling of causal openness in decision making than from any argument for the truth of that idea.[4] And, of course, even if the feeling is veridical, that does not entail that being a free agent *requires* such openness. That some agents make basically* free decisions is compatible with there being free agents who make no basically* free decisions and perform no basically* free actions.

Switching from incompatibilism to compatibilism in light of the imagined empirical discovery and holding on to one's incompatibilism are not the only options, of course. One might instead become an agnostic about incompatibilism. Such agnostics who know that our universe is deterministic do not have open to them the disjunctive thesis that either incompatibilism is true and some human beings have free will or compatibilism is true and some human beings have free will, where each disjunct is treated as a live option. (For, of course, if incompatibilism is true and our universe is deterministic, no human beings have free will.) Given their imagined knowledge and their agnosticism, they are committed to agnosticism about human free will. In this, they differ from agnostic autonomists (ch. 1), according to whom both disjuncts are live options.

Imagine now a very different empirical discovery: scientists discover that indeterministic brain processes of the sort required if modest libertarianism and DL are to have a chance of being true are common in human beings. What would *compatibilists* think after due reflection on this discovery? Compatibilism comes in different degrees of hardness. The hardest compatibilists contend that there can be free agents only in deterministic worlds. A less hard compatibilism than this requires that the internal workings of human brains be deterministic, even if our universe is indeterministic. Compatibilists of either of these kinds who believe that there are many free human agents and continue to be compatibilists would need either to give up that belief or to opt for a softer compatibilist view that allows for the possibility of free human beings whose brains work indeterministically in the discovered ways. If either DSL or the combination of modest and soft libertarianism hits its mark, it should persuade compatibilists that internal indeterminism is consistent with free agency. And, of course, compatibilism itself does not entail that there are no free and morally responsible indeterministic agents.

Might some compatibilists who reflect on the imagined discovery now under consideration become incompatibilists? Might they come to believe that they had been settling for too little—for something that falls short of free action and moral responsibility? Of course, this might happen. The more pertinent question is whether, partly in light of the imagined discovery, some compatibilists would be *justified* in becoming incompatibilists. In chapter 7 (sec. 4), I suggested that the more optimistic reflective agnostics are about indeterministic agents' prospects for free and morally responsible action, the more likely they are to have the intuition that, because of the way Ernie's zygote was produced in his deterministic universe, Ernie is neither morally responsible nor free—that is, that premise 1 of the zygote argument for incompatibilism is true. This might also be true of some compatibilists. The imagined scientific discovery can increase a person's estimate of the likelihood that some of us are free and morally responsible indeterministic agents, and the increased estimate might make premise 1 of the zygote argument seem more intuitive than it otherwise would. Now, what would *justify* incompatibilism is a sufficiently strong argument for it, and the most vulnerable feature of the zygote argument is premise 1. Increasing the justification for that premise would strengthen the argument. However, because whether or not premise 1 is true does not depend on how likely we are to be free and morally responsible indeterministic agents, the imagined discovery cannot make premise 1 seem more intuitive *by increasing the justification* for that premise.[5]

How would proponents of agnostic autonomism respond to the imagined discoveries? Again, the central positive claim that agnostic autonomists make is that the following disjunction is more credible than the thesis that no human beings ever act freely and morally responsibly: either compatibilism is true and there are free and morally responsible human beings or compatibilism is false and there are free and morally responsible human beings. The truth of the latter disjunct requires that our universe be indeterministic. If agnostic autonomists were to learn that, in fact, our universe is deterministic, they would probably become compatibilists. Whether they would be *justified* in becoming compatibilists depends on the strength of the arguments for and against compatibilism. I have suggested that if agnostic autonomists were to learn that indeterministic brain processes of the sort required if modest libertarianism and DL are to have a chance of being true are common in human beings, that would tend to make premise 1 of the zygote argument for incompatibilism seem more intuitive to them than it otherwise would. But, again, this imagined discovery would not contribute to the justification for that premise.

3. Conclusion

Although some word of mine will be my last word, I will never have the last word on a philosophical topic. Nor would I want to. My ultimate purpose in writing this book has been to help readers think more clearly about free will. My plan for doing that included, among other things, clarifying some of the central concepts, making vivid the most important conceptual obstacles for compatibilism and for libertarianism, arguing against various proposed accounts of free agency, and developing for consideration alternative collections of conceptually sufficient conditions for free agency.

I closed *Autonomous Agents* (Mele 1995) with an argument that a disjunction with compatibilist belief in human free will (or autonomy) and libertarianism as its disjuncts is more credible than the thesis that no human beings act freely (or autonomously). This time, I leave it to readers to make their own judgment about this; they will do that anyway! As I write this concluding chapter, ten years have passed since I wrote *Autonomous Agents*. If I am lucky enough to be alive and well ten years from now, perhaps I will take another shot at free will.

NOTES

1. A variant of 1a for morally responsible action includes the further condition that the *A*-ing has moral significance.

2. Recall Clarke's claim that "An agent's exercise of control in acting is an exercise of a positive power to determine what he does" (2002, p. 374). Control, for Clarke, is a power. The initiatory power that DL requires for basically* free decisions is essentially indeterministic.

3. For an instructive critical discussion of Strawson's appeal to heaven-and-hell responsibility, see Clarke 2005b, section 4.

4. I discuss this feeling and our experience of our own agency in Mele 1995, pp. 133–37, 246–49.

5. I am not excluding a kind of indirect dependence. Suppose that indeterministic agents' prospects for free and morally responsible actions are nil because free and morally responsible actions are conceptually impossible. That supposition bears on whether or not premise 1 is true, but not owing selectively to a truth about indeterministic agency.

References

Adams, Frederick, and A. Mele. 1992. "The Intention/Volition Debate." *Canadian Journal of Philosophy* 22: 323–38.

Almeida, Michael, and M. Bernstein. 2003. "Lucky Libertarianism." *Philosophical Studies* 113: 93–119.

Aristotle. 1915. *Nicomachean Ethics*. Vol. 9 of W. Ross, ed. *The Works of Aristotle*. London: Oxford University Press.

Arpaly, Nomy. 2003. *Unprincipled Virtue*. New York: Oxford University Press.

Audi, Robert. 1993. *Action, Intention, and Reason*. Ithaca, NY: Cornell University Press.

Austin, J. L. 1970. "Ifs and Cans." In J. Urmson and G. Warnock, eds. *Philosophical Papers*. Oxford: Oxford University Press.

Ayer, Alfred J. 1954. "Freedom and Necessity." In A. Ayer, *Philosophical Essays*. London: Macmillan.

Bailey, Ronald. 2003. "Freedom Evolves: Darwin + Hume = Daniel Dennett." *Reasonline*. http://reason.com/rb/rb021903.shtml.

Beebee, Helen, and A. Mele. 2002. "Humean Compatibilism." *Mind* 111: 201–24.

Berofsky, Bernard. 1995. *Liberation from Self*. New York: Cambridge University Press.

Brand, Myles. 1984. *Intending and Acting*. Cambridge, MA: MIT Press.

Bratman, Michael. 1987. *Intention, Plans, and Practical Reason*. Cambridge, MA: Harvard University Press.

Clarke, Randolph. 1997. "On the Possibility of Rational Free Action." *Philosophical Studies* 88: 37–57.

———. 2000. "Modest Libertarianism." *Philosophical Perspectives* 14: 21–45.

———. 2002. "Libertarian Views: Critical Survey of Noncausal and Event-causal Accounts of Free Agency." In R. Kane, ed. *The Oxford Handbook of Free Will*. New York: Oxford University Press.

———. 2003. *Libertarian Accounts of Free Will*. New York: Oxford University Press.

———. 2005a. "Agent Causation and the Problem of Luck." *Pacific Philosophical Quarterly* 86: 408–21.

———. 2005b. "On an Argument for the Impossibility of Moral Responsibility." *Midwest Studies in Philosophy* 29: 13–24.

Cohen, Daniel. In press. "Openness, Accidentality, and Responsibility." *Philosophical Studies*.

Coles, Michael, and M. Rugg. 1995. "Event-Related Brain Potentials: An Introduction." In M. Rugg and M. Coles, eds. *Electrophysiology of Mind*. Oxford: Oxford University Press.

Cuypers, Stefaan. In press. "The Trouble with Externalist Compatibilist Autonomy." *Philosophical Studies*.

Davidson, Donald. 1987. "Knowing One's Own Mind." *Proceedings and Addresses of the American Philosophical Association* 60: 441–58.

Day, Brian, J. Rothwell, P. Thompson, A. Maertens de Noordhout, K. Nakashima, K. Shannon, and C. Marsden. 1989. "Delay in the Execution of Voluntary Movement by Electrical or Magnetic Brain Stimulation in Intact Man." *Brain* 112: 649–63.

Della Rocca, Michael. 1998. "Frankfurt, Fischer and Flickers." *Noûs* 32: 99–105.

Dennett, Daniel. 1978. *Brainstorms*. Montgomery, VT: Bradford.

———. 1991. *Consciousness Explained*. Boston: Little, Brown.

———. 2003. *Freedom Evolves*. New York: Viking.

Double, Richard. 1991. *The Non-Reality of Free Will*. New York: Oxford University Press.

Ekstrom, Laura. 2000. *Free Will*. Boulder, CO: Westview.

Feinberg, Joel. 1986. *Harm to Self*. New York: Oxford University Press.

Fischer, John. 1982. "Responsibility and Control." *Journal of Philosophy* 79: 24–40.

———. 1994. *The Metaphysics of Free Will*. Cambridge, MA: Blackwell.

———. 1995. "Libertarianism and Avoidability: A Reply to Widerker." *Faith and Philosophy* 12: 119–25.

———. 2000. "Problems with Actual-Sequence Incompatibilism." *Journal of Ethics* 4: 323–28.

———. 2004. "Responsibility and Manipulation." *Journal of Ethics* 8: 145–77.

Fischer, John, and M. Ravizza 1998. *Responsibility and Control: A Theory of Moral Responsibility*. New York: Cambridge University Press.

———. 2000. "Replies." *Philosophy and Phenomenological Research* 61: 467–80.

Flanagan, Owen. 1996. *Self-Expressions*. New York: Oxford University Press.

Frankfurt, Harry. 1969. "Alternate Possibilities and Moral Responsibility." *Journal of Philosophy* 66: 829–39.

———. 1988. *The Importance of What We Care About*. Cambridge: Cambridge University Press.

———. 2002. "Reply to John Martin Fischer." In S. Buss and L. Overton, eds. *Contours of Agency.* Cambridge, MA: MIT Press.

Ginet, Carl. 1990. *On Action.* Cambridge: Cambridge University Press.

———. 1996. "In Defense of the Principle of Alternative Possibilities: Why I Don't Find Frankfurt's Argument Convincing." *Philosophical Perspectives* 10: 403–17.

———. 2003. "Libertarianism." In M. Loux and D. Zimmermann, eds. *The Oxford Handbook of Metaphysics.* New York: Oxford University Press.

Gomes, Gilberto. 1999. "Volition and the Readiness Potential." *Journal of Consciousness Studies* 6: 59–76.

Grünbaum, Adolph. 1971. "Free Will and the Laws of Human Behavior." *American Philosophical Quarterly* 8: 299–317.

Haggard, Patrick, and B. Libet. 2001. "Conscious Intention and Brain Activity." *Journal of Consciousness Studies* 8: 47–63.

Haggard, Patrick, and E. Magno. 1999. "Localising Awareness of Action with Transcranial Magnetic Stimulation." *Experimental Brain Research* 127: 102–7.

Haggard, Patrick, C. Newman, and E. Magno. 1999. "On the Perceived Time of Voluntary Actions." *British Journal of Psychology* 90: 291–303.

Haji, Ishtiyaque. 1996. "Moral Responsibility and the Problem of Induced Pro-Attitudes." *Dialogue* 35: 703–20.

———. 1999. "Indeterminism and Frankfurt-type Examples." *Philosophical Explorations* 2: 42–58.

Hitchcock, Christopher. 1999. "Contrastive Explanations and the Demons of Determinism." *British Journal for the Philosophy of Science* 50: 585–612.

Hobart, R. E. 1934. "Free Will as Involving Determinism and as Inconceivable without It." *Mind* 43: 1–27.

Hodgson, David. 2002. "Quantum Physics, Consciousness, and Free Will." In R. Kane, ed. *The Oxford Handbook of Free Will.* New York: Oxford University Press.

Honderich, Ted. 1988. *A Theory of Determinism.* Oxford: Clarendon.

Hume, David. 1739. *A Treatise of Human Nature.* Reprinted in L. Selby-Bigge, ed. *A Treatise of Human Nature.* Oxford: Clarendon, 1975.

Hurley, Susan. 2003. *Justice, Luck, and Knowledge.* Cambridge, MA: Harvard University Press.

Kane, Robert. 1985. *Free Will and Values.* Albany: State University of New York Press.

———. 1989. "Two Kinds of Incompatibilism." *Philosophy and Phenomenological Research* 50: 219–54.

———. 1996. *The Significance of Free Will.* New York: Oxford University Press.

———. 1999a. "On Free Will, Responsibility and Indeterminism: Responses to Clarke, Haji, and Mele." *Philosophical Explorations* 2: 105–21.

———. 1999b. "Responsibility, Luck and Chance: Reflections on Free Will and Indeterminism." *Journal of Philosophy* 96: 217–40.

———. 2000. "Responses to Bernard Berofsky, John Martin Fischer, and Galen Strawson." *Philosophy and Phenomenological Research* 60: 157–67.

———. 2002. "Some Neglected Pathways in the Free Will Labyrinth." In R. Kane, ed. *The Oxford Handbook of Free Will.* New York: Oxford University Press.

———. 2003. "Responsibility and Frankfurt-style Cases: A Response to Mele and Robb." In M. McKenna and D. Widerker, eds. *Freedom, Responsibility, and Agency.* Aldershot, England: Ashgate.

Kapitan, Tomis. 1996. "Incompatibilism and Ambiguity in the Practical Modalities." *Analysis* 56: 102–10.

———. 2000. "Autonomy and Manipulated Freedom." *Philosophical Perspectives* 14: 81–104.

Kaufman, Arnold. 1966. "Practical Decision." *Mind* 75: 25–44.

Keller, Ivonne, and H. Heckhausen 1990. "Readiness Potentials Preceding Spontaneous Motor Acts: Voluntary vs. Involuntary Control." *Electroencephalography and Clinical Neurophysiology* 76: 351–61.

Knobe, Joshua. In press. "The Concept of Intentional Action: A Case Study in the Uses of Folk Psychology." *Philosophical Studies.*

Lamb, James. 1993. "Evaluative Compatibilism and the Principle of Alternate Possibilities." *Journal of Philosophy* 90: 517–27.

Lewis, David. 1973. *Counterfactuals.* Cambridge, MA: Harvard University Press.

Libet, Benjamin. 1985. "Unconscious Cerebral Initiative and the Role of Conscious Will in Voluntary Action." *Behavioral and Brain Sciences* 8: 529–66.

———. 1989. "The Timing of a Subjective Experience." *Behavioral and Brain Sciences* 12: 183–84.

———. 1992. "The Neural Time-Factor in Perception, Volition and Free Will." *Revue de Métaphysique et de Morale* 2: 255–72.

———. 1999. "Do We Have Free Will?" *Journal of Consciousness Studies* 6: 47–57.

———. 2001. "Consciousness, Free Action and the Brain." *Journal of Consciousness Studies* 8: 59–65.

———. 2002. "The Timing of Mental Events: Libet's Experimental Findings and Their Implications." *Consciousness and Cognition* 11: 291–99.

———. 2004. *Mind Time.* Cambridge, MA: Harvard University Press.

Libet, Benjamin, C. Gleason, E. Wright, and D. Pearl. 1983. "Time of Unconscious Intention to Act in Relation to Onset of Cerebral Activity (Readiness-Potential)." *Brain* 106: 623–42.

Libet, Benjamin, E. Wright, and A. Curtis. 1983. "Preparation- or Intention-to-Act, in Relation to Pre-Event Potentials Recorded at the Vertex." *Electroencephalography and Clinical Neurophysiology* 56: 367–72.

Libet, Benjamin, E. Wright, and C. Gleason. 1982. "Readiness Potentials Preceding Unrestricted 'Spontaneous' vs. Pre-Planned Voluntary Acts." *Electroencephalography and Clinical Neurophysiology* 54: 322–35.

Malle, Bertram, and S. Nelson. 2003. "Judging *Mens Rea*: The Tension Between Folk Concepts and Legal Concepts of Intentionality." *Behavioral Sciences and the Law* 21: 563–80.

Marcel, Anthony. 2003. "The Sense of Agency: Awareness and Ownership of Action." In J. Roessler and N. Eilan, eds. *Agency and Self-Awareness.* Oxford: Clarendon.

McCann, Hugh. 1986a. "Intrinsic Intentionality." *Theory and Decision* 20: 247–73.

———. 1986b. "Rationality and the Range of Intention." *Midwest Studies in Philosophy* 10: 191–211.

McKenna, Michael. 1997. "Alternative Possibilities and the Failure of the Counterexample Strategy." *Journal of Social Philosophy* 28: 71–85.

———. 2000. "Excerpt's from John Martin Fischer's Discussion with Members of the Audience." *Journal of Ethics* 4: 408–17.

Mele, Alfred. 1987. *Irrationality.* New York: Oxford University Press.

———. 1992. *Springs of Action.* New York: Oxford University Press.

———. 1995. *Autonomous Agents.* New York: Oxford University Press.

———. 1996. "Soft Libertarianism and Frankfurt-style Scenarios." *Philosophical Topics* 24: 123–41.

———. 1997. "Strength of Motivation and Being in Control: Learning from Libet." *American Philosophical Quarterly* 34: 319–33.

———. 1999a. "Kane, Luck, and the Significance of Free Will." *Philosophical Explorations* 2: 96–104.

———. 1999b. "Ultimate Responsibility and Dumb Luck." *Social Philosophy and Policy* 16: 274–93.

———. 2000. "Reactive Attitudes, Reactivity, and Omissions." *Philosophy and Phenomenological Research* 61: 447–52.

———. 2002. "Akratics and Addicts." *American Philosophical Quarterly* 39: 153–67.

———. 2003a. *Motivation and Agency.* New York: Oxford University Press.

———. 2003b. "Agents' Abilities." *Noûs* 37: 447–70.

———. 2003c. Review of S. Buss and L. Overton, eds. *Contours of Agency* (MIT Press, 2002). *Australasian Journal of Philosophy* 81: 292–95.

———. 2004. "Can Libertarians Make Promises?" In J. Hyman and H. Steward, eds. *Action and Agency.* Cambridge: Cambridge University Press.

———. 2005a. "A Critique of Pereboom's 'Four-Case Argument' for Incompatibilism." *Analysis* 65: 75–80.

———. 2005b. "Libertarianism, Luck, and Control." *Pacific Philosophical Quarterly* 86: 395–421.

Mele, Alfred, and P. Moser. 1994. "Intentional Action." *Noûs* 28: 39–68.

Mele, Alfred, and D. Robb. 1998. "Rescuing Frankfurt-style Cases." *Philosophical Review* 107: 97–112.

———. 2003. "BBs, Magnets and Seesaws: The Metaphysics of Frankfurt-style Cases." In M. McKenna and D. Widerker, eds. *Freedom, Responsibility, and Agency.* Aldershot, England: Ashgate.

Mill, John Stuart. 1979. *An Examination of Sir William Hamilton's Philosophy.* J. Robson, ed. Toronto: Routledge and Kegan Paul.

Moore, G. E. 1912. *Ethics.* Oxford: Oxford University Press.

Nagel, Thomas. 1986. *The View from Nowhere.* New York: Oxford University Press.

Nahmias, Eddy, S. Morris, T. Nadelhoffer, and J. Turner. 2005. "Surveying Freedom: Folk Intuitions about Free Will and Moral Responsibility." *Philosophical Psychology* 18: 561–84.

Naylor, Marjory. 1984. "Frankfurt on the Principle of Alternate Possibilities." *Philosophical Studies* 46: 249–58.

Nowell-Smith, P. H. 1948. "Free Will and Moral Responsibility." *Mind* 57: 45–61.

O'Connor, Timothy. 2000. *Persons and Causes.* New York: Oxford University Press.

Pereboom, Derk. 2001. *Living Without Free Will.* Cambridge: Cambridge University Press.

Pink, Thomas. 1996. *The Psychology of Freedom.* Cambridge: Cambridge University Press.

Prinz, Wolfgang. 2003. "How Do We Know about Our Own Actions?" In S. Maasen, W. Prinz, and G. Roth, eds. *Voluntary Action.* Oxford: Oxford University Press.

Rosen, Gideon. 2002. "The Case for Incompatibilism." *Philosophy and Phenomenological Research* 64: 699–706.

Rosenthal, David. 2002. "The Timing of Conscious States." *Consciousness and Cognition* 11: 215–20.

Rowe, William. 1991. *Thomas Reid on Freedom and Morality.* Ithaca, NY: Cornell University Press.

Schlick, Moritz. 1962. *Problems of Ethics.* David Rynin, trans. New York: Dover.

Schrödinger, Erwin. 1983. "The Present Situation in Quantum Mechanics." In J. Wheeler and W. Zurek, eds. *Quantum Theory and Measurement.* Princeton, NJ: Princeton University Press.

Searle, John. 2001. *Rationality in Action.* Cambridge, MA: MIT Press.

Slote, Michael. 1982. "Selective Necessity and the Free-will Problem." *Journal of Philosophy* 79: 5–24.

Smart, J. J. C. 1961. "Free-Will, Praise, and Blame." *Mind* 70: 291–306.

Smith, Michael. 1997. "A Theory of Freedom and Responsibility." In G. Cullity, ed. *Ethics and Practical Reason.* New York: Clarendon.

———. 2003. "Rational Capacities." In S. Stroud and C. Tappolet, eds. *Weakness of Will and Practical Irrationality.* Oxford: Clarendon.

Spence, Sean, and C. Frith. 1999. "Towards a Functional Anatomy of Volition." *Journal of Consciousness Studies* 6: 11–29.

Strawson, Galen. 1986. *Freedom and Belief.* Oxford: Clarendon.
———. 1994. "The Impossibility of Moral Responsibility." *Philosophical Studies* 75: 5–24.
———. 2002. "The Bounds of Freedom." In R. Kane, ed. *The Oxford Handbook of Free Will.* New York: Oxford University Press.
Stump, Eleonore. 1990. "Intellect, Will and the Principle of Alternate Possibilities." In M. Beaty, ed. *Christian Theism and the Problems of Philosophy.* Notre Dame, IN: University of Notre Dame Press.
Stump, Eleonore, and N. Kretzmann. 1991. "Prophecy, Past Truth, and Eternity." *Philosophical Perspectives* 5: 395–424.
Taylor, Richard. 1966. *Action and Purpose.* Englewood Cliffs, NJ: Prentice-Hall.
Trevena, Judy, and J. Miller. 2002. "Cortical Movement Preparation before and after a Conscious Decision to Move." *Consciousness and Cognition* 11: 162–90.
van de Grind, Wim. 2002. "Physical, Neural, and Mental Timing." *Consciousness and Cognition* 11: 241–64.
van Inwagen, Peter. 1983. *An Essay on Free Will.* Oxford: Clarendon.
———. 2000. "Free Will Remains a Mystery." *Philosophical Perspectives* 14: 1–19.
Wallace, R. Jay. 2002. "Replies." *Philosophy and Phenomenological Research* 64: 707–27.
Waller, Bruce. 1988. "Free Will Gone Out of Control." *Behaviorism* 16: 149–57.
Watson, Gary. 1987. "Free Action and Free Will." *Mind* 96: 145–72.
Widerker, David. 1995. "Libertarianism and Frankfurt's Attack on the Principle of Alternative Possibilities." *Philosophical Review* 104: 247–61.
———. 2000. "Frankfurt's Attack on the Principle of Alternative Possibilities: A Further Look." *Philosophical Perspectives* 14: 181–201.
———. 2003. "Blameworthiness and Frankfurt's Argument Against the Principle of Alternative Possibilities." In M. McKenna and D. Widerker, eds. *Freedom, Responsibility, and Agency.* Aldershot, England: Ashgate.
Woolfolk, Robert, J. Doris, and J. Darley. In press. "Identification, and Social Situational Constraint, and Social Cognition." *Cognition.*
Wyma, Keith. 1997. "Moral Responsibility and Leeway for Action." *American Philosophical Quarterly* 34: 57–70.
Zagzebski, Linda. 1991. *The Dilemma of Freedom and Foreknowledge.* Oxford: Oxford University Press.
Zimmerman, Michael. 1988. *An Essay on Moral Responsibility.* Totowa, NJ: Rowman and Littlefield.

Index

220 • *Index*